on the lam

on the

lam

Narratives of Flight in J. Edgar Hoover's America

William Beverly

University Press of Mississippi / *Jackson*

www.upress.state.ms.us

Copyright © 2003
by University Press of Mississippi
All rights reserved
Manufactured in the United States
of America

Print-on-Demand Edition

∞

Library of Congress Cataloging-in-Publication

Beverly, William, 1965–
    On the lam : narratives of flight in J. Edgar Hoover's America / William Beverly.
        p. cm.
    Includes bibliographical references (p.) and index.
    ISBN 1-57806-537-2 (alk. paper)
1. American fiction—20th century—History and criticism. 2. Fugitives from
justice in literature. 3. Hoover, J. Edgar (John Edgar), 1895–1972—Influence.
4. Film noir—United States—History and criticism. 5. Justice, Administration of,
in motion pictures. 6. Fugitives from justice in motion pictures. 7. Justice,
Administration of, in literature. 8. Fugitive slaves in literature. 9. Criminals in
literature. 10. Narration (Rhetoric). I. Title.

PS374.F83B48 2003
813'.509355—dc21   2002010799

British Library Cataloging-in-Publication Data available

For my grandparents

contents

acknowledgments

This project began in the wonderfully creative atmosphere that prevailed in the English Department at the University of Florida in the mid-1990s, where I worked with an extraordinary group of mentors and colleagues. Daniel Cottom was the project's earliest supporter and most eloquent critic; I am first and foremost in his debt. David Leverenz, Phillip Wegner, Jeffrey Adler, and Susan Hegeman comprised a most insightful group of readers. The American literature discussion group directed by Anne Goodwyn Jones helped light the way toward this book; among that desperate band, I thank Gary Macdonald, Rhonda Morris, Betsy Nies, David Russell, Dina Smith, and Jim Watkins for their input and inspiration. I wish to acknowledge Anne Jones for her gracious loan of library work space and the University's College of Liberal Arts and Sciences for a 1996 fellowship that made a great difference.

More recently, Jeff Abernathy has provided valuable suggestions and spiritual kinship, and Dan Barden and Daniel Gutstein have afforded me access to research opportunities in Washington, D.C.

I wish to acknowledge H. Bruce Franklin, whose reading of the book inspired numerous improvements and transformed chapter 4. Among the editors at University Press of Mississippi, I thank Walter Biggins and Anne Stascavage. In particular, I am grateful to Seetha Srinivasan for her interest, her guidance, and her patience.

Elements of this book have been presented in different form at conferences sponsored by the Association for the Interdisciplinary Study of the Arts and the Modern Language Association.

During the development of this book, my friends and family have kindly listened to the same stories more than once; thanks to them for indulging me and to my parents for their apparently infinite patience.

In spite of its robbing her of a husband for countless hours, Deborah Ager has always encouraged my work on this project and eased its progress with wisdom and love.

This book is for my father's parents, William and Jane Anne Beverly, and in memory of my mother's, Jack and Leone Staples.

introduction

The Figure of the Fugitive

The lam story is surely one of America's great minor genres. From slave narratives to *Light in August* and *Beloved*, tales of flight occupy central places in its literary canon. Of the American Film Institute's 1998 list of "100 Greatest American Movies," four are fugitive stories, depicting a criminal's flight: *Bonnie and Clyde, Double Indemnity, North by Northwest*, and *Butch Cassidy and the Sundance Kid*. In the daily news as well, the manhunt has proven to be a most reliable headline maker. In the Lindbergh kidnapping, the aftermath of John Kennedy and Martin Luther King's deaths, and the bizarre freeway flight of O. J. Simpson, the hunt for the fugitive provides an uncommonly satisfying narrative structure among news items. Manhunts erupt from a distinct beginning, the commission of a crime or identification of a suspect; they match recognizable adversaries in deadly conflict; they barrel toward a climax, a shootout or arrest, or toward an eerie silence. If, as Elizabeth Kastor has written, the manhunt is "a perennial motif in American storytelling," it is because it is a strikingly good story.

Yet the fugitive has been too rarely discussed as a literary and cultural figure, despite the voluminous, often excellent critical attention paid to gangster and road stories, two narratives that flank the fugitive tale. At best, the twentieth-century fugitive has been classified as an enduring derivative of various nineteenth-century figures, the escaped slave or the Wild West outlaw, as in Phyllis Rauch Klotman's compendium *Another Man Gone: The Black Runner in Contemporary Afro-American Literature*. A variety of factors may have deterred critical juxtaposition of widely divergent fugitive texts: the disparateness of these texts, ranging from news copy and police bulletins to pulp and literary fiction, is one such factor. A tendency to depict, mythologize, and group white and black fugitives separately problematizes their comparison, despite the transgressive significance of figures such as Faulkner's Joe Christmas. Fugitives flee from different (and sometimes abhorrent) crimes, figure in different political dramas, and threaten or occupy different geographies. The genre is further complicated by innocent fugitives, those falsely accused—like *The Fugitive*'s Dr. Richard Kimble, or Peg, the screenwriter hero of Steve

Fisher's novel of workplace discipline, *I Wake up Screaming*—and those whose crimes contemporary readers tend to reject, like political refugees and slaves violating state and federal laws prohibiting their flight.

In order to render diverse historical and literary fugitive figures productive, *On the Lam* focuses on the tensions between gestures of flight (the lam) and police pursuit (the manhunt) in American texts from the twenty years between 1932 and 1952. Taken together, these texts reveal changes in the lam during a period of intense police modernization and reconfiguration. They trace an institutional effort to suture disparate jurisdictions and regions of the United States together into a coherent body, a national whole. From this effort sprang a transformed national geography of crime and police, as well as a nascent network of coordination and surveillance technologies that asserted policing power far beyond the presence of the policeman. In this sense, the cultural project these lam tales trace is specifically disciplinary; the deployment of technologies of registration and apprehension to which all American citizens increasingly became subject becomes also a critical locus of the formation of the modern American state. The fugitive figure's attempt to outdistance the police's gaze, to find a wilderness beyond the policed frontier, helped to inspire these national policing mechanisms and provides a sensitive record of their extension and effect across American culture.

That these effects reveal themselves consistently over the heterogeneous texts *On the Lam* discusses—autobiography, press accounts, film, and fiction, both canonical and long-neglected works—argues for the resounding success of police efforts to shape and dominate the discourses surrounding law and lawlessness at midcentury. In a 1934 speech before an International Association of Chiefs of Police crime conference, Franklin D. Roosevelt argued that manufacturing public consensus would be of paramount importance in modernizing and systematizing American law enforcement:

> An administrative structure that is perfect will still be ineffective in its results unless the people of the United States understand the larger purposes and cooperate with these purposes.

I ask you, therefore, to do all in your power to interpret the problem of crime to the people of this country. They must realize the many implications of that word "Crime." . . . It is your positive duty to keep before the country the facts in regard to crime as a whole—great crimes, lesser crimes and little crimes—to build up a body of public opinion which, I regret to be compelled to say, is not in this day and age sufficiently active or alive to the situation in which we find ourselves.

I want the backing of every man, every woman and every adolescent child in every state of the United States and in every county of every state—their backing for what you and the officers of law and order are trying to accomplish. (19)

Roosevelt found his champion in J. Edgar Hoover. Director of the Federal Bureau of Investigation from 1924 until his death in 1972, Hoover played a central role in revamping American law enforcement. He spearheaded lobbying efforts on behalf of federal and local police; built his Bureau's capacities for coordination, record keeping, forensic science, and detection; and amassed broad power and license for himself and his supporters. But his campaign to seize control of representations of crime and policing was perhaps his most impressive career accomplishment. Publishing prolifically, regularly contributing interviews or statements to other writings on crime, and intervening in the production of popular entertainments, Hoover and his ideas permeated discussions of crime issues throughout the twenty-year period of this study.

Roosevelt's conference address, like the New Deal itself, called for a spatial reimagination of the nation. In a basic sense this was consonant with the aims of the New Deal, whose programs extended federal influence to regions crippled by Depression poverty and isolated by uneven development. Government works projects asserted federal administration over a formerly local landscape; nationalization was carried on ideologically as well, as Christine Bold demonstrates in *The WPA Guides: Mapping America*, which illuminates the federal-regional conflicts surrounding the compiling of the Federal Writer's Project guidebook series. Insisting upon the acquiescence of "every county of every state" and alluding to the spread of crimes formerly concentrated in regions— "widespread drug peddling," "horrifying lynchings"—Roosevelt pointed at a goal which Hoover was diligent in pursuing: the diminishment of jurisdictional borders. The fugitive fleeing across those borders exposed outdated police practice and provided a clear test of a central government's ability to unite and oversee a spatially and administratively complex nation.

Thus the fugitive was valuable to Hoover in his moment, but the lam remains a useful cultural text to police today for other reasons. The criminal on the lam is particularly subject to representational mediation. After the event of crime precipitates the hunt for a culprit, and public concern and police information makes that apprehensive effort social as well, the police supply representations and narratives that stand in for the absent fugitive during his or her flight: identification orders, the "wanted" notices that festoon post office walls (and, more recently, the television and Internet); recountings of the crime; estimates of the fugitive's whereabouts, motives, associates, accomplices, and other criminal activity; warnings and precautions; solicitation of leads; news of sightings, encounters, or arrest; and, finally, reconstructions posed after apprehension, surrender, or death.

Via this discursive control, police not only shape cultural and legal reception of the manhunt but also influence the formation of myth. Richard Slotkin explains the role of myth succinctly: myth "expresses ideology in a narrative, rather than discursive or argumentative, structure," thus dodging critical analysis and naturalizing its ideological content (6). Recent scholarship has explored criminal narratives as a site for the production of social meaning; in *Inventing the Public Enemy: The Gangster in American Culture, 1918–1934*, David E. Ruth demonstrates the urban gangster figure's utility as a "vessel" through which Americans experienced new models of consumption and masculinity. Whereas Ruth moves from sociology and popular representations to Al Capone, positioned ambiguously between "cultural invention" and "flesh and blood," Claire Bond Potter's *War on Crime: Bandits, G-Men, and the Politics of Mass Culture* focuses on the superstructural "politics of myth and symbol" that aided the creation of the modern FBI. Linking the "production" of celebrity criminals to the "worship of data and information" and the privileging of penal punishment over social reform, she demonstrates that "confrontations between the G-man and the bandit . . . became arenas for articulating nationalist narratives about the benefits of an interventionist state" (4, 199). *On the Lam* discusses the fugitive similarly, as a figure whose irruption provides a dramatic stage on which the nation is continually reimagined and consensus around the meaning of law is recruited.

This meaning is also contested. Even as it enables police production of the fugitive, the lam's spotlighted absence also conduces to other mythic readings. Claire Bond Potter describes how the dearth of verifiable evidence (and the highly mediated nature of what little has survived) problematizes scholarly efforts to find solid ground in discussions of 1930s Texas outlaw Bonnie Parker. Potter writes, "Once Bonnie joined Clyde [Barrow] as a fugitive, she became an enemy of the state. She and Clyde exited the institutions and community structures that make it possible for historians to know an individual through documentary evidence. Thus, it becomes difficult to tell their story as more than a morality tale or a romantic tragedy" (91).

Certain historical circumstances and settings conduce to oppositional readings of the criminal. Eric Hobsbawm elucidates the figure of the social bandit, an oppositional hero designated out of the raw materials of violence or robbery when "a peasant society which knows of no better means of self-defence is in a condition of abnormal tension and disruption" (*Primitive* 5). One such bandit is Robin Hood; another sprawling legend has grown around American bandit Billy the Kid, who since his death has become "a flexible container" for mythic production, writes Stephen Tatum (11).

On the Lam details Hoover's efforts to circumscribe these mythic possibilities and gain control of what Hobsbawm calls the "few empty spaces of 'outback' or 'west.' . . . a spiritual Indian territory" that links an urban culture to a "sometimes imaginary heroic past" (*Bandits* 142). Chapters 1 and 3 discuss two fugitives, Robert Elliott Burns and John Dillinger, around whose lams a defiant romantic mythos was devised. Burns's effective defense of his flight from a Georgia chain gang depended upon the regional difference and the resultant instabilities in the cultural meaning of law that existed before Roosevelt and Hoover's initiatives. Dillinger, whose state-hopping 1934 lam Hoover used as evidence of the need to empower a national police, was mythologized by some as an emblem of local resistance to federal power.

Chapter 4 discusses a set of films that imagine flight in a networked nation. *They Live by Night, White Heat,* and *Gun Crazy,* all films noir made in 1948 or 1949, reflect a national surveillance capability designed to counter the mobility and anonymity of an increasingly motorized populace and to bear witness to the success of Hoover's postwar rearticulations of police and criminality. Finally, chapter 5 compares the perspectives of Richard Wright and Ralph Ellison on surveillance and flight, tracing a historical narrative that connects the black American's "place"—or lack of it—to the policing of slave geography in the antebellum South.

The slave narrative bookends this examination of twentieth-century texts. It is the form Burns invoked in framing his white flight narrative against the rule of Georgian law; in *Invisible Man,* the narrator's repression of the slave narrative's relevance impedes his responding realistically and sustainably to his cultural predicament, I argue. While many critics have recognized the fugitive slave narrative as a "canonical text," shaping African-American literary form, to echo Robert B. Stepto's assessment (ix), I argue that the slave narrative also functions as the crucial precursor to modern lam stories, prefiguring their tactics of flight, their strategies of surveillance, and to some degree their narrative structure. Furthermore, the light these two forms shed on each other illuminates the implications of criminality within the racial coding of American mobility: the degree to which traces of antebellum Southern constriction of black travel have persisted vis-à-vis the transparent yet profound privilege of the white traveler.

In the modern fugitive story, to go on the lam is to accept the possibility of never going home again. Seeking the holes, empty spaces, or borders of civil society, these fugitives also lose the other social designations that have marked and supported them. Through aliases, they discard their names; through flight, they abandon their homes. To cover their trails, they abandon (or murder) their spouses. They cannot practice their professions, or they have professions barely worth practicing. Yet despite Ralph Ellison's suggestion that the fugitive manages to endure on the borders of society by "running and dodging the forces of history" (441), this study finds fugitive stories to be intimately concerned with human and historical issues, commenting upon matters of gender, race, economy, sexuality, nation, work, and discipline. Fugitives are among the "transitory ones" Ellison's Invisible Man perceived in the subway, yet their flights chart enduring geographies of the American self's hinterlands and hiding places.

on the lam

1. robert elliott burns

The Slave Narrative's Pale Ghost

Drifting through Georgia in 1922, a shell-shocked veteran hitting rock bottom, "flat broke" and "disgusted with life," Robert Elliott Burns aided two threatening strangers in a grocery store stickup. The three armed robbers netted all of $5.80; arrested within the hour, each was sentenced to a term of hard labor. Burns got six to ten years. He was shipped to the Fulton County chain gang and fitted with shackles; at that time Georgia had no state penitentiary, and incarceration meant one was leased to chain gangs for long days of work in the blazing sun. After a few months on the gang, Burns cajoled a fellow convict into bending his ankle shackles with blows from a sledgehammer, risking not only punishment but a crippling injury. His gamble paid off: finding that the misshapen rings would slip off his ankles, he slipped away from the gang alone and ran, by his estimation, twenty-seven miles before flagging down a ride and then taking a train toward Tennessee.

I'm going to go get my money back with a lawsuit, like everyone in a civilized world.

—F. Lee Bailey, sentenced to a Florida jail for contempt of court, 1996

Burns landed in Chicago, his postwar malaise behind him. He began as a day laborer, then refurbished and leased apartments and founded the business magazine *Greater Chicago*. By 1929 he became a businessman of some note; however, the woman he had married and then divorced in Chicago betrayed him to the Georgia authorities, who demanded his arrest and filed to extradite him. Burns considered battling for his freedom in the Illinois courts but, promised an easy assignment, a pardon, and a quick release if he returned voluntarily to Georgia, he surrendered. To his horror, Georgia prison officials soon relocated him to the worst gang in the state, and it became quickly apparent that the deal was a sham.

After a hopeless year on the gang and the agonizing denial of his prison commission appeal, a desperate Burns escaped again, bribing a passerby and fleeing in the back of an automobile. With an enraged Georgia on his tail, he turned to a more mobile profession, writing.

In hiding, he wrote a serial account of his experiences which ran in *True Detective Mysteries* throughout 1931. The narrative was collected as *I Am a Fugitive from a Georgia Chain Gang!* and published in January 1932.

A mélange of biography, thriller, polemic, amateur regional sociology, and patriotic tract, *I Am a Fugitive* is a remarkable story and a remarkable rhetorical project. Uncommon is the criminal who takes the reins of authoring his own story. Even more so is the fugitive who manages, even while running, to become master of his own narrative, drowning out legal categorizations with his own justifications of his crime, his flight, and his defiance of law.

What is most surprising today, perhaps, about Burns's task is how successful he was. The book's most prominent reviews were positive and, more importantly, sympathetic: "The American public has been horrified by accounts in newspapers, magazines and books of the antiquated and inhuman methods employed by the State of Georgia in the management of convicted criminals," wrote the *New York Times Book Review* ("A Fugitive," 4). New Jersey's director of prison parole, Winthrop D. Lane, published two reviews commending the book and seconding its indictment of Southern penal practice, and the *Times Literary Supplement* chimed in warmly from London ("Sociology" 740).

Burns gained further vindication when his story was remade as a highly successful Warner Brothers motion picture starring Paul Muni, fresh from his triumph in *Scarface*. Burns traveled secretly to California to serve as a consultant to the Mervyn LeRoy–directed film, and he impressed its star deeply: according to the film's contemporary MGM/UA videotape packaging, Muni told Burns, "I don't want to imitate you, I want to be you." Released later in 1932, the film, *I Am a Fugitive from a Chain Gang!* was nominated for best picture and best actor Academy Awards; it won the National Board of Review's annual award for best picture. Its moody scenes and noirish closing have been praised by film critics, beginning, perhaps, with its 1939 identification as "an outstanding example of a social documentary film" by New York's Museum of Modern Art (V. G. Burns 322).

Politically as well, Burns seemed to hit his marks. He'd managed through his business success and personal energy to make influential connections in Chicago, and his 1929 arrest triggered the sending of "hundreds of letters and telegrams" to Illinois Governor Louis L. Emmerson. The list of supporters sending letters of introduction to his Georgia prison hearing included Franklin D. Roosevelt, Calvin Coolidge, New Jersey Governor Morgan F. Larson, and numerous other elected officials and business executives—even golf hero and Atlantan Bobby Jones. Though his suit failed, Burns's second escape took him to Newark, New Jersey, where in December 1932, with his book on the stands and his film in theaters, he was arrested again. Yet New Jersey Governor A. Harry Moore denied Georgia's extradition appeal in a dramatic December 21 hearing in the Trenton state assembly building attended by perhaps a thousand spectators. Representatives of the American Civil Liberties Union and the National Society of Penal Information testified on Burns's behalf, and Moore granted Burns effective asylum in New Jersey. Georgia remained adamant that Burns return; it was not until 1943, when Burns met with reformist Georgia Governor Ellis Arnall in New York City, that the end of his fugitive trail came into sight. In 1945, Burns surrendered to Georgia one last time for a trial in which his sentence was commuted to time already served. A full pardon for his crime was never granted.

Certainly Burns owed a measure of his success to his moment, when the projects of mapping the South in socioeconomic and cultural terms had pronounced Southern difference at the same time that H. L. Mencken's jeremiads and a steady stream of Southern prison scandals denounced it. As early as 1923, for example, *New York World* readers were scandalized by a hugely popular series of articles on the whipping death of North Dakotan Martin Tabert in the Florida work camp where he was atoning his train-hopping arrest (Tindall, *Emergence* 213). Features on Southern prison conditions ran regularly in the *Times*, though the charge was also leveled that Northern prisons were little better. Burns wrote to an audience ready, then, to hear the protest of an inmate against the system—particularly the South's system.

On the other hand, I would argue, Burns's story came at a moment when the public notions of crime and the criminal were shifting away from Prohibition's tolerance and tempered admiration toward more rigid, categorical vilification. As I discuss at more length in the next chapter, the 1930s arrived under a widespread cultural assumption— based more on hysteria, xenophobia, and a few high-profile crimes than any broadly representative statistic—that crime was threatening the everyday as never before. The year 1931 saw a peak in the production of violent gangster films, sparking outcry from church and police groups and spurring an era of self-censorship in the film industry.

Though it was published in 1932, at the height of the supposed "crime panic," I would posit that Burns's book succeeds in great part because it uses the lever of regional difference to upend definitions of crime and lawfulness, successfully identifying Burns as a fugitive from *injustice*. Burns works skillfully upon an audience and a form whose political might had reached an apex nearly a century earlier: the abolitionist North and its hunger for the narratives of runaway slaves.

Burns was no slave. He was white, a Brooklyn-raised Catholic of Irish extraction who'd attended New York public schools. Yet he faced a daunting, complex rhetorical situation: he was forced to plead his case against Georgia even as he admitted his original culpability and, furthermore, was forced to do so from hiding. Fighting out of this corner, the slave narrative presented him both a rich template and myth and a numerous, potent audience.

Reading any substantial number of slave narratives confirms the genre's commonplaces. "So similar was the structure of these narratives," writes Henry Louis Gates Jr., "that it sometimes seems to the modern reader that the slave authors were tracing a shared pattern, and then cutting that pattern from similar pieces of cloth. There can be little doubt that, when the ex-slave author decided to write his or her story, he or she did so only after reading, and rereading, the telling stories of other slave authors who preceded them" (*Classic Slave Narratives* x). Noting the "confining and two-dimensional" narrative pattern of the genre, Sterling Lecater Bland Jr. asserts the importance of the individual author's intent even within the broad social purposes proposed by genre; to read a slave narrative as an unartful, transparent account, unmediated by literary or rhetorical ambition and design, ignores or diminishes the self-authorization inherent in the narrative's writing, Bland insists (5, xiv–xv). The tendency to oversimplify the rhetorical ends and compositional subtleties of the slave narrator, attributing the texts instead to documentary impulse and a blunt polemical intent, may in fact root historically in antebellum racist skepticism about the very possibility of black literacy. William L. Andrews writes that even for Northerners, it was difficult to accept the notion that an author could spring from a race kept illiterate. The appearance of authenticity was a chief concern for authors and publishers of slave narratives (Andrews 2).

Burns's rhetorical position is as difficult. Because his book's form is autobiographical and some of his cliff-hanging chapters are successful as thrillers, he would seem at liberty to fashion and edit his tale. But because Burns presents the book as the "true story" of his "entire case" (6), an exhibit in a public debate, his narratorial credibility is essential, not only to representational questions but to legal ones. Yet his convict status compromises his ethos, and he cannot present his own best evidence—his reputation in today's community, his activities and companions of today—because of his ongoing need to evade arrest. Not only cannot he appear impartial; he cannot appear. Such is the paradoxical lot of the fugitive author: as he sought to regain his name, Burns worked menial jobs under an assumed identity.

For both slave authors and Burns, whose literary audiences doubled as potential defenders, questions of ethos were central. Slave authors' stories were conventionally introduced with testimonial corroborations of the author's character, eloquence, and literary will. Burns elicits an introduction from his own brother, Catholic Reverend Vincent

G. Burns. Reverend Burns affirms the book's veracity and his brother's character over a 28-page introduction (in his introduction to the 1997 edition, Matthew J. Mancini argues that Vincent Burns in fact authored the book in toto, xxi). The reverend's preface confirms through direct observation both his brother's specific incarceration and the generalized misery of the Southern bondsman, invoking the political sweep that underlay the narratives of individual slaves. In his introduction, Burns envisions *I Am a Fugitive* as a catalyst for reform, for "a wave of great indignation. . . . the public, once vividly conscious of the horrors and brutalities of chain-gang life, will rise in its wrath and force a clean-up" (35). Naming many famous supporters, including Carl Sandburg and Jane Addams, the Reverend Burns frames his brother as a patriot, possessed of "those qualities of courage, perseverance, industry, and honesty which lie close to the bed-rock of American life" (14). He also evokes the slave-narrative convention of the breakup of family with a sentimental portrait of the brothers' mother grieving over her son in chains.

A second motif of the slave jeremiad is the representation of slaves' injured humanity in "the hands of an inhumane system" (Andrews 15). "The gross wrong, fraud, and inhumanity of slavery," particularly his breaking by Mr. Covey, transforms the young Frederick Douglass "into a brute"; it is his discovery of physical defiance, in fact, that demonstrates "how a slave was made a man" (293–301). Leonard Black's 1847 account exemplifies such arguments:

> Slavery is a cruel system. The effects of it are scattered abroad throughout the land. It is the reigning evil of the country; yea, the mother of all evil. Why is it the mother of all evil? I answer in the language of Holy Writ, which saith, "Do unto all men as you would have them do unto you." It is not done. Again: "Love thy neighbor as thyself. This is the law and the prophets." It is not done. Reader,—where is the slaveholder who would wish his slaves to do to him as he does to them? There are none. Hence, then, the enormity of the evil.
>
> Dear reader: understand one thing. The slaves are taught ignorance as we teach our children knowledge. They are kept in darkness, and are borne

down under a cruel, cruel oppression! All human rights are denied them as citizens! They are not recognized as men! My old master frequently said, "he did not believe a d———d nigger had any soul!" They are made to undergo everything as a beast. Having a full, perfect, undeniable right to stand out before God as MEN, the cruel, God-defying white man, without semblance of right, with no pretence but might, has prostituted them to the base purpose of his cupidity, and his baser beastly passions, reducing them to mere things, mere chattels, to be bought and sold like hogs and sheep! (50–51)

Black, free in Massachusetts, underlines the condition of a freedman with his pronouns. It is Northern whites with whom he groups himself as "we," and souls still in slavery are "they" and "them." Invoking the Bible and demonstrating the hypocrisy of Christianity at once provides a proof for Northern readers and subordinates the condition of slave law to a higher authority, that of holy writ.

Burns makes explicit and vehement his comparison between slave-holding and prisons: "The chain gang is simply a vicious, medieval custom, inherited from the blackbirders and slave traders of the seventeenth and eighteenth centuries, and is so archaic and barbarous as to be a national disgrace" (57). "Prisoners and the slaves have always attempted to escape," he writes. "The battle has gone on for thousands of years. It will go on for thousands of years to come" (162). He postmarks the comparison for Northern consumption by insisting upon the Southernness of life on the gang and characterizing it as anachronistic and brutal, trading heavily in what George B. Tindall has called "the neo-abolitionist image of the benighted South" ("Benighted South," 281–94). The miserable gang food is identifiably Southern in character and is crudely made—"very bad coffee, a piece of hoe cake or fried dough, made of grease and white flour; and three small pieces of fried pork sides." Just to further sectionalize his distaste, Burns identifies sorghum as "Georgian." For dinner, each convict is given boiled, dried cowpeas, "not eaten anywhere else but in Georgia," Burns claims. He says, "They were unpalatable, full of sand and worms. . . . The corn pone was heavy, bitter, and also very unpalatable. And needless to say, the whole arrangement was unsanitary, and filthy" (52).

The unbearable filth of the gang is compounded by the presence of impoverished or archaic means of cleaning. "There were three tin basins for one hundred men to wash in—there were no towels—any old piece of cloth or an old bag was pressed into service by the few who did get time to wash," he notes of his first stay on the gang (52). Fulton County sleeping quarters feature "an iron cot, a dirty mattress, a still dirtier pillow, and a filthy blanket" (53); in Campbell County, the dirty bedding is decayed, "full of vermin" (59). By his return in 1929, conditions in Troup County have worsened: "Picture a man being ducked in water, clothes and all, then rolled in the dust while still wet, twice a day for six consecutive days, during which time he had not even washed his hands or changed his clothes, and there you have our condition. . . . the dust from the dirt road upon which we worked would settle on our bodies like frosting on a cake" (173).

Burns blames the gangs' horrid conditions on the "illiterate and coarse and brutal" guards (51), who absorb the first volley of a broad diminution of Georgian intellect and humaneness. Burns invited his Northern readers to imagine not the sentimentalized Dixie of intersectional reunion stories but the spiteful, intransigent, sadistic South of Secession. His mind of the South is slow moving ("like all Southerners," an unlucky barber is "infinitely slow"), "medieval," still vengeful over the Lost Cause, and "overloaded with traditions, sectional prejudices, and stubborn precedents" (193).

Like antebellum overseers whose excessive violence against slaves was punishable only as a crime against property, the guards dole out whippings and other punishments with little or no justification, and convicts' attempts to defend themselves are "drowned out." Whipped men bleed in their bunks without medicine, and convicts are painfully immobilized in the "jack," essentially a set of stocks, without the mandated examination and supervision of a county physician. They are baked in the sweatbox or forced to work with pickshacks attached to their legs.

Denied their state-mandated baths, beaten or tortured nightly, prisoners are "reduced to the same level, just animals," Burns laments (56).

Burns depicts the everyday racism of gang life. Blackboards are posted in gang encampments numbering white and black inmates separately, and Burns credits much of the camps' brutality to racism. Several lengthy anecdotes of exceptional brutality toward African-American prisoners amplify this point. One guard promises one convict to "break this limb on your damn Nigger hide," then beats him unconscious (157); another man, whose crime had been an infraction of Georgia's prohibition law, is routed from his bed and forced to work until he dies of sunstroke (188).

However, a rhetorical purpose runs through Burns's invocations of racism—not so much in his own ambivalent depictions of black prisoners, about which I will say more later, as in his remaking the object of Georgian racism in his own image. He directs the "traditions" of Georgian racism toward a Yankee object, so as to press the point of his polemic between the ribs of his Northern white readers: "Hatred of New York is found in direct expressions made to me by prisoners, guards, and free citizens while I was in Georgia, but I am not going to go into this further here because I believe it would only serve to stir up hatred. General accusations against me, and referring to all Northerners as well, were of an unprintable nature," he declares (196). Accounting for Southern bigotry against Northern whites, Burns conjectures that some of the depredations of Sherman's march to the sea "left scars on the hearts of these people. . . . this subconscious feeling is still struggling for expression" (196–97), and he warns, "If you were to visit Georgia and were arrested, accused of some violation of the law, the first question the Judge would ask you would be: 'Where do you come from?' and the next, 'What church do you go to?' If the answers to these questions brought out the fact that you were a Northern Catholic or a Jew, you would be in need of help" (197).

In such passages, Burns exacerbates the implied lawlessness of Georgian law by tossing in a broad-based religious intolerance sure to draw Northern notice. But more subtly, he characterizes a Southerner who is all "heart," full of "subconscious feeling" that Southern eloquence struggles to but cannot express. Thus the enigmatic Southerner becomes a proper object for Yankee intervention, for inquiry and analysis. The above passage, Burns's lengthiest discourse on the South, is prefaced by a statement of methodology which apes the discourse of anthropological inquiry. In analyzing the mind of the South, he clumsily stresses his ability to elaborate his own thinking process: "These doubts originated in my subconscious mind, and were supported by my mental analysis of the forces aligned against me and my surroundings" (193). Using his brain, not his heart, the Northern author works the South like a marionette upon strings of "inexplicability" and conjecture.

To support his condemnation of Georgian legal practice, Burns records the statements of ostensibly impartial lawmen. The baldest Yankee condemnation is voiced by Judge David of the Illinois Supreme Court: "Georgia—the Great State of Georgia—the home and birthplace of that vicious organization, the Ku Klux Klan. Where they sell the water of the Chattahoochee River at five dollars per gallon to baptize the ignorant and illiterate, that they may be initiated into the wonders of the Klan, and so continue their holy and Christian persecution of the Jew, the Catholic, and the Negro; and become acquainted with the fine art of lynching and midnight beatings and terrorism" (111–12).

If the judge's facts are shaky—generally the Klan is agreed to have formed around Pulaski, Tennessee—his Menckenian tone sympathizes with Burns's conflation of Southern law and vicious bigotry. Northern law's opposition to Georgia's prosecution is further established by the presence of lawyers and district attorneys among the figures writing letters for Burns's release in 1930.

It is Southern lawmen, however, who nail down Burns's point. His Georgia counsel is William Schley Howard, "the most powerful political figure and the ablest attorney in the State of Georgia" (124). But, as Howard makes clear, a capable legal defense provides no hedge against rampant corruption: "You are now in Georgia and things will have to be handled from the Georgia viewpoint" (133–34). Howard arranges $500 bribes to each prison commissioner to guarantee favorable handling of Burns's appeal. (Swallowing any distaste he felt, Burns calls these "gratuities"; the term spares him participation in a criminal act and casts him as the dominant partner in a relationship of service.)

Burns fashions practical criticisms of the appalling conditions and racist, counterproductive administration of chain gangs; in complaining of "many other violations of the state laws" in Troup County, he also demonstrates convict leasing's nominal and moral illegality. Thus he builds a case for sweeping penal reform in the South, playing to reform-minded readers such as John Spivak, author of *Georgia Nigger*, who testified on Burns's behalf at his December 21, 1932, extradition hearing.

Burns's personal objectives, however, could not be satisfied with mere prison reform. Understandably, writing after years of freedom and success in the North—his first escape freed him from 1922 to 1929, and his New Jersey residence had begun shortly after his 1930 escape—Burns shows little interest in returning to serve out his sentence in even a reformed and humane Southern penal system. So he seeks to justify his own freedom, despite his having committed and been convicted of a crime. In order to do so, Burns reinterprets the notion of penal justice away from punishment (which he terms "revenge") and toward correction.

But he takes it a step further. Having demeaned the authority of Georgian penal practice, Burns redirects readers' notions of *law* away from specifically legal definitions and toward the ostensible justice and manly individualism inherent in the industrial economy of the North. To do so benefits him doubly: it diminishes the juridical standard by which his record is tainted, and it proposes a new yardstick—putatively Northern in character—by which he has already proven himself.

Frederick Douglass recollects his arrival in New Bedford as an impressive display of the cultural and economic power of the North:

> I visited the wharves, to take a view of the shipping. Here I found myself surrounded with the strongest proofs of wealth. Lying at the wharves, and

riding in the stream, I saw many ships of the finest model, in the best order, and of the largest size. Upon the right and left, I was walled in by granite warehouses of the widest dimensions, stowed to their utmost capacity with the necessaries and comforts of life. Added to this, almost every body seemed to be at work, but noiselessly so, compared with what I had been accustomed to in Baltimore. There were no loud songs heard from those engaged in loading and unloading ships. I heard no deep oaths or horrid curses on the laborer. I saw no whipping of men; but all seemed to go smoothly on. Every man seemed to understand his work, and went at it with a sober, yet cheerful earnestness, which betokened the deep interest which he felt in what he was doing, as well as a sense of his own dignity as a man. To me this looked exceedingly strange. From the wharves I strolled around and over the town, gazing with wonder and admiration at the splendid churches, beautiful dwellings, and finely-cultivated gardens; evincing an amount of wealth, comfort, taste, and refinement, such as I had never seen in any part of slaveholding Maryland.

Everything looked clean, new, and beautiful. . . . The people looked more able, stronger, healthier, and happier, than those of Maryland. (323–24)

This revelatory passage correlates a labor force without slaves with multiple benefits: wealth, order, discipline, pleasure, beauty, and an individual laborer who is at once productive, well informed, and healthy. Douglass's cityscape follows close on the heels of his descriptions of slavery, but twice here he makes the contrast between Massachusetts and Maryland explicit. And the elevation in the station of the individual worker here benefits the employer and the city as a whole. Douglass sought work at once and sang the praises of a labor system that rewarded his diligence: "I found employment the third day after my arrival, in stowing a sloop with a load of oil. It was new, dirty, and hard work for me, but I went at it with a glad heart and a willing hand. I was now my own master. It was a happy moment, the rapture of which can be understood only by those who have been slaves" (324–25).

Burns effects a similar contrast between Georgia's visceral dirtiness and the conditions he experiences—working in a stockyard, no less—upon his escape to the North. At a wage of $3.20 a day, which two years earlier he had derided as "wage slavery—drudgery," Burns finds a hygienic reprieve from Georgia, even in coal-fogged, train-choked Chicago. Hand in hand with this cleanliness goes its intellectual and social stimulation—"$3.20 a day was all that any man could want. It meant a clean bed, clean clothes, soap and towels, clean teeth, recreational movies, books, libraries, lectures, walks through beautiful parks, museums, and the exhilaration of a great, growing, bustling city roaring all around, interesting and congenial people, things to see and do. In short, Life!" (83)

Thus many of the virtues of Northern wage earning specifically remedy Burns's complaints about chain-gang conditions. Not surprisingly, the hygienic and cultural superiority of Chicago is undergirded by its "growing, bustling" economy. Burns exemplifies William R. Taylor's Yankee archetype (Taylor 48): Burns sings the praises of Northern thought and action, of science and progress, and of the entrepreneurial principle that hard work can raise an individual to the top of society. (These contrast with what he represents of the Southern economy— chiefly blue-collar haunts such as farms, barbershops, and bus stations, as well as the thoroughly corrupt courts.)

Burns locates his redemption as a lawful citizen at the terminus of his first lam, in the commercial and civic spheres of Chicago. But it is as much his redemption as a *man*: his remembrance of the years between his return from Europe and his participation in the 1922 robbery evinces a deep emasculatory crisis. His "beautiful girl" had "married a war-time officer with a 'Sam Browne' belt." He loses his old job and can only get entry-level work, dismally inferior to "the wise guys [who] stayed home—landed the good jobs—or grew rich on war contracts" (38). Burns's protests come in terms that betray a petulant conviction that veterans should represent an elect class, a sort of battle-forged aristocracy: "We, who after all the ballyhoo is over, should get the most of our victory—we find we're only suckers, and get handed an existence instead of a competence" (39). To paint the category of veterans to which he belongs as "suckers"—connotative of fools, infants, parasites, or homosexuals—betrays the sense of deviance his initial failure provokes in him. More importantly, in so complaining, he accepts a passive role in defining his social place, which he sees "handed" to him, like a bonus or a discharge—an expectation which clashes with the mythos of self-interested competition that built and still runs the Northeastern economy into which he seeks to return.

Bitter, Burns begins to act upon his perceptions of deviance, forsaking social place as he moves to self-definition as an outcast. "I became a hobo," he explains, "just drifting along and around—here, there, anywhere—watching the world pass by, without taking any really active part in its march across the pages of time" (39). Fitfully conflating his lost romantic, vocational, and social places, Burns runs paranoid. He equates occupying one's proper (economic, social) place in the march with being active, worklike, with the activity of the industrial laborer; his postwar transit ends thus, collapsing into sour grapes at the feet of the progressive industrial economy, "watching the world pass by."

This abjuration of economic and social place soon snowballs, however, into a full-blown crisis of manliness. In the title of the book's first chapter, "The War Makes a Wanderer," Burns alludes to his descent into transiency. But his behavior before and during the 1922 robbery plays upon a second sense of "Wanderer," a self-coined nickname he mentions several times: on his travels, he is rudderless, without energy or convictions, incapable of making decisions. When he meets the men who will coerce him into robbery, he wonders "what it was all about" but allows food and comfort to take precedence over comprehending their proposal. "Let to-morrow take care of itself," he sighs (40). The narrator apologizes for the wanderer's weakness but externalizes its cause: "My morale had not been strengthened by my war experiences or my treatment when I got back" (44).

In the Atlanta robbery scene, Burns's passivity results in a harrowing demasculinization. As Flagg, the stickup's leader, proposes the crime, he suggests his own masculine potency and the feminizing humiliation that might meet Burns's refusal: "I got the rod in my pocket and I'll plug you if you try anything funny, see?" (44). At this, Burns folds down the middle: "Flagg won; and the Burns that was, lost," he mourns, explicitly gendering the moral, active self and the passive wanderer: "I might just as well be shot for a goose or a gander" (44).

Unmanned, Burns's perceptions become unreal; his experience of male lack triggers what Kaja Silverman calls "a loss of faith in the familiar and self-evident" (53). He goes through the inept stickup like a zombie: motions and objects seem unfamiliar to him, and he and the mute Moore move in a parody of impotence and homosexuality, while the hypermasculine Flagg, holding a gun, is a deadly penetrative force endangering them all: "Flagg covered the proprietor with his gun— Moore got to the cash register but couldn't open it. In a trance I walked toward the proprietor, who now had his hands above his head. Somehow I got through the process of feeling his pants pockets for the supposed roll. I was like one in a dream. I couldn't find a thing, and there I stood, between Flagg and the owner, right in the line of fire, should Flagg pull the trigger" (44).

Humiliating as it may be, this rift in Burns's character hedges his bets, casting him as pitiable, a victim of "Destiny and Circumstance." The victimization defense occurs to him quickly: at the sentencing hearing following his arrest, he claims a "mental attitude caused by the results of my treatment by society after my discharge from the war service" as a mitigating factor (46). In *I Am a Fugitive*, however, his defense strategy revolves around the vivid contrast between the weak drifter of 1922 and the energetic editor he became; Burns questions the applicability of that 1922 criminal record to the "reformed" individual of subsequent years. Devaluing his (criminal) record makes the "Wanderer" nickname and his genderized partitioning of self rhetorically necessary, for the principal argument he will use for his freedom becomes another such "record": his remarkable success in Chicago.

In Chicago between his 1922 escape and 1929, the fugitive Burns became an exemplary American entrepreneur, a business leader with enormous civic interest and commitment. Like Douglass and other slave narrators, he served as an orator for his cause, delivering "an average of five lectures each week" on "the great opportunity Chicago presented to the industrious, courageous, and honest thinker and worker" (93). And the Wanderer is banished: Burns's characterization of his ascent stresses and restresses his agency, dynamicism, and responsibility:

> It had become general knowledge that Burns's word was his bond. My credit was excellent. Banks cheerfully lent me money, which was always repaid on time. Concerns in the printing industry were eager to get my business and extend credit. I became a member of the Chicago Association of Commerce and also of the Chicago Real Estate Board.
>
> I stood for clean politics and clean business. I supported every worth-while civic achievement, cultural, charitable, commercial, and industrial. I helped sponsor the World Fair movement, supported it fearlessly and lectured for it often and without compensation of any kind. (93)

"Burns's word was his bond": in a phrase, Burns accomplishes an autocratic substitution, replacing Georgia's penal authority with his own ability to put himself into debt within the world of trade. Banks and creditors confirm his power of self-governance, and his civic activism and selfless contributions place him, within this balance sheet of socioeconomic value, in the black.

Yet his recovery from demasculinized criminal drifter to manly business leader suffers one notable relapse. In Chicago after his escape, Burns meets another unpleasant encumbrance: a wife. Emily Del Pino Pacheo, a once-divorced dinner waitress, takes him as boarder and soon as lover and husband (her second, he notes). Burns mystifies the "strange unknown power" that drives him toward Emily: "Now, here comes destiny again! What part did Fate have in causing me to turn into Ingleside Avenue, looking for a room? And why did I stop at 6444 Ingleside Avenue where a small sign read, 'Rooms to Let'?" (83). "Not being interested in any other woman, I accepted her with perhaps more than passing interest," he admits. "She admired me, looked up to me, believed in me. To her I was husband, lover and son" (85). Burns's syntactical passivity seems intended to reflect his disinterest in Emily, who, by contrast, is full of "tigerish ferocity" and "threw herself into the fight" for Burns's heart with "all the charm, power and strength her Latin temperament could muster" (85–86). But such passivity has meant trouble for Burns before. He seems to realize that his lingering with Emily presents a caveat to his commanding Northern identity. Emily links him doubly to his wanderer and criminal self: she alone in Chicago knows the truth, and by threatening to expose him if he should leave her, she pins him in the passive position of what he insists is an unwanted relationship. He despairs, "She knew my secret. My God! Must that ghost of the past always rise up before me; would it haunt me the rest of my days? Time was pressing and I needed a clear head for the day's activities" (91). Burns's resistance to Emily invokes "time," with its compulsion of "activity" and clear-headedness: the past becomes ghostly, unreal, horrible—like the chain gang in its horror. His liaison with Emily complicates his new, manly "record": he is constrained by his guilt, by an alliance he despises, and by a *woman*.

But for a time Burns represses the crisis by foregrounding the entrepreneurial aspects of their relationship over its sexual dimension—in effect, splitting the definition of marriage as he has done with the nation and himself. He cannot omit Emily from his narrative, for she will become his betrayer, but "living in sin" with her presents a representational dilemma. By 1925 she lives with him "as though she were my wife," he explains; "This you will please understand was not objectionable to me, but was absolutely voluntary on her part" (88). The illogically conjoined clauses suggest his dilemma: the record-building entrepreneur must not seem *too* helpless against Emily but at the same time must guard against the potential objection that he took advantage of a divorcée in order to shield his fugitive status. And if his unmanly lack of sexual agency or enthusiasm connotes a return to his wanderer persona, Burns counters with a dogged attention to *business* and an unremitting exactitude with financial (rather than feminine) figures—and the skill and effort he puts into them. The minutiae of their apartment-renting business is related so as to demonstrate his skill and Emily's lack of "business ability or shrewdness"; a deal she makes is "ridiculous" (89).

The apotheosis of his transformation of marriage into business is his separation and divorce from Emily. In this, ostensibly a final disentanglement from his passive, shameful self, he defines carefully the bonds that have tied him to her. "True, legally I was her husband, but morally I was not," he protests (95). Belittling an Illinois marriage certificate might trouble his simple privileging of Northern law over Southern, but in this analysis we also glimpse that his adherence to Yankee law is based not so much on its letter but its moral—and economic—spirit. His recounting of the events of the breakup paper over the legal and ethical ugliness of the divorce with a competing morality built upon square dealing, a fidelity that manifests itself in economic terms: "Her demands became so alarming that I left her home at 6444 and went to live at the Morrison Hotel. . . . I had been paying her back on the installment plan and had paid her about $500 at the time" (90–91).

If Emily is Burns's surrogate jailer, like the South in her "insane hatred" and administrative mediocrity, Burns seems appalled that she, like Georgia, resists the prospect of his "buying out." "Argument, logic, common sense, nothing moved her," he groans (91). But when he meets Lillian Salo and "love" forces him to leave Emily, he implies that her very life is owed to him in economic terms. Whereas in Georgia, during his second internment, he will later attempt to "buy out," here he argues that he has turned the tables of blackmail and debt. He has purchased *her*, he insinuates. "I found her in the cheapest ward," Burns writes, "dying from a major operation for rupture. If I had been wicked, a menace to society, a criminal, I would have left her to die. My secret would have been safe, and I would have been free from a tigerish, selfish, nagging woman who made life miserable for me. At this time, November, 1928, I had paid back every penny that was due her, and a great deal more. In fact, she had received almost $9,000 from me." "I visited her every day—brought flowers and fruits—and by prompt action on my party and the care I ordered and paid for, saved her life," he adds (96). When he and Emily demand vastly different alimony awards, Burns notes with satisfaction that the judge awards Emily even less than he had offered—his vindication.

He seems not to perceive the cruelty of bilking his ex-wife; the business of dealing with Emily is strictly business. "These pending legal actions were burdensome and troublesome," he reports dispassionately, "but I discarded them each evening as one takes off an office coat, when I went home to Lillian and our love nest" (105). Emily is a rogue stockholder, a mere legal affair, whereas the logic and power of an ideology that measures manliness by economic success allows—even encourages—him to live with Lillian out of wedlock, before the divorce, without a hint of moral "burden" or "trouble." He is simply asserting entrepreneurial initiative—opening a new agency, so to speak.

The complex enclosure Burns constructs around his Chicago self—involving masculine agency, a law that is economically motivated, and progress while divorcing passivity, Georgian "rules," and "that ghost of the past"—coalesces in the enclosure of his "private inner office," a sort of vaginal holding area for the publisher at the height of his potency. He cajoles Emily to divorce him and then makes her swear on the traditional icons that *she* worships—"the rosary beads of her religion"—to honor the divorce "and *not* to expose" him (101). Her betrayal—reporting him to Georgia authorities the same day she contracts not to—surfaces later. "Without waiting to be announced, she rushed into my private inner office, and leaving the door open, shrieked at the top of her voice, 'God damn you! I'm going to destroy you, or kill you!'" "The whole office force heard this tirade and was astonished," the publisher mourns paternalistically (101); his ex-partner/ex-wife is supposed to *wait* to be announced. Her grief, too, is subject to the Yankee commercial logic that Burns adopts as law.

The narration of Burns's two escapes from the gang yields the book's most thrilling moments. Contrasting the two escapes, however, one sees his second lam as a demonstration of his reform and mastery of Northern codes of commerce as well as an argument—even as he flees an armed camp—for his continued freedom.

Burns's 1922 escape depends on daring and perseverance: he runs away from shotgun fire and runs from late morning till five in the afternoon without a break. But in his northward passage, Burns also depends upon a series of favors and windfalls. First, there is "Sam," the black laborer, extraordinarily skilled with the 12-pound sledgehammer, who bends Burns's shackles against a railroad tie. Sam risks detection by guards as he helps Burns, but after his two pages of action and a cursory "Thanks, Sam," he is not spoken of again.

Other debts are incurred on his first run. To replace his gang "stripes," he steals a pair of overalls and a shirt from a clothesline at "a Negro shanty," probably a sharecropper's home (68–69). He accepts a ride and a ripe peach from "a young man in a Ford coupé" (69–70). And, bearing the few dollars he has from what his family has sent him, he seeks refuge in a cheap hotel, where, by coincidence, the clerk is a former gang mate of his. Burns shows his good character in this scene, refusing "whiskey or dope" and the affections of a pair of "broads" his friend produces. But he does accept a night's stay in his friend's room, and one of the two women tries to forge an alliance: "'Gee,' she said, 'you're what I call a real guy. I wish I could hook up with some man with guts like you, get out of this damn racket, and go straight once more. If I help you get out of Atlanta will you take me with you?'" (73) Burns explains the urgency of his flight, but "compromised by telling her that if she would help me and I got through o.k., I would send for her and help her go straight" (74). At this the woman gives him her bankroll, nine dollars, and a card with her name and address. She brings him a hot breakfast the next morning, and at the trolley he promises "to send for her." But the bargain comes to naught: "Alas! I could not keep my promise, for I lost the card with her address before I ever got settled" (75).

No such regrets haunt his second run north. By now Burns is the consummate businessman; his efforts to "buy out" through bribes have gone astray because in Georgia, as his attorney puts it, "there is many a slip twixt the cup and the lip" (133). Seeing his prison appeal denied and the quick release promised him on his extradition from Illinois slipping away, Burns begins putting a second escape plan into place. With money he has secreted in his clothes, he hires a local man to effect his escape from the gang by automobile. Though the Southerner balks twice and requires a greater payment than originally arranged, on the third try, he shows up, and Burns sprints from the gang to the waiting car, to be conveyed to the outskirts of Atlanta.

Throughout the remainder of his flight, Burns accepts no favors as he did in 1922; each interaction is paid in full, each transaction puts his fairness on display. He pays the "infinitely slow" barber (221); he waits fifteen minutes at a tailor's shop for change for a fifty-dollar bill (223); he pays a cashier at Rome, Georgia, soda fountain calmly, though two sheriffs are watching him (228). Most notably, he enlists a "stout buxom young lady about twenty-two years old" as camouflage on a train he takes to Cincinnati; in return for accompanying him off the train and to a hotel, he carries her baggage and chivalrously "leaves her in full possession of the room, allowing her enough time to bathe and change clothes" before she continues on to school in Chicago (235).

In many slave narratives, learning becomes a catalyst for self-discovery or escape. Slaves' acquisition of literacy empowered them to gain a greater understanding of the world that was shut off by slaveholders' injunctions to keep them illiterate; the faculty of reading also aided their escape and later aided those who penned their own accounts. For Frederick Douglass, reading was an illicit joy and a step to self-realization, and the discovery of a principled physical defiance was crucial, he wrote, to regaining "a sense of my own manhood" (298).

In a parallel fashion, the principle of square dealing becomes Burns's lesson and his salvation: it builds his power and record in Chicago, it displays his ethos during his second escape, and its practice supplies a route to freedom. Casting his commercial ethics and practice as a law higher than that of the court, he grounds his condemnation of the South and its penal authority in the scripture of entrepreneurialism.

Southern law is stale, dirty, driven by bigotry; Northern law is contemporary, scientific, driven by economic progress. Accordingly, Burns worries that his second detention in the South will render him obsolete once he returns to the fast-moving Chicago economy, "ignorant of the changes that would have taken place in society while I was in prison." Indeed, the stock market crashed while he was on the gang in 1929, taking what remained of his fortune with it.

The film *I Am a Fugitive from a Chain Gang!* capitalized on the similarities between slave narratives and Burns's story, devising a scene where black and white convicts dressed in stripes break rocks in a quarry, singing spirituals in a stirring quaver. It would be fair to conclude that, no matter how much the rhetoric and plot of his story owed the slave narrative, Burns's treatment of race is more ambivalent. He represents the plight of several much-abused black prisoners with detailed and sympathetic eloquence. However, later anecdotes betray Burns's subscription to stereotypes of the "quiet, simple, easygoing, harmless darkey," "niggers," and "illiterate Negroes" who leave "something in [their] footprints that a bloodhound enjoys" (161). If Burns planned to address his plaint to the remnants of Northern abolitionism, he aimed at their vigilance against Southern brutality rather than their interest in ending racism.

The lack of interest in Sam, his sledge-wielding benefactor in his first escape, suggests Burns's broader difficulties in empathizing with his fellow captors. Whereas escaped slaves looked South with pangs for the relatives and friends they left behind, Burns seems conscious of the delicate nature of his advocacy: those suffering the hardships of the gang are, after all, convicted criminals. Many, like the much-brutalized "Bounce" Murphy, who stole a pint of moonshine to earn his year of servitude, are serving for minor crimes, as Burns makes clear; still, they are convicts, and Burns, having risen from hobo to blue blood in just a few years, hedges his condemnation of the chain-gang system with a rigid resistance to identify with fellow convicts. Two coincidental meetings on New Jersey street corners illustrate: meeting an old acquaintance, a civil engineer who "belonged to the same club," leads to "a fine dinner topped off with good cigars" (247). In contrast, when by an even more outlandish coincidence Burns meets John Moore, the third member of his ill-fated 1922 holdup crew and himself a fugitive from the Fulton County gang, Burns offers a prudish lecture: "Moore, don't ever get in trouble again" (250). Burns limits their niceties to "a hearty handshake and a common knowledge of our common danger" (251). Accordingly, Burns seems reluctant to depict his own bodily agony as a convict, framing his anecdotes around other prisoners or the convicts as a population. Because Burns declines to identify himself as an ex-convict, his portrait of chain-gang life resounds with shudders rather than compassion.

Alex Lichtenstein observes that the outcry over Burns's antigang narrative was "ironic," for he spoke as a businessman only after dedicated social reformers and left-wing writers had tackled the topic (189). Burns had one advantage, however, over other writers: the pathos of having worked on a gang. His legacies are several. Although Mancini argues that Burns had little direct effect on prison reforms—he may have even hardened Georgian opposition to Northern criticism (xx–xxi)—his story, along with John L. Spivak's popular 1932 book *Georgia Nigger*, helped spark Northern concern about reform in the impoverished South on the eve of the New Deal. The extradition face-off that arose between New Jersey and Georgia also gave rise to a prickly exchange on states' rights. And the film of his story, in particular, staged a debate over the penal objectives of punishment and improvement, one that paralleled the rhetorical battle between abolitionists and slaveholders more than a half century earlier. Its memorable closing scene translates the horror of Burns's experience into an explicit denial of normative manhood, as his character greets his lost love from the murky shadows but cannot reclaim his romantic, social, or economic place.

Burns's initial redefinition of "record" did little to prevent Georgia from extraditing him in 1929: however real the expansive triumphs of Northern economics over Southern tradition may have been, the shell game of reconstituting his manhood in narrative did not take interstate extradition agreements out of effect. But his strategies after his second escape, which extend the partition in his self to a national schism, succeeded; three governors refused to allow Burns's extradition from Union, New Jersey. He worked there as a tax consultant—ironically, explaining and enforcing federal policies—until his death in 1955 ("R. E. Burns Dead," 33). Burns's later adherence to federal rule is hardly surprising; his social protest against the legal constraints upon him was driven by a conservatism that defended the very economy that law protects.

Thus it is with a certain irony we must read his revolutionary introduction to his "record of seven years of honest and industrious effort, wherein I gained an honored and creative place in society." "Let me bring out these self-evident truths," he begins this description of his entrepreneurial ascent (94). To so nakedly invoke the Declaration of Independence casts Georgia, Emily, and his wanderer self as King George in triplicate: three tyrannical monarchs imposing *taxation* upon a record that, he claims, is no longer an adequate *representation*. The flourish is an audacious one; imposing borders across his past and his nation, Burns declares independence from his guilt, aping the rhetoric of revolution. Yet his invention of a new self is eminently conservative. To solve his legal problems, this fugitive simply *becomes* America.

Burns's escapes across state lines capitalized upon a lack of coordination between states and a weak federal policing structure. By 1930, federal police had taken an interest in his highly publicized case: a "Department of Justice agent from Washington" complicates his efforts to find a stable job in New Jersey. Still, Burns was among the last fugitives for whom taking up residence in another state figured as a viable refuge, before the coming of the Roosevelt administration and the rise to prominence of J. Edgar Hoover's FBI—which I discuss in the next chapter—radically changed the landscape for the American fugitive.

2. j. edgar hoover and the federal discourse on crime

Longtime FBI director J. Edgar Hoover (1895–1972) has been variously, vividly, and sometimes viciously portrayed by critics and biographers as a policeman, a patriot, a reactionary, a blackmailer, a closeted homosexual. I, however, propose to discuss him first as a cartographer. Hoover was raised in a family of mapmakers close to the federal center, in Washington, D.C. From his birth in 1895 until his mother's death in 1938, he lived at just one address: 413 Seward Square, a short walk from the Capitol. The Hoovers were an old Washington family; both of his parents were born there, and his mother's family had lived on Seward Square since "well before the Civil War," reports biographer Richard Gid Powers (*Secrecy* 7).

> I have often wished, particularly since I entered public life, that there was some moral process parallel to the process of triangulation, so that the whereabouts, intellectually and spiritually, of some persons could be discovered with more particularity.
> —President Woodrow Wilson, 1916

Hoover's life's work shows the mark of his upbringing in Washington, where the very structures designed by the Framers and L'Enfant subsume the regional into the federal. One observes the nation's states making up the capital: in its street names, the license plates and tourists lining the Mall, and the gray-suited members of Congress filing into their desks, organized not by region but systematically by party and seniority.

The young Hoover showed a talent for such synthesis, simplification, and systematization: in 1913, to put himself through school, he took a $30-per-month job as an indexer at the Library of Congress (Demaris 4), where he became skilled in the Library's comprehensive subject-based numbering system that inventories and subdivides the whole of human knowledge. Over the years, Hoover mourned Washington's decline, and in particular, the Seward Square neighborhood's change from a homogeneous neighborhood of mostly white middle-class civil servants to, writes Powers, a rough, decaying, "predominantly black" district in Washington's most dangerous quadrant.

29

In his biography of Hoover, Powers conjures up this setting just before Hoover's death as a way, presumably, to attest to its seminal role in the director's thinking: "The old Seward Square home was gone, Seward Square itself widened, cut clear of greenery, a part of the city to be avoided at night . . . and yet those long-vanished institutions still lived on in him" (477). Indeed, the notion of "home" played an enduring role in Hoover's sentimental vision of an ideal America. In 1944, addressing a Boys Clubs of America audience on the subject of law enforcement, he mourned that "the home is not the same potent factor it once was" (Powers 260). And later, when anticommunism became the focus of his public efforts, he launched his 1958 book *Masters of Deceit* with a warning that Marxist doctrines "threaten the happiness of the community, the safety of every individual, and the continuance of every home and fireside" (vi).

Hoover's upbringing in a family of cartographers is, I would argue, a most suggestive influence upon the man and administrator he would become. Both his grandfather, John Thomas Hoover, and his father, Dickerson Hoover, worked in the print shop of the United States Coast and Geodetic Survey (USCGS). His father, a platemaker, served for a time as print shop chief and specialized in printing federally funded and commissioned "nautical charts and maps" that represented the knowledge gained by "explorations conducted at the agency's regional stations" (Powers, *Secrecy* 6; Theoharis and Cox 27).

Created in 1807 upon the request of Thomas Jefferson, the Coast Survey, as it was originally called, was commissioned to coordinate the mapping of America's coasts and borderlines. In a tumultuous first half century, the Survey suffered numerous departmental relocations and squabbles between the Navy and the Department of the Treasury, was twice investigated by Congress, and ceased to exist for one period of fourteen years; still, in 1871 the Survey saw its mandate significantly widened. Beginning that year, its mission was to include the mathematical fixing of "points and figures and areas" of terrestrial features (Hubbard and Baker 287–88), and it was renamed the Coast and

Geodetic Survey. The Survey's superintendent at the time was astronomer and mathematician Benjamin Peirce; his son, philosopher Charles Sanders Peirce, would later work for the USCGS, supervising work on his father's plan to achieve geodesic connection of preexisting East and West Coast surveys ("Peirce" 241–42).

The years of John Edgar Hoover's childhood were heady ones for the Survey. In 1897, T. C. Mendenhall and Otto H. Tittman described the Survey's completion of a longitudinal net across the United States in *National Geographic*: "Within the past year the Survey has completed and adjusted its primary longitude net covering the whole United States and fixing for all time the astronomical longitudes of the points included in it. . . . The adjustment of the triangulation along this great arc and the adoption of a homogeneous system of geographic coordinates will furnish the fundamental data for the coordination of all Government or State surveys for all time to come, if it be permitted to fallible human wisdom to make such an assertion" (297).

The culmination of Peirce's vision, the net along the thirty-ninth parallel covered forty-eight longitudinal degrees, two-fifteenths of the world's circumference. It was a crowning achievement for the Survey, producing the first scientific transcontinental map of the nation and laying the foundation for "all Government and State surveys for all time to come." After the line of precise levels connecting the Pacific Ocean with the Atlantic and the Gulf of Mexico was reported in the Survey superintendent's 1905 report ("Progress in Surveying" 110), ancillary surveys built upon the primary work as a building springs upward from its foundation. In 1916, William Henry Burger reported at the survey's centennial conference that

Since the completion of the two arcs mentioned, the Coast and Geodetic Survey has added many more arcs to its system, until the total length of the combined arcs is more than 150° of a great circle of the earth, or about three-sevenths of the circuit of the globe. Incorporated into the system and placed on one datum are also the many miles of coast triangulation of the Survey and much of the triangulation executed by the Lake Survey and by

the United States Engineers, until now the system stands without an equal
in any nation. (83)

But behind Mendenhall and Tittman's pride, one can also read an
institutional mind-set in which the fruits of research and surveillance,
rather than settling questions "for all time to come," engender and perpetuate their continuance. Even the geographers' caveat—"if it be permitted to fallible human wisdom to make such an assertion"—privileges
further geographic inquiry of the continent as inevitable, somehow
more fixed than even the human wisdom that conducts it. Indeed, a
1927 review recalibrated the Survey's picture of the nation, and following
improvements in surveying equipment and techniques and the addition of satellite imaging to the surveyor's palette, a 1971 Committee on
the North American Datum report renounced the possibility of surveying's end, prophesying, "It is obvious that a geodetic reference system
cannot be considered as something that, once accomplished, will serve
for all time; instead it is technologically and physically dynamic, with
ultimate obsolescence implicit from the moment of conception" (3).

In the first century of its existence, perhaps no figure was more central to establishing the Survey's excellence, and its aura, than Ferdinand
Rudolph Hassler, a Swiss engineer who was its superintendent from 1816
to 1818 and 1832 to 1843. Hassler scrambled for equipment and funding
and maintained a standard of using the most precise surveying techniques available, even as his tiny agency was shunted back and forth
between departments. Both Congressional investigations of the Survey
concluded that, though progress was slow, Hassler's leadership was
essentially faultless. Wrote Burger of Hassler, "To him belongs the
credit that to-day the operations of the Survey are bound together by
a trigonometric survey with long lines and executed by the most accurate instruments and the most refined methods, rather than being cor-
related by purely astronomical observations" (81). And, claimed Burger,
from Hassler's leadership had sprung a tradition of scientific excellence
that endured into the new century, extending Hassler's concern with

tools and techniques into scientific management and efficiency: "The work of the past was searched for the best in instruments and methods, field and office methods were standardized, limits of accuracy were set, and where it seemed advisable new methods and instruments were devised to meet the changing conditions of the work. This era may be characterized as a period of great speed and low costs, with the previous accuracy maintained" (83–84). At the same conference, President Wilson acknowledged the Survey's history by joking about its healthy Congressional funding; clearly it had mapped as well "the whereabouts of a great many committees of Congress and a great many other persons connected with the process of appropriating public moneys" ("Address by the President" 142). Indeed, the Survey's centennial conference, held at the Willard Hotel in Washington, claimed a handful of Congressmen in attendance, as well as a young New Yorker named Franklin Delano Roosevelt.

The imperative of surveying the nation and surveilling its minute geologic changes drove the Survey's work throughout the last few decades of the nineteenth century and the first years of the twentieth. The USCGS moved on into the body of the continent and across Alaska, simultaneously establishing a more global perspective and a detailed intimacy with the American terrain.

Thus I say that the unification and scientific refinement of *regional* representations into *national* maps had long been the family business for the Hoovers, a suturing of the nation's space. And in a very real sense, J. Edgar Hoover's efforts to federalize police communication and surveillance applied the nationalizing and mapping principles of his forefathers' work with the USCGS laterally to another medium.

Hoover first joined the Justice Department in the fall of 1917, shortly after he completed his master's in law at George Washington University. Several of the early incidents that advanced his career at the Justice Department show him enforcing national security through defining and managing national space. His first job in the Justice Department

involved processing the paperwork resulting from arrests of alien enemies during World War I. Woodrow Wilson's proclamation regarding
alien enemies, principally Germans, prohibited their owning guns,
explosives, radio transmitters, or ciphered or secret-writing documents.
Furthermore, they could not come within half a mile of military installations or munitions plants or other zones deemed sensitive by the federal government (the Capitol was one such area; its half-mile radius
would have included Seward Square).

This politicoethnic zoning preceded the operation that first made
Hoover a newsworthy name. On December 21, 1919, he presided over the
luridly staged "Red scare" deportations of Emma Goldman, Alexander
Berkman, and 249 aliens suspected of communism (Powers, *Secrecy*
82–89). The alien status of those deported—most but not all were
Russian—made more tenable the simplistic equation of political borders and national borders. The deportation proceeded upon the tacit
assertion of political homogeneity within American borders; political
"outsiders" found themselves forcibly removed to a space outside the
nation. Hoover's raids were met with a mixture of praise and outrage;
rarely again would the option of deportation be so readily, and spectac-
ularly, available to him.

Hoover's early success at creating a spectacle over the unknown
political or (il)legal practices of individuals initiated patterns of FBI
operation that persisted over decades. But until the Roosevelt administration, the Bureau was largely powerless, a specialized unit within the
Department of Justice with limited jurisdiction and a tight leash. Policing in America was still, for better or worse, a largely local endeavor. For
American citizens to accept the federal government as a policing
authority, their notions of what crime was—and what police could
be—would have to be redrawn.

Americans locate crime ambivalently today, both at the margins and
in the central, most developed parts of our landscape. But legality:
where, we might ask, is it sited? "Legal behavior" has not developed the
conventional episodic features of crime: the place, time, perpetrator,

victim, motive, and all the commonplaces of investigation and trial. Middle-class legality pervades, apparently, and it is putatively normative: the everyday. So whereas we frequently concede crime its "zones"— neighborhoods, cities, border and transition areas—conventional legality remains unmapped, at least insofar as legality is historically normative. Projects such as Michel de Certeau's *Arts de Faire* (*The Practice of Everyday Life*), which aspires to map the "everyday," demonstrate how our practices of mapping and classifying have long concentrated on the aberrant, the exceptional, the official—and how such episodic mapping tends to perpetuate itself, like the studies of the USCGS, for reasons of official and unofficial, scientific and voyeuristic interest.

The writings of Michel Foucault concur. Most notably, in *The History of Sexuality, Vol. I*, he argues that the knowledge—and power— gained from such projects of mapping made inroads upon formerly unarticulated panoplies of practices and behaviors, "officializing" categories of aberrancy and guaranteeing further investigations at those sites. The discourse on sex "stirred up people's fears; to the least oscillations of sexuality, it ascribed an imaginary dynasty of evils destined to be passed on for generations; it declared the furtive customs of the timid, and the most solitary of petty manias, dangerous for society. . . . In the name of a biological and historical urgency, it justified the racisms of the state, which at the time were on the horizon. It grounded them in 'truth,' " Foucault asserts (53–54). His analysis inverts what we might assume to be the case with the state's knowledge of behaviors and persons both "normative" and "deviant." He suggests that the project of identifying and mapping "perversions" made the deviant a more knowable domain than the normative. Legal behavior remains the body of behavior yet undivided, uncharted, less susceptible to the exercise and stratagems of power.

Thus the project of naming, inventorying, demarcating, and surveilling the deviant becomes a spotlight. Outside of its beam, the law-abiding citizen moves on, relatively unchecked. Yet this distinction is crucial, for upon it depends the liberty, life, and status of the individual; Joan Dayan has traced the application of "social death" to prisoners and their rendering into little more than slaves or shares of stock in a corporate penitentiary, and Foucalt elaborates the inquisitorial nature of criminal parole. Confusion between lawful and unlawful status propels the detective story, which milks suspense out of the temporary misrecognition of the guilty party, just as *North by Northwest* and *The Fugitive* trace the nightmare of the falsely accused.

Because this distinction is so powerful in actuality and in myth, demarcations of illegality figure in highly visible opposition to the categories that define citizenship. And this opposition is frequently enacted in geographic or geopolitical terms. Thus to site crime on our borders makes law-abiding citizens seem to stand together as a nation. To locate it in the wilderness insists upon the term "wilderness" and the obverse, the normalizing category of "settlement." And, in the present day, to observe it in our metropolises necessitates the development of terms that demarcate zones of illegality—"the inner city"—from the rest of the publicly used area: "downtown," "the urban area." "The thin blue line" of the police is a metaphor serving to compartmentalize legal from illegal persons and behaviors—as if such an ordering were spatially possible. Such is the value of the yellow crime scene tape that is unrolled, wrapped around signposts and trees, and left to flutter as a cordon around a house or stretch of street where a murder or robbery occurs. The tape warns people to stay out; in utilitarian terms, it preserves evidence, allows unencumbered investigation, shields victims and property from further scavenging or trauma. But as symbol, it reasserts the separation between the criminally tainted and the law-abiding normal—between the episodic and the everyday. Such geographical assertions and distinctions permeate the investigative and symbolic routines and rituals of our police.

Hoover's Red raids, in their invocation of "national security" as a cover for coercively proscribing certain behaviors and thus redefining lawful conduct on a nationwide basis, resembled Prohibition, the most profound and sweeping law-enforcement experiment in United States history. The Eighteenth Amendment belongs to a tradition of "socio-logical jurisprudence," writes Paul H. Murphy, wherein the federal government enacted law to "proscribe and limit evil behavior damaging to the broader society" (68–69). Murphy describes a temperance battle between centralizing and centrifugal forces: indeed, opposition to Prohibition was closely allied with the states' rights movement. A series of crises in the late 1910s had turned the tide toward the "drys." First, the United States Brewers' Association, since the Civil War the most effective lobbying agent for American brewery interests, suffered a 1916 scandal in which brewers were caught corrupting elections in Texas and Pennsylvania. Months later, the brewery-financed German-American Alliance was found to have engaged in "pro-German activities." In September 1916, Alien Property Custodian A. Mitchell Palmer charged American brewers before Congress with subsidizing pro-German press, illegal political influence, and unpatriotic activities (Kyvig 36–37). With World War I looming in the background, the patriotism that had always spoken, however insipidly, in the discourse of temperance crusaders was refigured into the more urgent duty of national defense; many drys believed, writes D. Leigh Colvin, "that from the standpoint of patriotism no greater service, outside the battlefield itself, could be performed than in overcoming the greatest enemy at home" (452).

Emergency wartime measures aided the passage of temporary temperance measures, inadvertently easing the transition to national prohibition—and justifying it, again via nationalistic discourse. The May 1917 Selective Draft Act forbade the selling, and later, any supplying, of liquor to soldiers in uniform; the August 1917 Food Control Act diverted distillery raw materials to food production. Some measures, such as the War Prohibition provisions of the August 1917 Agricultural Appropriation Bill, were designed to last only through the war. But within the life span of these statues, which gained public acquiescence due to the climate of national emergency, the Eighteenth Amendment was submitted (in December 1917). By the time lesser, temporary statutes had expired, the Volstead Act (which provided for the enforcement of war prohibition and, later, constitutional prohibition) had its teeth (Colvin 472–73). The Eighteenth Amendment was ratified by a 36th state in January 1919, two months after the Armistice and before many soldiers had returned from Europe, but the alibi of national defense that had helped create Prohibition rang hollow in the postwar world.

Temperance crusaders also hoped Prohibition would decrease American crime, and since initial resistance to Prohibition did not include rioting or labor strikes, early commentators called it a success. A 1925 number of the *North American Review* carried a series of articles arguing that Prohibition had cut crime: Richard J. Hopkins, a Kansas Supreme Court justice, alleged a "marked reduction in crime, especially in crimes of violence arising from uncontrollable anger, ill-will or other similar depraved emotions" (40). Colvin summarizes the effects of Prohibition in tipsy-sounding syntax: "The first year of national constitutional prohibition brought such a widespread compliance with the law that the results produced were so decisive and the benefits so extraordinary that they may be described as almost miraculous" (474). We now appreciate the naïveté of Colvin's 1926 account, but to be fair, public concern over bootlegging's outgrowths into organized crime did not peak until several years later.

If Prohibition sought to expel immorality from American space or at least public view, uniting the American nation in the sacrifice of personal liberty for what the Reverend Charles Stelzle called "the common good" (Kyvig 9), its failure brought a far graver insult to lines and divisions between legal and illegal conduct. The vision of a federally enforced "widespread compliance with the law"—a miraculous, crime-free national tableau—was replaced by images of the permeation of the American landscape by the newly criminalized offenses of alcohol consumption and bootlegging. Prohibition endangered law's very status by familiarizing ordinary citizens with its routine breakage. By 1929, the federal prohibition bureau had arrested over half a million people for violating the Volstead Act, which provided for the enforcement of the Eighteenth Amendment (Browning and Gerassi 366). Such enforcement was a practical impossibility.

The fourteen years of Prohibition gave American crime the conditions it needed to mature into a fully developed, largely integrated subeconomy that lurked in the spaces uncharted by the legal economy. In urban areas where a backyard still was not an option, illegal alcohol distributors found in common citizens' demand for liquor a black-market cash supply unrivaled until illegal drugs peaked in profitability half a century later. Supply networks and the official (albeit illegal) "licensing" needed to maintain them developed in patterns that paralleled the maturation of legal marketplaces. Bootleggers devised "storefronts" unregulated by police—the country still or the evasive man- about-town with pints in his pocket, like Joe Christmas and Joe Brown in Faulkner's *Light in August*. Or, more profitably, they arranged to fix their business within that regulatory gaze by bribe and other arrangements, as Al Capone did. (The cost of opening and maintaining markets could be passed on to consumers, who did not always enjoy the price-lowering benefits of a competitive market.) A bootlegger once explained the extraordinary collusion of lawbreakers, everyday citizens, and even the police during the period, "I couldn't exist if it weren't for the fact that I have the cooperation of the local police, the State constabulary, the municipal police, and 85 percent of the citizens. . . . Tell the average person that you've got a load of liquor in your car, and he'll hide you, lie for you, and help you" (Cashman x).

Demand for liquor—and the ingenuity and enterprise of those who satisfied it—decreased ordinary citizens' insistence upon a gap between lawful and unlawful activity, which had made the police nationally desirable since westward expansion. If the police functioned as "the thin blue line" protecting the social economy of the law-abiding public from what D. A. Miller has called, discussing Victorian literature, "the world of delinquency," bootlegging and illegal drinking scuffed breaks into that line of separation.

The spatial and cultural integration of bootlegging-related crime helped decrease the literal and moral distance between law-abiding citizens and more serious forms of criminal behavior. If citizens did not effectively object to the initial compromises between bootleggers and police, it may have been because allowing liquor into homes and discreet speakeasies seemed a relatively benign threat (or a welcome concession). Deviance, sociologist Howard S. Becker has argued, is not a quality inherent in acts but a consequence of rules and sanctions applied to an "offender." One might say that in Prohibition, laws were broken without widespread application of labels of deviance; thus a motorist speeding on a deserted road frequently does not incur social disapproval, even though she is breaking the law. But the speeder does so singularly, without assistance from other lawbreakers.

As bootleggers became more prosperous and well ensconced, they were prone to diversifying their criminal business into more serious operations. For example, Prohibition provided "a unique opportunity" for Italians and other immigrants to break the long-standing Irish monopoly on organized crime in Chicago, writes Sean Dennis Cashman (65). Al Capone gained the capital for his many businesses, legal and illegal, via bootlegging. By associating with bootleggers, Prohibition drinkers crossed the line into small-time illegality, and other, less benign criminal pleasures—prostitution and gambling, for example—seemed all the more accessible. That transgressing the law became a commonplace for Americans, making real (and fictionalized) criminals more familiar and seemingly more benign, problematized social divisions between lawful and unlawful conduct.

Simultaneously, popular notions of the criminal were transforming and undergoing inventory by psychology and criminology. Though deterministic theories of crime favoring ethnic and biological causes had enjoyed a brief vogue, by the mid-1920s they were fading away, overcome by a moralistic vision of criminality that conceded the criminal's relative normality and insisted upon his or her responsibility, writes David E. Ruth. While eugenicists envisioned crime as trapped in, or emanating from, lower-class urban ethnic neighborhoods and psychiatrists and social scientists envisioned a criminal whose difference could be objectively measured (and corrected or quarantined) well in advance of a crime, moralist explanations of crime affirmed that the boy next door—regardless of ethnicity, class, or neighborhood—faced the same moral challenges as anyone and possessed the same ability to succumb to criminal behavior (Ruth 12–34).

To develop the metaphor of the police as dividing line, we might say that the social landscape of the late 1920s reached a spatial crisis wherein crime and legality became intertwined—in actuality and, just as importantly, in the public mind. Clarence Darrow, writing in 1925, mourns that recent developments in court authority and specialization betray crime's inroads into home and family: "The creation of new courts, like 'Boys' Courts,' 'Juvenile Courts,' 'Courts of Domestic Relations,' 'Moral Courts,' with their array of 'Social Workers,' 'Parole Agents,' 'Watchers,' et cetera, shows the growth of crime and likewise the hopelessness of present methods to deal effectively with a great social question" (139).

Other observers described crime's growth in terms of geographical mobility and permeation. In 1927, a *Harper's* editorial reflected a growing conviction that "Among the busy marts of commerce, along the crowded highway the whisper goes forth that crime is rampant and banditry is rife. Rumors of it have even crept into the newspapers" (Levy 262). An October 29, 1930, *New York Times* editorial item titled "Chicago Afraid of Herself" attributed the "dimmed radiance of first-night jewels" at Chicago's opera season premiere to the rumored gangster threat to even the highest echelons: "innocent dwellers in London and Paris—even New York" share the impression that "every Chicagoan packs a 'gat' and that the surviving citizens must be very quick on the trigger" ("Chicago Afraid" 24). Clearly, the perception was that crimes more serious than bootlegging were on the move, penetrating heretofore inviolate sectors of society.

Such impressions were—and remain—difficult to confirm. As late as 1929, no method existed for the accurate compilation of national crime data and statistics. The National Crime Commission could not comment officially on former attorney general George Wickersham's assertion that "a certain new and reckless disregard of human life is apparent in some of our large cities" ("Wickersham Would Change" 1).

With or without official statistics, however, crime paranoia was swept onto the front pages by President Herbert Hoover's tense twenty-five-minute speech to an Associated Press meeting on April 22, 1929. Hoover called law and crime "the dominant issue before the American people," warning, "A surprising number of our people, otherwise of responsibility in the community, have drifted into the extraordinary notion that laws are made for those who choose to obey them. And in addition, our law-enforcement machinery is suffering from many infirmities arising out of its technicalities, its circumlocutions, its involved procedures, and too often, I regret, from inefficient and delinquent officials" ("Text of President Hoover's Address" 2). America was facing, said President Hoover, "the possibility that respect for law as law is fading from the sensibilities of our people." The President's discussion of the crime problem invoked explicit spatial metaphors: "we are not suffering from an ephemeral crime wave but from a subsidence of our foundations." Rather than as a "wave"—originating from without and indeed "ephemeral" in its retreat and return—Hoover mapped contemporary American crime as tenacious, possibly permanent. He located its effects beneath our feet, our homes. "No part of the country, rural or urban, is immune," he added; "Life and property are relatively more unsafe than in any other civilized country in the world" (2).

Reactions to the speech echoed the President's message that crime had become a national concern. The *Kansas City Star* called it "one of the most arresting and impressive addresses made to the American people in many years," and the *Philadelphia Public Ledger* agreed that crime had become "a great national emergency" ("Press Comment" 28). Various respondents, including Senator William Cabell Bruce, lodged objections against two of Hoover's points: first, that only 8 percent of reported felony convictions in 1928 could be traced directly to the Volstead Act, and second, that there was no need for increased federal involvement in crime fighting ("Bruce Takes Issue" 3). Bruce pointed out that in some jurisdictions, bootlegging-related crimes totaled 80 percent of all convictions: "It is true that there was too much crime in the United States before the adoption of the Eighteenth Amendment, but beyond all question it is the general spirit of lawlessness borne by such an imbecilic and tyrannous statute such as the Volstead Act which is responsible for the rampant crime which pervades throughout the country at present" (3).

In the wake of the President's speech, tabulation of American crime began in earnest. By the fall of 1930, the Bureau of Investigation had coordinated local surveys from 772 cities that showed that "all offenses known to police" had risen from the year before. A 10 percent rise was measured in one month between July and August 1930 ("Crime Rise This Year" 12).

The thin blue line separating the middle class from the world of delinquency was thus crowded from both sides—by an increased tolerance of lawbreaking from one side, by more socially integrated criminal enterprises from the other. At the same time, police toleration of and interaction with bootleggers made the utility and integrity of a protective police border less effective—and its maintenance at public expense more debatable.

The tension between police's prescribed roles and their perceived irrelevance made its mark in the era's popular entertainments. During the Herbert Hoover administration, representations of the police often underplayed or ridiculed their authority. The inept, dour-faced Keystone Kops had starred in Mack Sennett farces from 1914 until the early 1920s; Sennett, a veteran of burlesque comedy, conceived the Kops when Los Angeles police arrived to end two of his actors' playful interference with a Shriners parade. (Ironically, from their ranks came film star Roscoe "Fatty" Arbuckle, later tried and acquitted for a rape and murder of which most observers thought him guilty.) But after the Kops' heyday, to depict American policemen as inept was no longer a matter of farce. Hollywood films painted police as "incompetent, corrupt and impotent," whereas the anarchic criminal reigned in bloody, amoral crime dramas (Powers, *Secrecy* 177). The many gangster films that thrilled early-'30s audiences have been ably enumerated and analyzed by Richard Gid Powers, Andrew Bergman, and David E. Ruth.

As glamorous, socially mobile gangster heroes, including Paul Muni's *Scarface* and Jimmy Cagney's *Public Enemy*, drew large audiences and provoked dozens of imitators and knockoffs, the film industry sensed the possibility of regulation or boycotts and sought to censor itself, but to little avail. A Chicago censoring agency reported "that nearly half the cuts it made in films between 1930 and 1931 were for 'showing disrespect for law enforcement' and for 'glorification of the gangster or outlaw.'" A New York censor board asked director Howard Hawks to change *Scarface*'s climactic killing of the title character from gangland revenge to shooting by police, presumably to lend some semblance of authority to much-embattled New York City police forces (Bergman 4–17). But public regard for police was so low—and the possibilities represented by the Prohibition-era gangster figure so glamorous and seductive—that filmmakers could not bring themselves to shelve their profitable crime-flick projects. In response to the language in the Association of Motion Picture Producers code condemning the portrayal of "activities of American gangsters, armed and in violent conflict with the law or law-enforcement officers" (Martin 289), filmmakers simply omitted police—or, worse, eliminated "conflict" between gangster and police interests.

Consequently, what had been designed to prevent cinematic devaluation of the law resulted in unflattering depictions of lawmen. "In film after film," reports Andrew Bergman, "in *Little Caesar, City Streets* and *The Secret Six*, the police are dreary operatives, slow-talking and vengeful, obvious heavies. Sometimes they never appear at all" (13). In 1931, at the height of the gangster-film craze, filmic police functioned as mere accomplices to gang rule, suggesting deep disillusion with governmental authority. In *The Secret Six*, only a vigilante group of masked townspeople fight gangster activity; their police are in league with the thugs.

The film was loosely based on the vigilante Chicago Crime Commission, which operated apart from Chicago police and whose members maintained anonymity for fear of underworld revenge (Powers, *G-Men* 23).

By 1932, spurred in part by the murder of the child of Charles Lindbergh—kidnapped, significantly, from the bedroom of the Lindberghs' New Jersey home—grassroots pressure against media glorification of crime began to accumulate. Roman Catholic bishops and the professional association of the nation's chiefs of police led a drive for what Monsignor Giovanni Cicognani called "the purification of the cinema," and the *New York Herald-Tribune* was ludicrously calling the Lindbergh kidnapping "a challenge to the whole order of the nation" (Powers, *Secrecy* 175). That year, public discourse swung toward invoking national power against crime itself, broadly defined, seeking a "war on crime" even as it disavowed confidence in the police who presumably would lead such a war.

Simultaneously, the election campaign of 1932, waged against the backdrop of the Great Depression, counterposed incumbent Herbert Hoover's conservative response to Democratic challenger and New York Governor Franklin D. Roosevelt's aggressive philosophy of works programs and employment stimulus. Roosevelt's victory—he claimed 59 percent of the popular vote and a 472 to 59 electoral landslide and was accompanied to Washington by a new Democratic Congress that favored, and swiftly achieved, Prohibition's repeal—bespoke the suffering nation's readiness to embrace a more interventionist government. The sense of fiscal emergency, coupled with perceived failure of the Hoover administration to sweep the house clean of incompetent and corrupt police, made for an atmosphere in which the first white-hatted hopeful riding in on a horse would become sheriff by popular acclaim. In both the administrative and mythological senses, J. Edgar Hoover made sure that that hero came from his agency.

Hoover's importance to this project has roots in his frantic, and frequently successful, effort to marshal law and law enforcement back from the disorder of the late 1920s and early 1930s. His appropriation of scientific and organizational methods and discourse made the young federal agency's authority seem natural, progressive, destined not to successful coexistence with local jurisdictions but to ascendancy over them. By authorizing his own bureau at the expense of local and state agencies, Hoover managed to conflate law enforcement with his own visions of nationalism: for example, his involving the agency in the pursuit of American communists and his advocacy of legislation that made communism illegal or unfavorable. He figured centrally, then, in disseminating a discourse on crime that used cartography to prescribe law enforcement antidotes. His discourse, and the federal policies it accompanied or made possible, changed the ground on which criminals walked (or fled) in the mid–twentieth century.

Created in 1908 by Attorney General Charles J. Bonaparte, the Bureau's early role was to supplement, not to interact with or coordinate, state and local jurisdictions. The Bureau of Investigation (its first name; it became the FBI in 1935) was charged with detecting and prosecuting "crimes against the United States"; initially, this included interstate shipment of "stolen goods, contraceptives, obscene books, and prizefight films, and the transportation of liquor into dry States" (Lowenthal 13). Over the next dozen years, Congress granted the Bureau additional duties: the Mann Act of 1910, a response to the "white slave scare" of that year, the 1914 Harrison Narcotics Act, and the 1919 Dyer Act, which forbade the transport of stolen autos across state lines, fell under its purview. The President or Attorney General could also summon the Bureau for political reasons: against anarchists, communists, or radicals, as occurred in the 1919 Goldman/Berkman deportations; or against strikers, as happened in 1922, when the Bureau helped arrest over 1,200 striking railroad workers (Powers, *Secrecy* 139–40). But its powers were severely limited; agents were forbidden to carry guns until 1933. Even Don Whitehead, in his enthusiastic *The FBI Story*, calls the early FBI "small and inept" (14).

In order to secure credibility for the Bureau and for himself, Hoover first had to isolate his agency from the popular perception that lawmen were lazy, corrupt, and ultimately indistinguishable from the criminals they were commissioned to fight. (A grand jury had declared as much in 1928, declaring the Chicago Police Department "rotten to the core" [Tannenbaum 156].) Toward this end, Hoover redesigned the federal agent toward a physical, intellectual, moral, and procedural ideal. He did so by effecting a prompt break with the old-style gumshoe detective image of his predecessor, William J. Burns, a Harding appointee who was forced to resign under Calvin Coolidge's reform-minded federal housecleaning, in favor of the scientific-management style of new Attorney General Harlan F. Stone (Powers, *Secrecy* 144–46). Hoover broke with the Bureau's pre-1924 personnel by cutting staff from a 1920 peak of 1,127 to 581; he slashed the number of agents from 579 to 339. By doing so, Hoover identified himself with Coolidge's anticorruption measures and at the same time made the Bureau more efficient in appearance, if not actual function. In 1924, when he took over the Bureau, field offices numbered fifty-three; by 1932, there were only twenty-two (Powers, *Secrecy* 151).

In a May 1925 memo to Special Agents in Charge (SACs, the commanders of the Bureau's local offices), Hoover insisted that a contrast be asserted between the reputations of Bureau agents and those of other government or law agents. "This Bureau cannot afford to have a public scandal visited upon it in the view of the all too numerous attacks made . . . during the past few years. I do not want this Bureau to be referred to in terms I have frequently heard used against other government agencies," he commanded (Whitehead 70–71). Hoover's memo reasserted the line between lawful and unlawful conduct, forbidding the use of alcohol and other intoxicants by agents "to any degree or extent upon any occasion." For those agents who survived Hoover's cuts or were hired under his administration, stringent and meticulous standards were enforced. Publicly, Hoover required agents to hold a law degree (to prepare them to execute arrest and evidential procedures flawlessly) or an accounting degree (because many Bureau cases required knowledge of accounting practices and procedures).

While this requirement had been on the books before Hoover, it had not been enforced. This idealized agent may have been more mythical than actual: Curt Gentry points out that several of the lawmen Hoover hired during the mid-1930s had no college education and met few of the Bureau's requirements. Their terms of service with the Bureau went "unpublicized" (169–70).

Officially, at least, Hoover remapped the federal agent's appearance, demeanor, and procedure according to detailed manuals, the use of which he defended vigorously. For years agents grumbled about the Bureau's appearance standards, which dictated not only their dress code and the emblematic hat but also a maximum weight—which Hoover exceeded for many of his years as director. Revolts against his leadership frequently noted agents' dislike for his strictness and intense demand for loyalty (Powers, *Secrecy* 151–55). Paperwork increased exponentially and became more rigorously formatted; routinely conducted inventories and inspections checked the accountability and condition of FBI equipment. FBI informational packets still trumpet the surprisingly bookish, intricate requirements of gun-toting special agents (United States, *FBI Facts* 5; *99 Facts* 6). (Gentry also quotes Charles Winstead, an old-school Bureau agent who survived Hoover's cuts despite failing to meet many of his requirements: "The first thing you've got to do," he told new agents at the remote New Mexico office to which he had been assigned, "is unlearn everything they taught you at the Seat of Government. The second is to get rid of those damn manuals" [170].)

Richard Gid Powers sees ethnic connotations in Hoover's redrawing of the federal agent: "Hoover was the first non-Catholic director in some time, and this was noted with approval in respectable circles. The Irish cop had a shabby image, and Hoover's predecessor was almost a caricature of that stereotype. Although there is no evidence that Hoover was overtly anti-Catholic or anti-Semitic, it is clear that his Protestant, Masonic, Sunday school image represented, in his own eyes and in the opinion of others, a considerable step up the ethnic status ladder for the Bureau" (*Secrecy* 152).

Elsewhere, Hoover's intensely detailed redrawing of the FBI agent has helped to justify various homoerotic readings (for example, Athan Theoharis's *J. Edgar Hoover, Sex, and Crime: An Historical Antidote*) of his relationships with other men, especially lifetime friend and companion Clyde Tolson. Whether we read his installation of a conformist discipline into all elements of the agency's personnel and practice as fetishistic or merely practical, his re-creation of the federal agent is a microcosmic—but crucial—first step in his discursive redrawing of crime, policing, and Americanism.

Most important, however, in Hoover's reconfiguration of the Bureau was his championing of its national fingerprint registry and forensics labs. As early as 1925 Hoover promoted the fingerprint bureau among lawmen, arguing that "the rock of universal cooperation" was the foundation of improved crime detection (Powers, *Secrecy* 149–50). Extant Department of Justice records were combined with the Washington fingerprint collection of the International Association of Chiefs of Police and the Department of Justice's Leavenworth, Kansas, fingerprint records in 1923; the resulting consolidation was funded in July 1924 and housed at 1800 Pennsylvania Avenue, two blocks west of the White House (Hoover, "National Bureau" 12). In the 1930s, however, the fingerprint registry became at once an exhibit of the Bureau's scientific prowess and of the value of federally coordinated police records. Through fingerprints, the FBI could identify criminals from disparate jurisdictions, an ability that figured prominently in its self-promotion—and growing public enthusiasm.

In 1933, Bureau fingerprint detectives received 2,200 fingerprints per day; 45 percent of prints received matched already cataloged sets, and the Bureau reported matches back to local officers within thirty-six hours (Hibbs 35). The registry's national scope and swift response became the central exhibit of the Bureau's potential. "When one of his automobile thieves in his twelfth district brings an automobile from Kansas, Arkansas, or Oklahoma into Missouri the officers there catch him and fingerprint him, and they send those fingerprints up here to

J. Edgar Hoover. He checks them up with his classified list and locates the criminal, and usually he finds that for fifteen years the accused has been violating the laws of the United States," argued Texas Representative Thomas Blanton on the floor of the House on January 4, 1933. "Does not my friend from Missouri think it is worth while for the officers of his district to have access to this information?" (*Congressional Record* 1375). Hoover volunteered the use of FBI records and facilities to any and all state and local lawmen—a shrewd concession, for those who did not gratefully accept the federal agency's assistance appeared ungrateful or negligent.

To supplement his concern over the figure of the federal agent and the technical capabilities of his agency, Hoover monitored and altered the details of Bureau discourse. He was notorious in the agency's early days for wanting to review—and edit—every piece of information released to the press and public. Until Franklin D. Roosevelt expanded the agency's jurisdiction in the early 1930s to include investigation of various high-profile criminal matters, public interest in agency affairs was low, and such information could be easily monitored. For Hoover, little separation existed between the agency's administrative and public-relations efforts. He insisted upon and maintained a central role in both, and his personal scrapbooks, preserved by the National Archives, demonstrate the exquisite care with which he reviewed and preserved even the most banal mentions of his Bureau in the nation's press.

Under the supervision of Roosevelt attorney general Homer Cummings, Hoover and the Bureau took advantage of the rehabilitation of law enforcement that was a component of the public backlash against the gangster-film heyday of 1931. By late 1934, movie producers admitted that "self-regulation" had been a flop (in moral terms, perhaps; it had, for a time, been immensely profitable) and submitted to the oversight of a censor who could block distribution to films that broke the guidelines of a stiffened production code (Powers, *G-Men* 67–69). This code promised that in American movies, "crime will be shown to be *wrong* and that the criminal life will be loathed and that the law will *at all times prevail*" (Martin 114). The code also specified that the "presentation of crimes ... must not arouse sympathy *with* the criminal as *against* those who must punish crime" (Martin 118).

This rehabilitation moved slowly at first. The lingering public distaste for local police, even in the face of this federal rehabilitation, illustrates the degree to which the older police bureaucracies had lost their credibility as protectors and exemplars of legal and moral standards. It was as difficult to dispel popular notions of police corruption as it was to weed out the corruption itself. Hoover's sweeping and public directives toward discipline and professionalism gave federal agents a leg up in the rehabilitative process. Roosevelt's 1933 merger of three federal agencies into a "super police force," although it did not in itself contribute to the Bureau's internal reforms, allowed Cummings to publicly introduce Hoover's agency as the "new" Division of Investigation (Powers, *Secrecy* 183–84), a title that would change to the Federal Bureau of Investigation in 1934. The Memphis arrest of kidnapper George "Machine Gun" Kelly in October of that year provided a well-timed publicity windfall for the Bureau.

When Hollywood cinema shifted from gangster stars to police stars, it was the newly glamorized FBI that "found itself elevated to guardianship of the public good," writes Andrew Bergman (84). The Hoover-led FBI became, according to Richard Gid Powers in *G-Men: The FBI in American Popular Culture*, the best survey of the Bureau's media heyday, "one of the greatest publicity-generating machines the country had ever seen" (95). A 1939 American Institute of Public Opinion poll claimed that 80 percent of respondents thought Hoover had done an "excellent" or "good" job as "head of the G-men"; only 7 percent answered "fair" and 1 percent "poor" (Cantril 557). Hoover's showmanship moved spectators both high and low and easily outlasted the effects of Prohibition and the Depression; V. O. Key wrote in 1947, "So effective has been his continuing [publicity] campaign that when Mr. Hoover makes a request of Congress newspaper editors all over the land editorialize in support of his position" (Keller 24). Gallup polls done in 1950 and 1953 found overwhelming support for Hoover among both political parties and independents (Gallup 891, 1197–98).

Hoover regarded the swelling interest in his agency's policing activities as both a boon and a threat. Though the 1934 surrender to production codes had for a time banished the gangster from the screen, producers sought—and found—a loophole that allowed their reappearance. Spurred by concern from the International Association of Chiefs of Police and the immense profitability of crime films, the studios got permission to make a "limited number" of gangster films glorifying federal crime-fighting activity. Hoover monitored these images fanatically. He responded with a broad-based public relations campaign in which certain representations were certified as "authentic" and others were discredited. "Unauthorized" representations of Bureau agents and business infuriated him. When former ace agent Melvin Purvis— who led the hunt for and killing of John Dillinger—involved himself with children's clubs and radio shows and wrote articles about his career, Hoover bitterly disowned Purvis, publicly reassigning credit for the fatal shots to another agent, Sam Cowley, whom he called the man with "the deepest notch on his gun in the world" (Powers, *Secrecy* 192). (William C. Sullivan's bitter 1971 memoir claims that, in fact, Charles Winstead killed Dillinger [19].) Whenever the Bureau could commandeer control of a story representing its work, it did; when Purvis attempted to land jobs as a consultant on motion pictures, Hoover commanded the head of the Los Angeles FBI office to offer the Bureau's assistance and endorsement, gratis (Powers, *Secrecy* 222–25). Furthermore, even though it was wildly successful, Hoover had reacted with tight-lipped disapproval to the 1935 film *G-Men* (this nickname, short for "Government Men," was the title of numerous entertainments). By casting the charismatic Jimmy Cagney as Agent Brick Davis, *G-Men* reversed the trend of four years earlier, when charismatic actors such as Cagney, Paul Muni, and Edward G. Robinson represented gangsters.

In place of "unofficial" representations of the Bureau and its agents, Hoover moved quickly to supply official substitutes—including himself. His involvement with media representations of his Bureau took numerous forms. According to Powers, public ignorance about the role of the FBI began to vanish after Hoover established working relationships with several writers. Most prominent among them were former *Washington Star* reporter Rex Collier and Courtney Ryley Cooper, who between 1933 and 1940 wrote twenty-four fictionalized accounts of FBI cases as well as four movies and three books (not including *Persons in Hiding*, published under Hoover's name in 1938). In the introduction to Hoover's 1938 *Persons in Hiding*, Cooper manages to lionize Hoover individually without betraying the scientific-management principles that Hoover held high:

> It is nothing for him to work from fourteen to sixteen hours a day. His brain is one of the most rapidly functioning mechanisms I have ever encountered; I have seen him direct the handling of four big criminal cases simultaneously, veering from one telephone to another as he commanded the hunt, instantly freeing his mind from the concentration of one case that he might give his entire attention to the other. His associates believe that he possesses a sixth sense which allows him instantly to find the flaw in seeming perfection. (ix)

In 1935, Hoover managed to gain editorial control over yet another *G-Men*—this one a weekly radio program—in exchange for assuring its officiality; he then rewrote facts to craft narratives of FBI heroism. Hoover also managed, by "authorizing" the production of a number of sensational films about the agency, to gain partial control of Hollywood's representation of Bureau agents and business. The poster for the film version of *Persons in Hiding* blurts, "She's the woman behind the killer behind the gun! J. Edgar Hoover* tells her amazing story in 'Persons in Hiding.'" Typically, the asterisk assured officiality: "Director of the Federal Bureau of Investigation," it explained below. Although the plots often bore little resemblance to actual events, similar attributions of authenticity were made in advertising for *Undercover Doctor* and *Queen of the Mob*. For a 1936 film titled *You Can't Get Away with It*, Hoover himself shouldered a tommy gun and acted for the cameras.

The implausibility of this bit of work in a "crime exposé" that billed itself as "Actual scenes . . . actual G-Men . . . life in the raw!" led Hoover, perhaps, to his involvement as a gun-toting participant in several 1936 raids and arrests. Perhaps the raids assuaged Hoover's insecurities as well as his vanities: he suffered an April 10, 1936, taunting from Senator Kenneth D. McKellar, who asked pointedly, "Did you ever make an arrest?" in response to Hoover's request for an appropriations increase. McKellar forced Hoover to admit that he had never received any formal criminology training, nor had he any police experience (Nash, *Citizen* 56).

Hoover's design also included the Bureau's physical self-presentation. Mindful that the FBI needed a central office worthy of its carefully groomed image, Hoover helped design a tour of the Bureau's Washington, D.C., headquarters that presented an image consistent with his vision. This tour, stressing the bureau's heroic triumphs and up-to-the-minute innovations, is still among the capital's main tourist attractions (Powers, *G-Men* 94–112; Powers, *Secrecy* 179–227).

In the popular media, Hoover's public-relations efforts effected two changes. They helped turn public sympathy back toward the lawman. Simultaneously, they privileged the federal lawman over the local police. By 1935, "with actors like Jimmy Cagney and Edward G. Robinson playing agents of the Federal Bureau of Investigation, the law had a new vibrancy and toughness; it again became the focus of films, and was something to identify with," writes Andrew Bergman, and the "thick-headed law officers and shyster-ridden legal codes" of the old (failed) legal regime were replaced by the new agents and procedures of the G-Man (83). Hoover's control of media representations of the FBI allowed him to distance the mythical G-Man from older, presumably more corrupt law-enforcement agencies. Hoover "skillfully manipulated the media," writes Lawrence M. Friedman; "The FBI was fearless, incorruptible, efficient, bold—a magnificent army in the war against crime. Or so it seemed" (271). He "made the Bureau's great cases demonstrate the virtues that FBI defended, the vices it warred against, and the irresistible power of its scientific crime-fighting methods," writes Powers (*Secrecy* 141). Although the Bureau had been around since before Prohibition, by presenting itself as a new, compact force of unimpeachable integrity, it was able to start with a clean slate, attacking the criminality that had arisen during the 1920s without bearing responsibility for its rise.

> *In the meantime, at Main Haven, the racing G-boat had summoned aid. Wires were humming with the news. The Chief himself had dictated crisp orders! Men were appearing instantly as if from the ground itself. From barber shops, boat yards, and the grocery store, came men who had worked for a day or so now as common working men but who were highly trained law officers awaiting this very summons!*
> —Warren F. Robinson, *The G-Man's Son at Porpoise Island* (1937)

Courtney Ryley Cooper's Bureau-sanctioned accounts of FBI landmark moments illustrate Hoover's criminal cartography. Cooper's stories have been described by Powers as "pulp," "a judicious mixture of mystery, action, struggles between clear-cut good and evil, and rapid shifts of scene to exotic locales" (*G-Men* 99–100). Within these narratives Cooper disseminates the Bureau line, describing its agents, laboratories and methods in the officious, friendly tone of a corporate tour guide. The rolling action casts awed glances at the FBI's technical and organizational innovations: the equipment issued each officer, the coordination of communication between jurisdictions and offices, the teamwork of field agents and investigative scientists, the renowned national fingerprint registry. Most of all, it trumpets the genius and persistence of Hoover, who wrote the introduction to *Ten Thousand Public Enemies*.

Such mid-1930s FBI discourse outlines a two front war, a geographer's battle plan, against the new, cash-rich criminal element. The offensives it proposes will be fought both at home and in the hinterlands. At home, Cooper maps the interpenetration of the post-bootlegging criminal economy and everyday business. The opening of the FBI-commissioned *Ten Thousand Public Enemies* (1935) depicts a social landscape in which the taint of criminality is in every setting, "mixed" and "intertwined" with our bodies and our monetary trans-actions. Yet no gray area exists between the clearly identified criminal entities and the first-person-plural coupling of narrator and reader. In these close, sweaty quarters, at least crime is again *crime*.

> Criminals do not spend their lives in secretiveness and solitude. They are all about us, and, paradoxically, the more desperate they are, the more likely they are to be in places where they will mix with those who obey the laws. Our daily lives are intertwined with crime and its perpetrators. The dreamy-eyed manicurist who files away so enthusiastically at your nails may be thinking only of closing time, when she can hurry to meet the man whose "moll" she will eventually become, arranging his hide-outs, carrying his gun for him, fainting at the scene of a burglary to confuse pursuit. Provided this manicurist works in a shop of heavy patronage, it is almost certain that the very instruments which shape your finger nails have performed the same service for men who have known the cell block and the mess hall of prisons. Your tip after a hotel meal clinks in the same pocket with the gratuity of murderers and kidnappers. (3–4)

Here the insistent, analytical voice of the Bureau ("it is almost certain") counterpoints the inability of the reader to distinguish the criminal from the lawful. Criminals are dreamy eyed; they give tips. And the scuffed line does not stop with the service trades; criminals have also developed an industrial power that rivals that of the legal economy. Cooper admires the custom construction of an armor-plated car for criminal use; the car is equipped with gun compartments, blowout-proof tires, and bulletproof windows, yet the manufacturer's insignia and all other markings that indicate the car's ordinariness have been painstakingly replaced. Again, the general public is depicted as inca-pable of "telling the difference": "I believe I am a fairly close observer; yet I have ridden in armored cars and not realized the fact until I have rolled down the windows," he reports. "Where is it all done? Many law-enforcement officers would like to know. They can't find out." (36–37).

In Cooper's post-Repeal geography of crime, the threatening taint of criminality is essentially discrete from yet interspersed with and indistinguishable from the populace. If "the more desperate" flock to public places, then the thin blue line between legality and delinquency has vanished or has become a Möbius strip; the criminals seem to be those we most trust. Like an epidemic or a rapist, the formerly discrete and distanced criminal element intrudes into the spaces of the everyday, threatening the borders of our own bodies. No wonder, then, that the Bureau's enduring pairing of discourses of scientific analysis and sociopolitical regulation did not draw more criticism. As Prohibition ended and Americans attempted to close ranks against crime, these vertigo-inducing discourses of infection made the overstated scientism of FBI practice seem a prophylactic necessity. Years later, Hoover would warn Americans similarly to "open our eyes" and "inform ourselves about Communism" (Hoover, *Masters* 9). To inform oneself frequently led, of course, to informing on others.

Cooper's modeling of underworld hierarchies upon the legitimate economy dramatizes and amplifies the eerie proximity of criminals. To become a criminal, Cooper explains at one point, one uses the same skills and undergoes the same processes as another person climbing a corporate ladder.

> To the law-abiding it perhaps seems a difficult process for a man to become a member of a notorious gang. In reality, its counterpart in ordinary life would be that of the ambitious young man who works in the grocery store in a small town and who knows everyone. He is alert and eager, he forms friendships easily and impresses those whom he knows as a person with executive ability. Soon another and bigger grocery starts down the street, and a surprised town finds the young man is one of the partners. It is exactly the same in crime. (10)

This business metaphor is only one mapping tactic locating criminality and legality side by side. Cooper's first-chapter analysis of the landscape of American crime, built upon data from Bureau files, divides "public enemies" from lesser offenders, but it then ties each criminal to the hierarchy by metaphorizing crime as an educational institution in which promotion and graduation occur in an orderly, routine fashion. "The dangerous criminal becomes such by a process of education," Cooper asserts. "In practically every instance, he begins in a petty way, slowly becoming more vicious, until at last he is classed as a mad dog" (6). Just as in contemporary cockroach-control advertisements, the criminals you could see indicated the hidden presence of many more—"A gang, it might be added, usually is composed of from five to eight principals, with at least four minor characters or hangers-on for each major member. Therefore, this file of ten thousand names in reality means an army of criminals far greater than the numerical strength as indicated by the cards. These are the post-graduates of crime. The remainder of the three million might be called the general student body" (6). Ominously, the underworld organizes as a "file," an "army," and though its end products are "mad dogs," the criminal "educational process" appropriates the means by which everyday legality reproduces its knowledge and ensures individual and societal progress. Cooper paints American criminality as a culture in development—occupying the same ground as the reader's culture and presumably bound for conflict.

His portrait foreshadows a battle, then, that will be fought on that shared ground. The organization and technology used in such a war must match or overpower those of the criminal enemy; Cooper suggests that older, more entrenched forms of law enforcement—local and state agencies—are useless by dint of their toleration of and failure to respond progressively to more sophisticated criminals. In 1935, Cooper and Hoover thought of the "army of crime" as a "grass-roots organization," notes Powers; such a metaphor places the fault for well-entrenched criminal networks upon local police forces and exonerates the FBI, which emerges as the one law enforcement power sophisticated enough to fight modern crime (*Secrecy* 199). Such an argument, Powers proposes, also helped Hoover "avoid unwanted organized crime jurisdiction"; Hoover's denial that the Mafia existed in America and his refusal to investigate or intercede in its activities has been called "the greatest, most obvious and most inexplicable failure of the FBI" (Cook 140).

Accordingly, in his introduction to *Ten Thousand Public Enemies*, J. Edgar Hoover endorses "a newer order of law enforcement." He condemns the "morass of ineffectual laws" that predate the Bureau's rise or that complicate its mission at the local level. "A barbed wire entanglement of various factors" stops law enforcement officers, he warns: the "maze of politics," the "impediment thrown up by well-meaning but non-thinking folk." In these metaphors, the police and populace obstruct: they figure as ramparts or thickets which prevent the clean, total sweep of criminals that presumably the FBI's science and national jurisdiction could achieve (vii–viii).

Hoover denied that the FBI intended to usurp policing power— "Let's get this Scotland Yard business straightened out," he protests in a 1933 *Country Gentleman* article titled "Is the Sheriff a Back Number?" "We in the Division of Investigation are not advocating that its functions be extended. If the suggestion comes from the outside, we'll be happy and eager to take on any job that is assigned us" (35). But just as quickly, he rationalizes this usurpation via the discourse of technological elitism. "There is nothing which can take the place of local forces properly equipped to deal with local crime," he assures Cooper's readers; "However, day by day, crime is laughing at localities" (viii). At the height of the Depression, little hope existed of "properly" equipping local police, as Hoover had already acknowledged: "the great problem" of a police officer lies "in reaching a position from which capture is possible" (vii). Under the guise of cooperation, Hoover's introduction justifies the nationalization of policing networks and perpetuates the stereotype of the inept local lawman.

The terms of this bicultural interpenetration describe illegality's threatening integration and slippery mobility. "There is the vast maze of hide-outs, tuck-aways, apartments, hoodlum hotels and hoodlum camps where wanted men may be sheltered for a price and no one the wiser," writes Hoover ("Foreword," viii). This curious, somewhat paradoxical pairing of integration and mobility matches perfectly Hoover's arguments for the FBI's primacy: that its scientific methods of detection and nationwide jurisdiction are appropriate, progressive responses to a more dangerous, resourceful world of delinquency.

This mobility opens the second front of the battle proposed by FBI-approved discourses of the 1930s. The automobile—and the development of restaurants, service stations, motels, and lodges to accommodate auto travelers—established a mobility that frustrated local police: "no matter how efficient, [they] cannot be expected to catch criminals when, almost immediately, they vanish from [local officials'] jurisdiction. Detectives cannot amass protective knowledge about persons they never before have seen" (Cooper, *Ten Thousand* 51). The incremental spread of formal law and policing across the United States, as well as the realities of police funding, gave rise to the jurisdictional system whereby a lawman's power stopped at the border of his locality. "What is done in Brownville is, generally speaking, of no concern to Smithton," Harvard law professor Sheldon Glueck complained to the attorney general's 1934 crime conference (54). This second spatial aspect to post-Prohibition crime also invited a specifically federal response—in this case, the Bureau's ability to coordinate manhunts across multiple jurisdictions.

"There was a time," reminisces Cooper, "when crime was a haphazard affair. Then it was a problem of the community. Crooks traveled about only at intervals and held to certain constricted avenues of law infractions. All that has been changed. Speedy automobiles and airplanes have widened both the field of acquaintanceship and of activity. The old-time specialist has, to a degree, vanished; a man no longer is a safecracker and nothing else; he is an all-round criminal and he uses the nation for his field" (48–49). Cooper gives as an example the story of bank robber Charles Erb Redding:

Time after time, this man had left his filling station in Salt Lake, driven across Utah, through Nevada and California into Los Angeles, there robbed a bank, and driven the thousand miles back to his legitimate business. Not once had he even stayed overnight in the California city.

Thus crime has taken on shuttle-like proportions; men living in one State and committing crimes a thousand miles away, mobsters of one city in direct touch with the mobsters of another, bank robbers hurrying from place to place by fast automobile or airplane that they may contact lawyers, doctors, face lifters, hair dyers, brokers for stolen bonds, purveyors of kidnap money, dealers in gangster guns. (51)

Here, metaphors of mobility and infestation cross. The portability of 1930s crime, Cooper suggests, opens up "constricted avenues" and specific criminal "intervals." As the "field" of illegalities widens, the recognizable criminal "vanishes" into a support network of allies that begins with the pillars of the legitimate economy—lawyers, doctors— and extends in a continuum into "purveyors of kidnap money, dealers in gangster guns."

Cooper makes a disorienting pastiche of several dozen of the most notable crimes and criminal figures of the period, using acquaintances between crooks as transitional devices that, as well, suggest the interconnection of the underworld. Moving breathlessly from character to character and state to state, as if to dizzy the reader, Cooper's style mimics the mobility afforded criminals by their automobiles.

This was a gay meeting in Kansas City. Everybody was glad to see everybody else, and asked innumerable questions. Where was Bernard Phillips now? Still in Leavenworth? And how were Durrill and Thayer and Kelly getting along? All swell fellows. The party grew so jovial that it was decided to go somewhere and celebrate. A stop was made at the farm near Joplin. Then Jelly and the Farmers and the Harmons went to Hot Springs, Arkansas, where they rented a house and stayed nearly six weeks. One day Charlie and his wife had a spat. She went back to her house in Chicago. The farm called Deafy and Esther. Frank Nash and Charlie Harmon were left together. So they went out and robbed a bank.

It was good to have real money again. Charlie wanted to return to Chicago and square up with Paula. Frank Nash saw him to the station and then went back to the Farmers and to his bootlegging.

There was a reconciliation in Chicago; Paula Harmon closed her house of prostitution and went to St. Paul with Charlie. St. Paul was a grand town in those days; crooks told each other that the liquor business had effected certain tie-ups by which a big-timer in any of the tougher rackets could see the right person and be assured of a quiet, undisturbed life. (215–16)

The whirling mobility suggested by such a passage, Cooper suggests, outstrips the capabilities of local police. The Charles F. Urschel kidnapping of 1933 came as Franklin D. Roosevelt was empowering federal police with a package of crime bills. Urschel, a wealthy oil wildcatter, was released after eight days, but the investigation and capture of the kidnappers made the news daily between July 22 and mid-October. The police work was shared between federal and local sources: husband-and-wife kidnappers George "Machine Gun" and Kathryn Kelly were in fact arrested by a Memphis police sergeant on October 26. But Hoover's retellings of the story stressed the Bureau's role in the kidnappers' capture. Powers's note on this discrepancy is useful:

In the early accounts of the story, the AP gave credit for the capture to the Memphis detectives. The *Washington Star*'s rewrites made Hoover's special agent in charge, William Rorer, the hero of the case (*New York Journal*, Sept. 26, 1933, p. 1, and *Washington Star*, Sept. 26, 1933, p. 1). The *Star*'s rewrite of the AP story added that SAC Rorer immediately telephoned word of the capture to Hoover. The *Star*'s own story said that Rorer was carrying out "Hoover's plan" and that the key to the capture was a planeload of agents from around the country who had converged on Memphis when the Bureau learned of Kelly's whereabouts. (*Secrecy* 530)

According to hostile FBI historian Jay Robert Nash, Hoover fabricated Machine Gun Kelly's legendary cry of "Don't shoot, G-Men, don't shoot!" (*Citizen* 36–37). After Walter Winchell and other newspaper and radio commentators popularized the expression (Gentry 178), the story passed into the realm of truth in biographies such as Gentry's and Ralph de Toledano's. However, the phrase appears nowhere in the *New York Times, Time,* or many other periodicals as they report the capture. Powers points out that the Urschel case made a particularly valuable story for the Bureau in that it involved multiple states: Urschel was abducted in Oklahoma and held hostage in Texas, where kidnapper Harvey Bailey was arrested. But the *Times* was wowed by the Bureau's multimodal investigation and deduction, which, Powers adds, was one of Hoover's early successes at controlling the very narrative of a case (*Secrecy* 186–87). While blindfolded and tied, Urschel had tricked his captors into telling him the time as a plane passed overhead each day.

> Federal agents began a systematic check of all airline schedules in an attempt to identify the plane. . . . At first they thought he had been hidden in Southern Oklahoma, but their check-up proved this to have been impossible.
> They decided it must have been in the American Airways route between Amarillo and Fort Worth, probably nearer the latter city. Then they interviewed pilots and ground radio operators and learned that on the day Urschel had missed the plane, the pilot had swerved from his course because of bad weather.
> This left a comparatively small area, which was carefully searched with binoculars from the air and also from the ground. ("Urschel Abductor Captured" 1)

The story became hallowed in FBI history. Cooper's account in *Ten Thousand Public Enemies* stresses the complexity of both crime and investigation, narrating the arrests of various other criminals who had associated with Bailey or the Kellys or who had received or helped launder ransom money. Cooper salutes local police agencies for their cooperation but reiterates the federal force's necessity:

> So the raids began. One arrest led to another—in Minnesota, where ransom money had been passed; in Colorado, Tennessee, Texas, Illinois and other places where, working with the aid of local authorities, criminals were rounded up. . . .
> The wide range of this case is an excellent example of how the Division of Investigation, with field offices located at strategic points throughout the United States, can pursue a gang of criminals in as many as thirty points at the same time, especially when given the splendid cooperation of local police units, such as was evidenced in the Urschel case.
> Had this kidnapping been wholly a state matter in which the Oklahoma City police solely were given the job of tracking down the kidnappers, it is

doubtful if there could have been as complete a solution of the crime. (290–91)

Several critics have proposed that the Urschel investigation is a largely fabricated legend. William J. Helmer contests the account of the Memphis Kelly arrests but also questions the veracity of the story of locating the Paradise, Texas, ranch where Urschel was held; far from deducing the ranch's whereabouts, Helmer argues, the FBI actually based its investigation on informant leads (Girardin 6)—an ostensibly less "modern" investigation and one that, in its evocation of the elbow-rubbing camaraderie between police and bootleggers in the 1920s, would run counter to the image the Bureau was building. Not only did major FBI investigations have to succeed to meet Hoover's standard, but they also had to be rendered productive in terms of shaping the Bureau's mandate.

Spurious or not, Hoover's revision of the social cartography of lawlessness successfully built support around federal policing. By imagining and disseminating a geography that placed criminals both in secure places near us and in the transitory spaces between communities and jurisdictions, Hoover and FBI discourse shaped American notions of the law enforcement techniques and resources necessary to fight crime.

In 1933 and 1934, representations of crime and criminals shifted, David E. Ruth notes, from predominantly urban lawlessness—bootleggers, gangsters, Al Capone, and the Lindbergh kidnapping—to encompass rural crime, particularly the bandits who wreaked havoc on small banks across the Midwest and Great Plains. Hoover led Hollywood to these hinterlands bandits, notes Ruth; while filmmakers' sudden interest in "hopeless farmers and dejected migrants" and the rural outlaw may reveal changing social concerns and an effort to come to grips with the ravages of the Depression (145–46), for Hoover the shift was entirely productive. His examples—the "tramp or petty thief" in Des Moines who may be guilty of "more than one murder in various sections of the country" (Hoover, "In the Fight" 3)—relocate crime into the heartland and make it an undeniably American phenomenon, one that unitary policing is impotent to counteract. Simultaneously, the example of the wandering felon authorizes a broad project of identification and record keeping, presumably coordinated at a central hub: "It is manifestly impracticable for the police authorities in that section to make inquiries of every town in the United States or of the civilized world as to the criminal record of this individual" (Hoover, "In the Fight" 3). The identification and registration functions of the Bureau became a means of plotting an individual, an inward gaze that did not limit itself to lawbreakers. Fugitives, for their part, tested the Bureau's outward reach, its aspiration to map and police the far-flung nation. No outlaw engaged the machinery—or the legend—of the young Bureau as fully as John Dillinger, the Indiana-born bank robber whose 1934 lam I discuss in chapter 3.

3. "this sure keeps a fellow moving"

The Making of John Dillinger

Indiana outlaw John Dillinger is perhaps the best-remembered of the Midwestern desperadoes of the early 1930s; only Bonnie Parker and Clyde Barrow come close, in large part due to Arthur Penn's 1967 film *Bonnie and Clyde*. Yet a raft of contemporaries had bloodier, more notorious careers than did Dillinger: Ma Barker and her gang, Barrow and Parker, George "Baby Face" Nelson, Charles "Pretty Boy" Floyd, Alvin Karpis. Even some of Dillinger's closest criminal associates had longer rap sheets, including Harry "Pete" Pierpont, Homer Van Meter, and John Hamilton. But none have longer reputations.

> If John Dillinger had been the son of a Mellon or a Morgan, he would not be a bandit. . . . Why are you worrying so much about bandits? Why don't you worry about bank failures? Why don't you worry about money being in the hands of too few people?
> —Clarence Darrow

> Great desperadoes from little urchins grow.
> —a *Time* photo caption

Dillinger's enduring fame has much to do with the attention he garnered in news accounts as well as his penetration of other media: the Library of Congress Archive of Folk Song lists two commercial recordings and thirteen items of sheet music and lead sheets with "Dillinger" in the title, all copyrighted in 1934 and 1935. Several films and biographies have retold Dillinger's life, and a public museum in Crown Point, Indiana, preserves the outlaw's memory.

Dillinger's enduring notoriety has also sprung from his enshrinement as an FBI trophy. A 1937 *New Yorker* profile describes the Bureau display case in the anteroom to J. Edgar Hoover's office:

> In the anteroom where visitors wait to be admitted to the Director's presence the most compelling decorative object is a startling white plaster facsimile of John Dillinger's death mask. It stares, empty-eyed, from under the glass of a display case. There are other exhibit cases in the anteroom, but this one, like a prize scalp, is significantly located closest to the Director's office. Grouped about the mask are souvenirs of the memorable night when the spectacular outlaw was cornered and shot down after he had emerged from a motion-picture theatre in Chicago. (Alexander 21)

Hoover made a great public show of execrating Dillinger. Hoover's 1938 book *Persons in Hiding* calls Dillinger a "foul murderer" (93) and "a cheap, boastful, selfish, tight-fisted plug-ugly" (303). Jay Robert Nash calls Dillinger "Hoover's personal nemesis" (*Citizen* 41). Indeed, Hoover issued an unprecedented "public enemy number one" alert for Dillinger in 1934, placing a "shoot to kill" order and a $10,000 dead-or-alive bounty on his head. He found Dillinger sympathizers "infuriating" despite his own "repugnant fascination" for the outlaw, and he scowled after Dillinger's death that "there is no romance in a dead rat" (de Toledano 113–14). Hoover's "hatred" of Dillinger continued to grow "beyond all reason" over decades, report Athan Theoharis and John Stuart Cox. Hoover cursed Dillinger with Martin Luther King Jr., whom the FBI director despised, "in a kind of involuntary incantation, as if all the world's evil had been reposed in their two vile bodies." It was as if the director had fallen "negatively in love," Theoharis and Cox write suggestively (360).

Why would Dillinger have troubled Hoover so, even after his 1934 rampage ended happily for the FBI, the prolepsis of pursuit had been closed, and the death mask became a display trophy for the director? After all, the two complemented each other marvelously as cat and mouse. Hoover biographer Ralph de Toledano notes that Dillinger, a fine baseball player, "could have been a successful lawyer, businessman, or master mechanic. He had more than average intelligence and great manual dexterity. He liked people and people liked him" (113). Many eyewitnesses to his robberies lauded his organizational ability and coolness under pressure. And, like Hoover, Dillinger understood public relations: an avid newspaper reader, he monitored his position relative to the police and the law-abiding majority (Girardin 189, 198). A letter Dillinger supposedly wrote in May 1934 to automaker Henry Ford exhibits a sardonic awareness of his public allure:

> Hello Old Pal:
> Arrived here at 10 AM today. Would like to drop in and see you.
> You have a wonderful car. Been driving it for three weeks. Its [*sic*] a treat to drive one.

Your Slogan should be.

Drive a Ford and watch the other cars fall behind you. I can make any other car take a Ford's dust.

Bye-Bye

John Dillinger (Toland 301)

Even if a forgery, as G. Russell Girardin suggests (283), the letter attests to the considerable place Dillinger occupied in the public imagination during his 1934 heyday.

The director's scorn may have been righteous indignation or show business; certainly "the Boy Scout," as his enemies called Hoover, generated plenty of both. To draw—and to *talk*—a hard line against criminals was Hoover's job. I agree with William J. Helmer's argument that Dillinger and Hoover "became a study in mutual mythmaking," that the defeat of Dillinger rewarded Hoover with prestige that he "would forever wear before critics like a bulletproof vest" (Girardin 269). Discussing the "structural utility" of wrongdoers, sociologist Orrin E. Klapp pairs villainous types with types of heroes and assigns each dyad a linking theme; for example, conformers combat outlaws, rebels, and corrupters over the issue of "conformity." "There is a kind of teamwork between heroes and villains," he writes (66–67). "The villain is a functional character, and ritual is a social device for repeating his functions again and again. He often serves society, for example, as a scapegoat or safety valve for aggression, or as a perfected hate-symbol building morale for law enforcement and other actions. Oddly, he serves society by deviating from its mores" (51). Klapp's simple binarism comments acutely on the relationship between police and criminals. Cops need crooks to keep working. The criminal is essential to definitions of lawfulness as well as law enforcement. In naming and pursuing a criminal, law enforcement defines itself and its dyadic opposite, and apprehending that criminal spells the end of a particular performance of thematic difference—or, as Lacan would have it, of desire.

Though their scathing Hoover biography has shortcomings as an authoritative source (they ignore the murder of William P. O'Malley,

by most accounts Dillinger's one verifiable killing, apparently to mini-
mize Dillinger's importance), Athan G. Theoharis and John Stuart Cox
propose that Dillinger's menacing reputation was in fact a product of
the very Justice Department publicity Hoover helped orchestrate. They
call Dillinger "a comparative nonentity" who "had held up several
Midwestern banks . . . but at no time, then or later, committed a known
capital offense. . . . He seems, on the contrary, to have been chosen
solely for his star quality" (123). Such a reading suggests that the
Bureau, to continue its expansion under the new Roosevelt administration, looked for a nemesis and, to some degree, manufactured one.

If one accepts such a reading of the outlaw as star, then Dillinger's
story confirms the ideological utility of criminals, and in particular, of
the selection of certain types of villains for the public staging of morality plays. Images of criminals, just like images of the police, needed
mediation, as they do still. "The average police officer has become a
knowledge worker," writes Renee Goldsmith Kasinsky (203). "In the past
few decades the police profession has become much more involved with
the news media, which has been accompanied by an increase in their
political power, personnel, and fiscal power. They have made an effort to
control their environment through a proactive strategy of selectively dis-
closing knowledge about organizational activities and of defining their
public image" (207). But these possibilities do not explain Hoover's fixation; to suggest that Dillinger's fame was puppeted in order to increase
the value of his eventual capture makes the notion of Hoover execrating
the outlaw after thirty years seem even more unlikely.

Hoover's frustration, I will argue, has roots also in Dillinger's success at drawing out their battle and humiliating the FBI, which led
national media to construct Dillinger as a foil to the director and his
steps toward national policing. Early in 1934, Dillinger seemed perfectly
cast for the role of testing the police's ability to pursue and apprehend.
Furthermore, his escape from an Indiana jail evoked derision for the
local police who guarded him, aligning him directly opposite the federal bureau's interstate jurisdiction. Dillinger proved unpredictably

charismatic, and the popular press and law-abiding public joined in his defiance of Hoover's nationalistic strategies. Dillinger also defied Hoover's attempts to redefine the criminal and the law-abiding citizen as mutually structuring and opposed categories. With the aid of popular media representations that aestheticized him and repressed the danger he posed, he briefly became more popular than his G-man pursuers. Somehow, even as he flitted from state to state, he managed to escape to some degree his deserved reputation as a cosmopolitan, mobile fugitive, taking on a comfortable public persona as an Indiana farm boy. Toward the end of his lam, the outlaw inspired a craze I will call Dillinger spotting; he managed to frustrate the Bureau's efforts to keep track of him while at the same time gleefully inviting the citizenry— who in Cooper's discourse are upbraided for their inability to spot crime even in their own backyards—to follow his progress. Whereas Hoover's first steps toward what Robert J. Corber has called "a national security state" focused on recovering, analyzing, categorizing, and empowering various forms of knowledge (fingerprints, local police records, membership lists and practices of "subversive" organizations, and so on), Dillinger's lam showed the limitations of even a full-out FBI manhunt's ability to keep legend from overrunning the facts.

Born in 1903, Dillinger was the smart but delinquent son of a grocer and farmer. He was a Navy deserter and estranged from his father when, on September 6, 1924, bored and drunk, he and a local ne'er-do-well tried to rob a storekeeper in his hometown of Mooresville, Indiana. When the victim struggled, Dillinger's gun went off harmlessly; frightened, he ran for the getaway car, which wasn't there. Tried without a lawyer, Dillinger wound up serving nearly nine years of a ten-year sentence; his older partner received half that. Dillinger was paroled on May 22, 1933, so he could visit his mother's sickbed, but she died shortly before he arrived (Toland 3–14; Girardin 9–22).

Dillinger emerged from prison bitter and well connected. Clearly, he had become a classmate in what Courtney Ryley Cooper called the "general student body" of American crime, a gangster, not a loner. Arrested in Dayton, Ohio, on September 23, 1933, for bank robbery, he had only to wait three weeks before fellow Indiana ex-convicts Harry Pierpont, Charles Makley, and John Hamilton—whose September 26, 1933, escapes from the Michigan City jail he had designed and set into motion—arrived to break him out, killing Sheriff Jess Sarber in the raid.

In popular news accounts of Dillinger, we can see how the language that formed his legend conformed to, then broke from, the period's dominant discourses about crime and criminals. Reports of his exploits before January 25, 1934, are nondescript, statistical, blandly condemnatory accounts of gangsterism, painting the Dillinger gang as the "corporate" type described by Cooper and Hoover. The gang's reputation was as yet small, though a four-paragraph Associated Press report printed in the *New York Times* on January 12 describes with some irony a "box score" of killings (gang members vs. policemen) kept on the wall by an Indiana State Police patrolman who himself was killed during the capture of one of the felons Dillinger helped escape from Michigan City ("Indiana Police" 15). Stories characterize the gang only indirectly: the gang is neither prominent enough nor available enough to describe. A December 26 *New York Times* story coaxes some memorable copy out of captured gangster Edward Shouse, who calls the gang "kill-crazy," but in speaking further about the group, with whom he escaped from the Michigan City prison, Shouse recycles crime-story clichés, identifying the gang only as desperate outcasts. "The others, too, would rather die than be brought back here," he tells a sergeant, "They'll shoot it out to the last bullet." Beyond calling the group "the Dillinger gang," the article makes no distinctions among the six gangsters named, who, Shouse insists, speak "of little else than killing policemen." Thus the robbery becomes a standard exhibit for post-Prohibition police discourse: the faceless gangsters are anticops, cop killers. If Shouse characterizes the group, he does so only by invoking a direct opposition between "kill-crazy" felons and the "married men with families" whom they threaten ("Dillinger's Gang Called" 28).

The tenor of early Dillinger coverage is exemplified by reports of the gang's January 15 robbery of the East Chicago First National Bank. During this robbery, Dillinger shot policeman William P. O'Malley, by most accounts Dillinger's only killing. The *Chicago Daily Tribune* recognized him as "notorious," "Indiana's most dangerous outlaw." But as yet his criminal menace remains rather abstract; the method of the heist and estimates of its take figure more prominently than any glimpse of the outlaw himself. This front-page *Tribune* story—the second-biggest of its day, headed by "Dillinger Robs Bank, Kills Policeman"—doesn't even focus primarily upon Dillinger. It features other gang members, including John Hamilton, who had killed a Chicago officer a few weeks before. Dillinger and Hamilton are lumped together as having "been identified by policemen who had seen both many times" ("Dillinger Robs Bank" 1).

As the edited, reprinted story appears outside Chicago, Dillinger's ostensible ringleadership recedes further. *New York Times* headlines read:

OUTLAWS ROB BANK, KILL A POLICEMAN
Band Believed to Be Dillinger Gang Shoots Way through 8
Officers in East Chicago.
LEADER USES MACHINE GUN
Sprays Victim at Door and Flees in Car—Used Banker as
Cover.

Though the header names Dillinger as the robbery's leader, the plural and collective nouns—"outlaws," "band," "gang"—downplay his celebrity. (The headline's "Believed to Be" guards cautiously against mistaken attribution of the robbery, a sign that the Dillinger gang's work might yet be mistaken for other gangs'.) The *Times* coverage was nothing special; notice of a Philadelphia bank robbery for $21,140—Dillinger took almost the same amount, $20,376—appears next to the East Chicago report and occupies nearly as much space, although in Philadelphia no officers were injured or killed ("3 Bandits Seize" 42). In these colorless articles, even the eulogy of the slain officer that ends the *Tribune* article comes off as dry and official.

Even with Dillinger momentarily visible, newspaper coverage of the gang's January robberies shies dutifully away from the sort of portraiture that might be taken by censorious readers as glorification of the gangster. Both *Times* and *Tribune* stories include the long narrative of banker Edward L. Steck, who describes Dillinger as "a terrible man." There is a studied grimness to Steck's imagery; he metaphorizes the robbers' operation as procedural, even automatic. Even the killing of policemen becomes but a stroke in the mechanical cycle of robbery: "While Hamilton, the second man, was getting the money Dillinger glanced out the doorway and saw other policemen congregating. Instead of appearing frightened, he called out to the money-gatherer: 'There's been an alarm and the police are outside. But don't hurry. Get all that dough. We'll kill all these coppers and get away. Take your time'" ("Dillinger Robs Bank" 1).

Dillinger's gang are no mad dogs; like the G-men themselves, they work through a situation according to the manual. Steck's account echoes Courtney Ryley Cooper's dread about the mechanics and organization of modern bank robbery. The gang's weapons reinforce this impression: after "electrifying" the crowd, Dillinger shoots O'Malley with a "machine gun," and the gang escapes behind "bullet proof vests" in an automobile with "bulletproof glass." During the getaway, the wounded Hamilton's condition cannot be ascertained (such are the complications of reporting on fugitives), whereas the getaway *machine's* collision with another car fills nearly a paragraph (4). And the gang's trademark maneuver of using bank officials or passersby to shield themselves from police fire becomes emblematic of inhuman use of humans: Steck characterizes hostage banker Walter Spencer as "protective covering," as little more than electrical insulation. The gang's procedure reduces victims to inert objects or machine parts, effecting a dehumanizing process. This dreadful imagery aligns the group with the mechanistic criminality Cooper maps in his 1930s FBI stories. However, one might also compare the gang's procedure to Hoover's scientific-management style; presumably only the distinction between threatening criminal and protecting policeman exonerates the FBI from the same repulsed public reaction.

The nature of Dillinger coverage changes profoundly with his January 25, 1934, capture in Tucson, Arizona. No longer a fugitive, his status as reportable object changes. No more can reporters parlay the factual details of his robberies into constructions of "the notorious outlaw"; the crimes end, and practically speaking, the outlaw becomes visible, quotable. Soon he is available via pretrial appearances, even jailhouse interviews, which he granted amiably to curious reporters. The easy access provided to Dillinger by his Arizona captors and Indiana jailors suggests that the police considered the specter of the outlaw in a jail cell an image of immense strategic value in the war against crime. He was a big fish to land. Furthermore, according to the representational economy of Hollywood production codes, apprehension permitted a different sort of coverage. According to Olga J. Martin, because of the prohibition of gangster characters and warfare, "the types who are to portray the robbers should not be of the hard-boiled, tough-looking gangster type. They must, of course, be apprehended and punished" (146). Dillinger's apprehension, then, made his retroactive construction as a character permissible. Furthermore, he represented the criminal type the codes preferred: they mandated banishment of the "hard-looking, foul-speaking type, eager to kill" and his replacement by the racketeerish "gentleman with at least a surface polish ... softspoken and businesslike in his conversation rather than 'tough'" (133). Imprisoned, Dillinger could be made to fulfill the "crime doesn't pay" denouement held paramount by these production codes, and by police from Cummings and Hoover on down. Consequently, Dillinger's intelligence and dry, articulate speech appeared useful to police; they lent a tragic sense to his choice of a criminal "career."

After his Tucson capture, no longer was Dillinger a composite of statistical accountings of value stolen and casualties inflicted, nor an object of an eyewitness account favoring narrative rather than description. He became a character, quotable and knowable. After walking straight into a police stakeout, unaware that henchmen Charles Makley, Pete Pierpont, and Russell Clark have already been arrested, Dillinger launches a lament that delights the small-town police who had surprised him: " 'My God,' he cried. 'How did you know I was in town? I'll be the laughingstock of the country. How could a hick town police force ever suspect me?' " ("Catch Dillinger" 1). He had, in fact, already been taken twice by local forces: by Mooresville police following the bungled robbery in 1924 and by the Dayton police in 1933.

Yet Dillinger's lament redefined him as a national outlaw, one whose mobility ostensibly overpowered the resources and capabilities of local police, one whose reputation transcends region. Legend has it that he took a great pleasure in taunting Indiana State Police Captain Matt Leach; according to John Toland, Dillinger sent Leach a Christmas package containing the 1862 book *How to Become a Detective* (Girardin 38; Toland 157). The "hick town" disparagements envision Dillinger, in other words, as the very outlaw the federal agency was designed to apprehend.

David E. Ruth argues that the popular gangster figure served in the 1920s and 1930s as a "vessel" for communicating "a multitude of messages, some contradictory, for a public still adjusting to the city" (4). The Dillinger of January 1934 exhibited some of the hallmarks of the urban gangster: conspicuous consumption and, in particular, extraordinary sexual power and liberty. The *Chicago Daily Tribune*'s account of the Tucson arrest draws attention to Dillinger's speech and body; before police guns surround him, he appears a well-dressed, self-assured desperado, endowed with several phallic signifiers:

Dillinger, the bold leader, was the last of the four to be arrested. Apparently not knowing that the others had been caught, he drove up tonight to the residence he rented only three days ago. With him in his car was a handsomely dressed blonde about 35 years old, who later identified herself as Anne Martin, his sweetheart.

Stepping from the car, with a baby machine gun only partly hidden under his coat, Dillinger walked up to the porch of the house. As he inserted his key in the lock of his front door, fifteen Arizona policemen and deputy sheriffs stepped from the shrubbery in which they had been concealed. ("Catch Dillinger" 1)

Boldness, car, house, blonde sweetheart, machine gun too big to hide, key: such details about Dillinger had never before been available to *Tribune* reporters. Presumably supplied via wire by Tucson police, these details paint the picture of a hypermasculine outlaw. Other periodicals echo this note: *Newsweek* calls him "suave and slim" ("Public Enemies" 14), and the *New York Times* refers to the outlaw's "aplomb" ("22 Who Saw Dillinger" 3). Department of Justice agent C. J. Endres told press that $40,000 in cash was seized at the Tucson hideout, as well as $4,000 in diamonds, five machine guns, and other weapons ("Dillinger Gang Guarded" 1).

But apprehension by the local police unmans the star outlaw. Under the subheading "Submits to Handcuffs," the *Tribune* story continues:

Dillinger whirled about, but before he could pull the trigger of his deadly machine gun—said to be the one with which he shot Policeman William P. O'Malley to death . . . the police were upon him. Obediently he dropped the wicked looking gun and submitted to being handcuffed.

Less than a minute later the attractive Miss Martin, screaming, had been taken into custody. Dillinger, venting a stream of oaths and shaking with rage and fear, was led to police headquarters, where he was identified through fingerprints. His bravado deserted him. (1)

Capture effects a reversal: the police strip Dillinger of his physical and sexual force and assurance, rendering him an obedient, shivering creature. His bravado is identified as a facade, and force and initiative shifts dutifully to the police, who identify and remove the outlaw after springing "upon him" in a sexual or predatory fashion. A January 30 *Tribune* article makes explicit the contrast between the police's physical command of Dillinger and the outlaw's loss of bodily control: on the plane, his hands are manacled, and his feet, East Chicago police chief Nicholas Makar promises heartily, will be "locked in braces." The same paragraph notes that "the bandit leader was trembling slightly; one lip kept twitching. His debonair spirit of the morning . . . had disappeared" ("Speed Dillinger" 2). "Dillinger Gang Guarded by Own Machine Guns," crowed a January 27 *Los Angeles Times* headline; in later stories, the paper reinscribed the police's mastery, noting on January 28 that Dillinger "complained bitterly" ("Police Hunt" 2) and that he "scratched, kicked and screamed" when taken from his Tucson cell to return to face capital charges in Indiana ("Dillinger Sped" 2). Capture allowed daily papers to begin filling in the hitherto missing details of the bandit's shadowy celebrity. And, indeed, this celebrity had taken hold; as the extradition flight progressed eastward to Indiana, a procession that one-upped in speed and glamour the rampage of the gang, crowds of onlookers flocked to each refueling stop to try to catch a glimpse of the outlaw ("Meek Dillinger" 2).

This sharpening of focus around reportable detail, I would argue, did not initially contravene the tonal constrictions that police and church groups imposed upon representations of criminals following the crime panic of 1929–30 and the gangster-film glut of 1931. Presumably, the condition of captivity foreclosed the narratives of public menace and flight from apprehension he posed. Simply to subject Dillinger to description made clear that the quarry had been trapped. Thus the map that appears on page 2 of the January 30 *Tribune* (headed by "Scene of Capture") is a triumphant one. With its arrow ("Tucson") showing a small city at the junction of railroad lines, it spells a rare triumph for much-maligned local police against an automobile-era fugitive.

Tucson police capitalized upon their catch by allowing reporters and photographers opportunity to meet the criminal. He issued statements in the Pima County Jail and, after Arizona Governor E. B. Moeur visited the gang on January 26, cell block interviews were granted to newsmen, many of whom had traveled from Indiana or Chicago to meet the gangsters. Dillinger talked "at some length with Tubby Toms of the *Indianapolis News*" and "another newsman," report Robert Cromie and Joseph Pinkston in their biography of Dillinger (144). A *Chicago Times*

photographer purchased the four vacant seats on the plane that extradited Dillinger from St. Louis to Chicago in order to shut out his competitors and talk to the "very quiet and congenial" gunman (Cromie
and Pinkston 147).

Dillinger's panic at being captured and extradited didn't last long.
The *Tribune's* January 31 account of Dillinger's extradition to Chicago
has him "screaming and fighting" on the airstrip in Tucson, "manacled
and meek" and "shivering" at the airport in Chicago, but fully composed
upon his well-attended and much-photographed internment in the
Lake County jail at Crown Point, Indiana.

> Hardly had the iron doors clanged behind him when the outlaw, no
> longer glum and morose, but rather smiling and alert, posed for pictures
> with his principal guards and Prosecutor Robert G. Estill, who is to ask a
> jury of Lake County residents to send him to the electric chair for the
> O'Malley murder.
>
> Next, with an air that demonstrated him to be as mild a mannered man
> as ever shot up a bank, he submitted to general interviewing. Gone were the
> snarls with which he had greeted the Arizona police. His talk was full of
> praise, even for the Chicago policemen whom he had described in Tucson
> as "the dumbest in the world." There were verbal bouquets for the "nice
> fellows" who had accompanied him on the plane trip and an admission:
> "I like Mr. Estill and Mrs. Holley [the sheriff] seems like a fine lady."
> ("Meek Dillinger" 1)

A battery of photographs taken the night of his arrival in Crown
Point, Indiana became the biggest story of his six-week incarceration.
Reprinted widely—including in the *New York Times* and on the cover
of *Newsweek*—the photos show Dillinger posing with a small group of
officials, including prosecutor Estill and Sheriff Lillian Holley with one
elbow propped on Estill's near shoulder and Estill's arm draped around
his neck in what the *Times* called "a pally sort of way" ("Prosecutor
Posing" 3). Cromie and Pinkston argue that the prosecutor, "weary from
the trip to Tucson and back," "responded automatically" when a Chicago
photographer asked the group to stand close together (150–51). But the

public response to this ostensible show of camaraderie was immediate and scathing. Frank J. Loesch, head of the vigilante Chicago Crime Commission (made more respectable and less anonymous by its success against racketeers, memorialized in *The Secret Six*), blasted Estill, "Perhaps it isn't unethical, but it is certain that such familiarity breeds contempt for law enforcement in the minds of criminals" ("Prosecutor Posing" 3). Later that year, Estill lost in primary elections for his job—thanks largely to his opponent's campaign strategy of distributing copies of "the fatal picture" ("Primaries" 8).

Expecting a publicity windfall, local lawmen had failed to anticipate the risk in allowing newsmen access to Dillinger after he had regained his composure. Perhaps because so many criminals issued only ineloquent or surly denials, juvenile or profane humor, or other undistinguished behavior, to grant pressmen access to prominent "collars" rarely endangered the police's image. After all, the occasional prisoner with appeal and eloquence could be made to reiterate the very moral Ralph de Toledano draws from Dillinger: a wrong turn into crime had damned a smart boy.

But Estill's momentary lapse of judgment refueled perceptions that local police were too mild on dangerous criminals. While Arizona police had captured Dillinger, for their part, Indiana police had done little to slow the gang's robbery spree or to prevent their 1933 Michigan City jailbreak. Photographs of the prosecutor with his arm around the outlaw raised questions of police motives and competence, questions that flared after Dillinger's subsequent escape.

The police also seemed to ignore the possibility that the outlaw would prove a more compelling interpreter of his own story than they. On the surface, Dillinger's January 30 responses to "a dozen interviewers" at Crown Point fit with Hoover's model of the modern criminal. He admitted that his first imprisonment acquainted him with a network of "good fellows." Now safely ensconced in a cell, the outlaw reminisced about his gang's free range through public—ostensibly "legal"—space: "Those were exciting times. We moved from house to house, rented one, stayed a few days and moved on when the neighborhood got hot. But we used to go to the downtown theaters whenever we wanted to" ("Meek Dillinger" 2).

However, within these replies, which were snapped up by eager reporters, Dillinger managed to subvert Hoover's scripts of "educated" and "incorporated" criminals' proximity and resemblance to the populace. "I don't have many bad habits," he told a reporter who offered him a cigarette. "I don't smoke and I don't drink. About the only bad habit I've got is robbing banks" ("Dillinger Back" 3). Unlike Hoover's rhetoric of criminal infection, Dillinger's account abjures threatening the public. He stresses his origin *among* the public: "I am not a bad fellow, ladies and gentlemen. I was just an unfortunate boy who got started wrong." Dillinger directs his gang's menace instead at policemen and bankers at a historical moment when both groups' public images were compromised. He admits that henchman John Hamilton (now dead) had killed a policeman and answers a question about how long it took to "clean out a bank," "O, about a minute and 40 seconds flat" ("Meek Dillinger" 2). Carefully circumscribing his targets, Dillinger positions his gang shrewdly and manages to skew the binary between legality and illegality that Hoover was working to reimpose.

The interview's end betrays how thoroughly Dillinger's self-repositioning worked on a writer for the *Daily Tribune*:

> Something like a tear glistened in one eye as the interviewers left. Outside stood deputy sheriffs with machine guns poised to repel any attack that his friends might make in the hope of releasing him. In the corridor, constantly watching, was an armed man ready to kill Dillinger if he showed any signs of attempting to escape. In the jail dining room were the 32 Chicago policemen, commanded by Capt. Stege, enjoying the dinner and the half barrel of beer furnished by Deputy Sheriff Carroll Holley. ("Meek Dillinger" 2)

Like the central image of the eloquent man behind bars, the paragraph responds dutifully to a "crime doesn't pay" template. Yet after the corny poignancy of the "tear," the article reverses the representational politics of Dillinger's story. Whereas in Shouse's January statement the police had been "married men with families" and the gang a terrifying, machinelike force, suddenly Dillinger is the round, human character. The multitude of policemen surveilling the building take on an eerie anonymity, the mechanics of their roles (and weapons) far more visible than their faces or names. The Orwellian juxtaposition of this malevolent, dehumanized functionality with the feast in the dining room (complete with alcohol—Repeal had been achieved less than two months before), where the off-guard officers revel only yards away from the seriousness of the prison watch, cuts the police no favors. They have no opportunity to retort.

Intentionally or not, such coverage rearticulated Dillinger as popular entertainment, repressing any threat he posed to citizens and substituting a contest of charisma, a staged drama of anecdotes, one-liners, and threats between gangsters and lawmen.

Dillinger's subsequent escape from Crown Point, then, on March 3, 1934, put the press into a high hilarity. By most reports, Dillinger—called "John the Whittler" by his fellow convicts—fashioned a fake gun out of spare wood, stained it black with shoe polish, and used it to disarm the deputy nearest his cell. Then he systematically disarmed the guards and locked them in cells, without firing a shot. He took only one accomplice, an obscure black murderer named Herbert Youngblood who was captured in Michigan within a week. Dillinger even seized two machine guns from the "escape proof" jail, kidnapped a deputy and a mechanic who were working on a brand-new V-8 Ford, and then stole that car—Sheriff Lillian Holley's own—to get away.

Howls of derision rained down on Indiana's lawmen from near and far. Reportage and editorials alike luxuriated in the locals' embarrassment, repeating Dillinger's wisecracks to the caged guards: "If you aren't hick cops, I'm the chief of police," the *Miami Herald* quotes him as saying ("Dillinger Gets Out" 1). Most papers donated their own insults as well: the *Herald* calls the Crown Point police "nitwit guards," "incompetent officials," " 'hick' cops," "amateurish," and "weak-kneed and mentally disabled men" ("In Today's News" 6). In the *Literary Digest*, they are "wooden-headed" ("Crime-Ridden America" 39). The *Los Angeles Times* credits the escape to "plenty" of police "stupidity and cowardice": "In England, or even in New Jersey, he would have been hanged by this time; Indiana had not even put him on trial" ("Dillinger's Escape" 4). "Three spectacular robberies in different parts of the country which followed almost immediately may, or may not, have been inspired by the laxness of Indiana authorities," it editorialized a week later (Editorial, 12). Sheriff Holley's disgust became a parody of ineffectuality: "If I ever see John Dillinger again," she promised, "I'll shoot him dead with my own pistol" ("Three States" 1). The *Baltimore Sun* called her "hysterical" ("Gone Again" 8), and a *Cumberland Evening Times* front-page photo spread ran a profile view of Dillinger next to a photo of Holley in the jailhouse, cut one inch longer so as to display her long dress ("Noted Killer" 1). The *New York Times* reprinted its "pally" photograph of Dillinger and Estill together, revisiting the controversy of a month earlier. As for Estill, he credited the escape to "just damn dumbness" on the part of the guards ("Dillinger's Trail Lost" 1).

Many articles extend their condemnation of Indiana officials to local and state law enforcement officers across the country. Although it notes that Lillian Holley was the "actual sheriff, having been elected," the *Literary Digest* wails,

> Without the note of rather forlorn hope that the very depth of the humiliation might germinate a seed of reform, the total reaction would be one of unmitigated despair over the sorry mess of county jail management throughout the three thousand and more counties of the forty-eight States, with their army of political sheriffs and sheriffs' wives or widows, blonde or brunette, each with her star, her pistol and her vanity case. Which is not to imply that the feminine incumbents of shrieval functions throughout this fair land have done very much worse than some of the men, because that would be impossible. ("Crime-Ridden America" 39)

The normally male sheriff finds himself syntactically obliterated by feminine detail, the pairing of "her pistol and her vanity case."

Collier's editorialized about "the weakness and ineptness of our local governmental machinery" under a page-wide cartoon where an oversized pointing hand ("Dillinger") surprises two huddled, corpulent figures ("Law Enforcement" and "Politics"). About our "too weak, too clumsy, too contemptible" police, it complained, "In most states, politics, not fitness, selects sheriffs, jailers, prison guards and the entire aggregation of law enforcers. We seldom ask if a prison warden is qualified by education, character, prior experience or any other relevant factors to manage the institution we commit to his care. . . . the voters of Lake County, and Lake County is not unique, had a cheap regard for their law-enforcing agencies" ("Stop Encouraging Bandits!" 70). "Milksop enforcement . . . lady finger and pink tea caliber of law enforcement," sniffed the *Miami Herald* ("Milksop Enforcement" 6).

Opportunistically, *Collier's* uses the episode to plead for reform not of the purportedly corrupt local and state policing system but via laws "vastly extending the police power and the police operation of the national government." "Soon government belongs only to those capable of exercising it," its argument goes, comparing local prison administration unfavorably to the leadership of "a modern school, a hospital, or an efficient technical business." *Collier's* calls for the supersession of "scientific" federal police control over the "political" jurisdiction of the sheriff: "John Dillinger was able to run from state to state because in various places he knew refuge would be afforded even though he was a murderer and a thief. Refuge was available because local government here and there was weak, complacent" (70).

A serendipitously timed *Saturday Evening Post* article, appearing on March 10, less than a week after Crown Point, dramatized the problem in language that mimicked Courtney Ryley Cooper's. Author Albert W. Atwood first frames crime as a sociological problem involving "the whole structure of society"; more sympathetic to the predicament of local officers, Atwood traces their ineffectiveness to the limitations of local jurisdiction.

The criminal seeking refuge crosses county and state lines at will, but for the officer, appointed and paid to safeguard society, these boundaries rise as

impassable barriers. It is necessary in extradition to secure the consent of
the governor of the state to which the fugitive has fled, and if the latter
fights the process, an incredible amount of red tape is involved. . . .

Not only must constables, sheriffs, city police, county police and even
state police stop dead at the boundaries of the forty-eight sovereign states
but, as a matter of right, the chief of police in one city cannot demand
help from the police of another city, even in the same state (23, 82)

Characteristically, J. Edgar Hoover did not let the moment slip away.
The theft of the Ford and its transport over the state line into Illinois—
a violation of the 1919 Dyer Act—presented the Bureau its jurisdictional
opportunity. Remarkably, Dillinger had never before committed a crime
that invoked federal jurisdiction, since bank robbery had not yet been
made a federal crime at the time of his Tucson arrest. Such condemnations of local police presented the symbolic opportunity. There could
not have been better tinder for the efforts of Cummings and Hoover to
kindle public and political opinion toward federal law enforcement.
"The crook fraternity as a class notoriously has a far healthier respect for
Uncle Sam and the long arm of the law than for mere State jurisdictions," opined the *Washington Evening Star* (Editorial, A-8).

On March 19 and 20, Homer Cummings outlined a "Twelve Point
Anticrime Program" to Congress that included increased federal jurisdiction and powers. "Crime has become a business—a cold, hard, cal-
culating enterprise," he declared. Cummings's request to Congress
made the opposition of local and national policing strategies explicit,
advocating control of "those who deliberately take advantage of the
protection presently afforded them by State lines" ("Federal 'Teeth'"
46). On May 3, he asked the Congressional Budget Office to finance
"fast armored cars, airplanes, machine guns and special rifles" for the
federal arsenal, thereby procuring technological muscle to back up
Hoover's organization and jurisdiction ("Air, Land, Sea Drive" 1). The
Houston Post endorsed the federal drive, claiming that federal crime
empowerment would "be welcomed even in commonwealths that
have been the most ardent champions of constitutional States' rights
guarantees" ("States' Rights" 6).

Dillinger's calm escape and his abandonment of local and state jurisdiction shaped the identity of the forces that would be called to head off his flight. Sheriff Holley's promise to "shoot him dead" made little sense in the eye-for-an-eye logic of revenge. In contrast, Hoover's federal force—which, if it had had little to do with Dillinger's January capture, at least had played no part in his ill-fated incarceration—already had mobilized a rhetoric of scientific, infallible methods and interstate jurisdiction to which Dillinger's interstate rampage posed a legal and symbolic affront. In this sense, Dillinger was the first modern American fugitive—the man in flight across a nation whose internal borders ostensibly had been erased.

After painting charismatic portraits of the outlaw in January, news-papers seemed reluctant after the Crown Point escape to discard the image they had made of Dillinger and shift him dutifully into the role of public enemy. Perhaps journalists who feared restrictions on their own representational freedoms decided to stand firm on their coverage of Dillinger. Perhaps it was a less principled, more visceral sympathy that writers felt for the bandit. After all, the police had invited the press into the jail and helped to create the articulate Dillinger image.

Almost certainly, his jailhouse charisma made ignoring the outlaw an unprofitable editorial stance. Writing about the national press's eager reprinting of lurid crime-scene and morgue photos following Dillinger's death, the stern-faced *Literary Digest* alluded to the "likeli-hood of attracting circulation": "The decision was easy, let us assume, in the case of the typical tabloid; not so easy, it may be imagined, for papers like the *Chicago Daily News* and the *Cleveland News*. However, they, too, struck a balance in favor of the ghastly display as against the protest of sensitive readers, and for the same reason—circulation. The moral imperative, if they entertained it, was a pietistic afterthought" ("At the Observation Post" 11).

For whatever reason, the stories in which writers retell Dillinger's escape from Crown Point leak an ambivalence that deflates their rote condemnations of the outlaw. The *Tribune* called him "the calm, humorously cynical bandit" and credited the escape to "his own desperate courage" ("Three States" 1). Many articles downplayed the danger Dillinger might pose the populace—after all, he dropped his hostages off on an Illinois roadside unharmed, apologizing for not giving them carfare home. Instead, the attractive aspects of Dillinger's demeanor dominate these accounts. The eloquence and patience that had made him seem an attractive, valuable prize while in custody now came back to taunt the police: "Keep your noses clean," he tells his Indiana hostages upon releasing them ("Escape Is Pictured" 8). Several *New York Times* headlines, "Dillinger 'Rose' in 6-Month Spurt" and "Dillinger Escapes; His Pistol Wooden," reinscribe and extend the phallic power that capture had briefly cost him. The *Tribune* notes how "carefully" he locks the jail's doors, how he counseled the deputy (who tried to crash the getaway car into another to thwart the escape) " 'Take your time, take your time. . . . Thirty miles an hour is enough. There's no hurry' " ("Three States" 2). Here Dillinger becomes the patient, paternal figure, admonishing *the police* to follow the traffic laws.

An indicative treatment is the *Miami Herald*'s March 4 story. Initially, it acknowledges a responsibility to tell the story as a tragedy in law and order, a story of "ruthless killers," but this duty is acknowledged in a subordinate clause. Then the alternative, "forbidden" version—as if the story were a fiction, unthreatening to its reader—dominates the narrative's tonal aspects. About "America's arch-desperado" and "his most spectacular jail escape"—phrases that magnify the story instead of ruing it—the *Herald* wrote,

> Were not Dillinger, particularly, and the negro Youngblood as well, known as ruthless killers, the whole affair might well have been taken from a film scenario of the old "Keystone Kops."
> Dillinger evidently viewed his achievement in that light, for as he walked back past the guards who ignominiously were chafing behind the bars where he had locked them, he called out to them:
> "I certainly fooled you lugs that time. If you aren't hick cops, I'm the chief of police."

Then he threw down the wooden pistol in front of them. ("Dillinger Gets Out" 1)

To allude to the Keystone Kops evokes comedy but also benign textuality, as if the Dillinger episode is purely an entertainment spectacle. Accordingly, Dillinger's behavior in this anecdote (the details of which vary substantially from paper to paper) tends toward the theatrical: "that light," "he called out," and the triumphant display of the wooden gun. For the *Herald*, Dillinger's escape amounts to little more than a staged humiliation of the local police.

As I have said, Dillinger's Crown Point escape positioned him, both symbolically and legally, as the FBI's ideal fugitive nemesis. He dragged his last lam out for four and a half months, despite intense publicity, nationwide manhunts, and generous rewards. As the year wore on and several FBI ambushes came excruciatingly close to arresting or killing Dillinger, the Bureau itself felt the sting of ridicule and more substantial criticism. Their near misses were seen as failures, their deliberate detective work as time wasting. The FBI had chosen its enemy carefully but had underestimated the difficulty of the showdown.

While the eyes of the nation focused upon the battle, Dillinger's public profile changed in several crucial ways. Partly through his own actions and partly via popular mythologization, his identity became more local—even as he circulated through vast expanses of the American landscape.

Secondly, his reputation for politeness and amicability grew, even in the light of continued criminal activity and bullet-punctuated escapes. Dillinger became aestheticized, we might say, through individual anecdotes and textual and historical comparisons carried out even as the manhunt chased him down. He quite successfully managed to escape the monotonic typing that nineteenth-century criminologists and Hoover alike sought to impose upon criminals.

Thirdly, as a fugitive, Dillinger managed to make frequent public appearances at various points on the national map. The flurry of sightings imputed to the outlaw suggest a mobility that opposed pre-cisely the FBI's ostensible closing of interjurisdictional gaps, its pan-continental gaze.

Furthermore, authentic sightings were accompanied—and are still, in most histories of the period—by a string of false sightings and naive recognitions. In the Middle West in the early summer of 1934, Dillinger inspired a sort of revelry—an emotional, hallucinatory fixation on the outlaw and the stories he engendered. Whether rooted in paranoia, boredom, honest misrecognition or just an idle desire to get one's name in the paper, this craze proposed a popular-discursive opposition to exactly the sort of painstaking, authenticating imperative represented by Hoover's FBI. The false alarm does not contribute to the official—that is, police-maintained—chronology of an outlaw's deeds. It does, however, stage the possibility of resistance to the Hooverian project, the scientific management of information about criminals. At a historical moment when the FBI first promoted the possibility of a national law enforcement net, the false sighting affirms that even a highly sought person—"America's most wanted"—could both exist and elude.

When taken as a group, moreover, the questionable veracity of each sighting makes the next one (in whatever town) all the more possible. If Dillinger can be everywhere, why not here? Ultimately, the false sighting becomes a trope within the Dillinger history, one that biogra-phers have had trouble negotiating. Episodes taken as fact in the Toland and Cromie/Pinkston Dillinger biographies are given the lie by Girardin's 1937 articles. Yet Girardin's "authentic" sources are fre-quently Chicago organized-crime figures, and Helmer's annotations of Girardin's text cast further doubt on details of what may be the most convincing of the existing Dillinger histories. The false sighting erodes the very determinants of identity that the FBI promised to make indeli-ble: was it Dillinger? Wasn't it? If such a proposal seems specious, con-sider Dillinger's own efforts around the matter. In late May, in Chicago, he and Homer Van Meter underwent plastic surgery to change their faces and alter their fingerprints—according to FBI science, the very

authenticators of identity. These private machinations toward redrawing one's identity—Dillinger hungered to "live like other people," reports
Girardin (139)—mirror Hoover's redrawing of the Bureau agent and of
the identity of crime and police in America. They also helped lend plau-
sibility to rumors (repeated by Jay Robert Nash in *The Dillinger Dossier*)
that a look-alike, in fact, had been set up to take the police's bullets and
that Dillinger managed to outlive his own apprehension and death. In
some versions of his own legend, Dillinger managed the Tom Sawyer
trick of attending his own funeral via the newspapers.

In the wake of Crown Point, the *New York Times* seems determined
to resist the previously prevalent coding of Dillinger as a "national"
criminal opposed by "hick cops." Rewritten *Times* headlines over a
reprinted *Chicago Daily Tribune* story suddenly describe him as an
"Indiana Farm Boy, Now 31 Years Old." The "small Indiana farm" is
mentioned again in the lead paragraph and again in the third:
"Dillinger as a youth left the farm, which his father still tills at the age
of 73" ("Dillinger 'Rose'" 2). Though G. Russell Girardin has argued
that the wooden gun used in the escape was smuggled in to Dillinger, a
jailhouse tale about his "whittling a bit of broomstick with a jackknife"
appeared quickly in press accounts. Disregarding the implausibility of
prison guards allowing an accused murderer to keep a knife in his cell,
Newsweek writes, "'I'm going to shoot my way out of this,' [Dillinger]
told his cell mates. 'Listen to John the Whittler,' they snickered" ("Public Enemy" 10). The rural folk craft of "whittling" contrasts with the
more urban, artisanal possibilities of "carving" or "machining." In the
same article, Dillinger is quoted twice as singing snatches of cowboy
songs: "Git along, little dogie, git along," he tells the prison guard who
drives the getaway car, adding, "I'm going to the last round-up."

This challenge to Dillinger's cosmopolitan image, initiated by such
terms as "farm boy" and "whittling," is mirrored in the emergence of
John Dillinger Sr. as a commentator on and minor character in his son's
flight. In reports immediately after the Crown Point escape, Dillinger
Sr. professes worry over his son, but his "mingled feelings of happiness

and grief" help excuse the excitement and pleasure many observers doubtless felt:

> "It makes me feel a little better, of course," [the elder Dillinger] said. "But at the same time I will be constantly worried that he will get into more trouble or be killed.
>
> "John was kind of reckless and if he got the chance to get away he'd take it," the aged farmer, a respected citizen in his community, said.
>
> The elder Dillinger sat by a radio tonight listening for news of the hunt for his son. ("John Dillinger Sr. Glad" 3)

A "respected citizen in his community," the heretofore anonymous Dillinger Sr. manages to affix the aura of local origin to his son without evoking the bumbling incompetence of the Crown Point police. Subsequently, as Dillinger Sr.'s formerly "mingled" feelings turn to unreserved public loyalty to his son, the familial connection becomes a source of pathos that further scrambles the vilification of "Wanted" posters and federal bounties. "He has horse sense," Dillinger Sr. told *Time*; "John is a country boy, and likes to get back here once in a while for good green vegetables and home-cooked meals" ("Bad Man" 19).

Dillinger Sr.'s reluctance to tell the police about his son's daring April visit to Mooresville counterposes a curmudgeonly country wisdom to the interrogatory imperative of the FBI: "In Mooresville, John Dillinger Sr.—his farmer 'Paw' who doesn't 'aim to tell no lies' but 'didn't tell police because they didn't ask me'—said sure, John was home for a ham and green vegetable dinner Apr. 8. After the gunman left, his home-town friends got up a petition asking Gov. Paul McNutt to offer Dillinger amnesty because 'he has never manifested a vicious, revengeful, or a blood-thirsty disposition'" ("Crime: Dillinger's Latest" 10). Although Governor McNutt, still stinging from the humiliation suffered by his state police, denied the petition, John Dillinger Sr.'s dignity and independence as he was pictured by many American newspapers make his loyalty to his son seem acceptable. Pressmen pursuing the Dillinger story to Mooresville seem charmed by the outlaw's father. Dillinger Sr.'s frequently reprinted photograph depicts him in the field with a simple plow, durable and dignified, the fallow earth beneath him in clods. His presence in news of his son communicates not the acquiescence to criminal intimidation Hoover excoriated America for but instead a well-spoken and unashamed family partisanship. Even Clarence Darrow, whose fiery *Washington Post* editorial eschewed romanticizing Dillinger, mentions his early, local crimes and rural upbringing rather than focusing on his recent rampage ("Dillinger Just Pawn," 11).

The April 8 foray onto his father's farm—it soon became a family reunion, as "car after car of relatives drove up that Sunday" while FBI agents surveilled the farm with frequent drive-bys (Toland 254)—became another in a string of humiliations for both Midwestern police and federal agents. It was not until over two weeks later that the *Indianapolis Star* reported that the reunion had taken place; papers such as the *Miami Herald*, then, could run the photograph of the senior Dillinger and notice of the Mooresville visit—about which "authorities were quite perturbed"—concurrently with notice of the disastrous FBI raid on the Little Bohemia resort in Mercer, Wisconsin ("Dillinger's Father" 7). A week after reporting the reunion in its April 28 issue, *Newsweek* ran an International news service photo of Dillinger Sr. and reported that his farm had been quarantined for measles ("Crime: Congress Speeds" 12). This kept reporters away for a while, presumably to J. Edgar Hoover's relief.

By July 7, the interaction between father and son had taken on the exquisitely staged appearance of a soldier-abroad melodrama.

On his Mooresville, Ind., farm, the bandit's father last week handed Indianapolis Star reporters a batch of son-to-father letters. One thanked the honest father for a loan of $10. Another, from Chicago, showed the soft, sentimental side of young Dillinger. It read:

"Dad: I got here alright and found I still have some friends. . . . Would like to have stayed longer at home (on Apr. 8) I enjoyed seeing you and the girls so much. I have been over lots of country but home always looks good to me. Tell that little Frances (his half-sister) to keep smiling. This sure keeps a fellow moving. . . . Hope everybody is well. Johnnie." ("Crime: Dillinger and Company" 9–10)

Dillinger's "soft, sentimental" optimism romanticizes home, as if duty has compelled the outlaw to take to the "country." An April 28 *Newsweek* illustration suggested that Dillinger's national audience responded in kind. Above a caption mentioning the "Home-cooked Meal" Dillinger shared with his father, a Pennsylvania tavern keeper's turnpike billboard read, "Hello Dillinger—You'll like Lee Hoffman's food."

While this reversion to local-hero status seemed to renege on the globetrotting-criminal image that invited the FBI's pursuit, Dillinger's character was undergoing other, simultaneous makeovers in the popular press. I have suggested that he was aestheticized—a term about which postcolonial critic David Spurr writes, "The aesthetic qualities of media form allow for an interest on the part of the media audience which depends on a certain detachment from the real conditions that constitute the object of representation" (44). Though "real condition," which Spurr derives from Marx, becomes a potentially troublesome term here, the reality of Dillinger's lam—the menace he posed in carnage and larceny to a broad public—became, apparently, old news as 1934 wore on. Details released about him become more and more detached from asserting his criminality, less and less moored in the context of the battle between law and order which was being waged, in bullets and verdicts and words, simultaneously across the country. Discussing the *Washington Post*'s aestheticized discourse about the plight of Haitian refugees, Spurr argues, "When the picturesque and the melodramatic are given prominence, they displace the historical dimension, isolating the story *as* story from the relations of political and economic power that provide a more meaningful context for understanding poverty" (48).

I would argue that during Dillinger's post–Crown Point lam, mass-media aesthetics saw superior dramatic potential in Dillinger's side of the story. Thus reporters rendered him "picturesque" and "melodramatic."

Numerous examples might be drawn from a notorious *Time* story of May 7, 1934, which included more than three pages of captioned illustrations. A typical phrase claims that Dillinger's career has "reached unmatched heights of daredevil ruthlessness." The *Time* writer's "heights" and "daredevil" mitigate the actual threat of Dillinger's "ruthlessness" into something exciting, theatrical, and dangerous only to the daredevil himself ("Bad Man" 18). The burst of descriptive and storytelling energy that characterizes many Dillinger stories seems to indicate that reporters seized a reprieve from the tonal moorings of the cops-and-robbers establishment line.

In divorcing Dillinger from the "real" threat his lam posed to citizens during 1934, press commentary aestheticizes the outlaw by invoking narrative and textuality. Like the *Herald*, the *Washington Post* describes the March 3 escape as a "Mack Sennett–like comedy"—remarking, incongruously, that the "desperado's strange escapade is too vicious for levity" ("Not a Comedy" 8). On March 4, the *Times* wrote that the Crown Point escape "rivals the exploits of the *heroes* of Wild West *thrillers*" ("Dillinger Escapes Jail" 1, emphasis added). The *Tribune* notes Dillinger's role in "three escape plots" ("Dillinger Plays a Part" 2); the *Post* grumbles that "It's always the same. Give a man the *title* of desperado and what have you? A *legend* almost overnight" ("Two Crimes Solved?" 8, emphasis added). The *Post* pins two recently noticed thefts on Dillinger, who "has read all the Nick Carter–like stories that have been written around his name." A recurrent insistence on textuality and narrative highlights the ways in which police discourses about criminality could not operate without interference and contestation from previously established narrative forms, both of the detective and of the honorable outlaw, Robin Hood variety.

Time's May 7 piece borrows the tactic of framing Dillinger within a narrative structure, detailing Dillinger's criminal coming-of-age in a series of contrived "chapters":

First chapter of the Dillinger career was the sordid story of a boy gone wrong. In 1924 he began with a petty robbery, was identified after a grocery

store hold-up at Mooresville outside of Indianapolis. For that he got a
sentence of from 10 to 20 years. And the chapter ended with him in
the Indiana State Penitentiary after he had proved too tough a customer
to be handled in the reformatory.

Chapter No. 2 began last May when, thanks to the intercession of his
honest farmer father and the judge who sentenced him, he was set free and
went home. But prison had not cured him, for now friends were the hardest
of hard criminals. ("Bad Man" 18)

The device of the chapter structure asserts a familiar and comforting
pattern: that of the sentimental or moral novel wherein evil is punished
and good gets its reward. Furthermore, the invocation of fictional convention *mimics* fiction and its assurance, "It's just a story," containing or
concealing the real threat Dillinger posed to Midwesterners.

In the same vein, many articles contextualize Dillinger against a history of memorable figures and escape stories. Occasionally these comparisons are exacting and uncomplimentary: a March 4 *Tribune* article
compares Dillinger's escape to that of "Terrible Tommy" O'Connor,
who killed a policeman in 1921 but escaped four days before he was to
be hanged. However, this violent precursor is described in terms of his
ability to draw attention and inspire speculation: O'Connor, "now 45
years old unless he is dead, still gives police throughout the country an
occasional thrill as new reports are raised that he has been found"
("Dillinger Break Recalls" 3).

More frequently, papers compared Dillinger to Wild West figures.
Such juxtapositions conceded Dillinger his outlaw status but simultaneously problematized the remapping of the outlaw sought by Hoover.
On March 10, the *Times* marks a transition from "big-town gangster"
to "old-style bandit," from "Chicago to the Bad Lands of Oklahoma"
("Hardly a Crime Wave" 6). Dillinger was in fact not far from Chicago
that day; there are no authoritative reports of him operating that far
south or west after his Tucson arrest (Girardin 274–76).

Elsewhere on March 4, the *Tribune* wildly overstated Dillinger's menace. "Through a series of lurid and bloody crimes," it crowed, "Dillinger

has achieved a notoriety which has made him preeminent among criminals of his time. Beside him Gerald Chapman, the notorious jail breaker, is less villainous. He is today what Dick Turpin, the English highwayman, and Jesse James, the American road agent, were to the public of their day" ("Steps" 2). Significantly, the *Tribune*'s evocation of Jesse James ties Dillinger into a tradition of Western outlaw heroism described by Richard Slotkin in *Gunfighter Nation*. James was appropriated and heroized by Missouri journalists, then by "cheap literature" that had after 1875 "abandoned Indian-war settings in favor of conflicts between 'outlaws' and 'detectives,' and the struggle between classes" (127): "It was not his true and *local* history that made him a modern and *American* social bandit but the pseudo-history that was fabricated for him in the mythic space of the dime novel. It was not the historical (and now defunct) Jesse James that the Postmaster General banned, but his fictional incarnation. When he became a subject for national media, the form and meaning of his social banditry were transformed and enlarged" (128).

Slotkin's point prefigures Spurr's postcolonial analysis of American aestheticization of Haiti. Slotkin opposes local history ("true" here) to the "pseudo-history" that results when a figure such as Jesse James comes to occupy a supplemental "mythic space" that erupts from public discourse occurring around an unlocatable figure. "Social bandit" is Eric Hobsbawm's term for a peasant outlaw regarded by the state as a criminal but who is considered a hero or liberator by his or her people (*Primitive* 7). James, who fought for the Confederacy during the Civil War and then in Missouri against the Reconstruction government, was mythologized as a defender of local and regional rights against the federal government, which was hated in Missouri for its 1860s repression of suspected "guerrillas." James's mythologization was so successful that a series of amnesty bills were proposed in the state legislature, "often in the teeth of new evidence of the Gang's criminality" (Slotkin 134). A month after this article appeared in the *Tribune*, the citizens of Mooresville began their amnesty petition, drawing on and revivifying the pseudo-history already forming around their most notorious native son.

The *Tribune's* March 4 remapping of Dillinger into the tradition of social banditry anticipates the tinctures of heroism that characterize public discourse about the outlaw later that year, as when a caption to a *Time* photograph of the young Dillinger would juxtapose him with Tom Sawyer, Abe Lincoln, and Jesse James all at once: innocence, restlessness, honor, honesty, leadership, principle, bravery, local heroism ("Bad Man" 19). The *Tribune's* comparison implies a recognition of contemporary Hooverian nation mapping. Intuitively or intentionally, it charts Dillinger as an emblem of local resistance to federal power's consolidation of regions and "wilderness."

Other allusions to Western heroes recast the articulate jailbird into another form. On March 11, the *Times* published an article which announced in its subheading, "Dillinger Case True to Old Frontier Types." Although Dillinger has been called "the country's worst outlaw since Jesse James," the *Times* notes,

> His escape technique reminds readers of frontier records chiefly of Black Bart. That stage robber always worked with an unloaded shotgun. He was educated, and believed the "moral effect" of an empty gun at a victim's head was just as good for purposes of brigandage. . . . it is the old Wild West stage, train and bank-robbing outlaw that the Dillinger type of public enemy resembles. Black Bart had the Dillinger self-possession. He had left his Illinois home "to collect a living." Between robberies he would swagger round San Francisco, a dandy with a cane and diamond stickpin. Challenges to express drivers, written in rhyme and pinned to a tree, and a lost silk handkerchief that was traced to the laundry he patronized, led to Black Bart's capture. ("Bandit's Escape in Tradition" 14)

Thus the *Times* placed Dillinger into a stylish bandit tradition. (Bart also resembled Bonnie Parker, shot to death in 1934, in his habit of writing poetry.) The comparison's imputation of nonviolence to Dillinger is particularly shaky, given the murders his gang did commit in the act of robbery.

Like the *Tribune*'s references to Jesse James, the *Times*'s comparison of Dillinger to Black Bart carries complex implications. Each comparison invites the federals' pursuit; historically, James challenged the federal government's jurisdiction, whereas the effete Black Bart's "technique" and insistence on "moral effect" connote a cerebral criminality well matched to the investigative might of the Bureau. At the same time, the sympathetic, principled James and the deliberative Bart subvert the Bureau's remapping and valuation of criminals. Bart's forbearance of force and insistence instead on "moral effect" and "collect[ing] a living" depict a different "educated" criminal—one steeped not in rude jailhouse know-how but in a less morally absolutist vision of economic law.

Thus Dillinger's place on the other side of the thin blue line becomes not a savage's lair but a bohemian's necessary exile, marked by exhibitionistic, "swaggering" reappearances. Like Bart, Dillinger dresses suavely. Newspapers increasingly mentioned Dillinger's many sweethearts, and each Dillinger biography features photos of the outlaw's "girls." Dillinger's girlfriend Evelyn Frechette is described by *Newsweek* as "a Titian-haired beauty" in the midst of an action sequence detailing an escape from St. Paul police ("Dillinger: The Killer" 10). *Time*'s glamour treatment highlights the sexual liberties of Dillinger's fugitive status. The gang "made themselves comfortable with cards, women, dancing and drink," reads the main caption. "To be plentifully loved and diligently hunted is the lot of desperadoes," begins the caption to a photo showing three stylishly dressed women—"shame-faced girls"—who had participated in the "rendezvous" at Little Bohemia and were now in the custody of federal agents. Another photo shows "Dillinger's boudoir," where "he slept the sleep of the hunted"—but this photo, next to that of the women, shows unmade double beds, a magazine loose on the floor. The juxtaposition paints fugitive life as a sexual rampage with willing, attractive women—and the room where the outlaw sleeps is memorialized as such, as are rooms in the East where George Washington once slept—but Dillinger's "boudoirs" are photographed in their humid morning-after disarray ("Bad Man" 20). Clearly, a fascination with the possibilities of individualistic masculine potency underlies this bohemian reading of the fugitive outlaw.

John Toland's biography of Dillinger depicts, however fancifully, the young Hoosier in the hayloft of his father's barn, educating himself in the representational economies of outlawry by reading "volume after volume of Wild West stories. His favorite hero was Jesse James and he would bore Hobson with involved accounts of the famous gunman's Robin Hood qualities; he seemed obsessed not only by Jesse's courage and daring but also by his kindness to women and children" (10). This tidbit, appearing in the first chapter of a sequential biography, suggests that even dispassionate observers such as Toland have felt the urge to cast Dillinger as a sort of Robin Hood figure.

The connection is made explicit elsewhere. *Time* captions photos of the gang's Little Bohemia hideaway, "Under the greenwood tree lived Robin Hood. And John Dillinger stopped to rest at a roadhouse in the woods" ("Bad Man" 20). Hoover's introduction to Cooper's *Ten Thousand Public Enemies* answers *Time* tartly, "There is the innate urge of human nature to picture the widely-publicized criminal in the role of a Robin Hood when the facts reveal him as exactly the opposite" (vii). In the dark Depression climate, where "traditional" ways of "making a living" became less efficacious, the transformation of criminal into Robin Hood—the substitution Hoover so despised—answered the mood of an economically damaged nation in which many had become the Sherwoodian "poor." Where many Americans suddenly had less investment in the economic status quo that categories of "crime" and "legality" helped protect, a less absolutist, morally ambiguous figure such as Robin Hood found social currency wherever he (or she) could be projected. And despite production codes that complicated the representation of criminals, Robin Hood stories were produced fairly regularly during the 1930s. They include *The Lash* (1930), Michael Curtiz's *Adventures of Robin Hood* (1938), and William Witney's *Zorro Rides Again* (1937), which uses temporal and cultural anachronism to defer censorship of a morally ambiguous crime story. *The Vanishing Frontier* (1932) and *Robin Hood of El Dorado* (1936) reset Robin Hood stories in the American West, suggesting that the imaginative link between the West and economic salvation that drives *The Grapes of Wrath* also fostered the development of American social banditry. Dillinger cut a figure of undeniable potency in a nation emasculated by the Depression; though years of rampant unemployment and poverty had helped elect Roosevelt and sanction broadened federal powers, they may have also left a nation hungry for figures of successful self-reliance.

I include here in its entirety a June 27 *New York Times* item titled "Asks Capital for Horse So He Can Get Dillinger."

> An old plainsman has learned, to his disgust, that the Department of Justice hasn't got a horse.
>
> Eyes alight with the prospect of capturing John Dillinger and a $10,000 reward, he approached J. Edgar Hoover, director of investigation.
>
> "I learned to shoot under Buffalo Bill," the hard-bitten son of the West said; "all I need is a horse."
>
> Mr. Hoover had to tell him that the department had no horses. (40)

For at least this news reader, the Western aestheticization of Dillinger worked. The "hard-bitten" plainsman presents the law enforcement of another time; the pitying "had to tell him" lays to rest an entire tactical and technological era. But the plainsman's proposal confirms that the popular press managed over several months to successfully connect a bank-robbing gangster to Wild West mythology. "Perhaps the underworld has taken in our imaginations the place of the old frontier," former Secretary of State Henry L. Stimson conceded at the Attorney General's crime conference in December 1934. "But it is certainly not right for such a spirit to be fanned up artificially by the engines of a sensational press" (9). Likening criminality to a mythic meeting place between civilization and "savagery," Stimson fails to account for the ways in which the extension of federal policing itself was driving a new set of "frontiers" toward the nation's physical limits.

Frequent reports of the Dillinger manhunt's size and strength seem intended to reassure any still-wary reader of the inevitable closure of the story. They also promise swift and excessive pursuit to other jail-breakers; the coordination of a multistate task force was one of the earliest such efforts for the FBI, and the effort may have deserved being called the "country's greatest manhunt." Immediately after the March 3 escape, the *Tribune* reports, "Several thousand policemen in Illinois, Indiana, and Ohio last night were conducting a widespread hunt for John Dillinger" ("Three States" 1). A day later, the *Times* hints at the extension of the manhunt, in geographical and tactical terms: "Dillinger Eludes Hunt in 4 States; 'Kill' Order Issued." "Cordon Is Thrown over Roads in Ohio, Missouri, Illinois, and Indiana; Two Suspects Escape Net," the subhead read ("Dillinger Eludes Hunt" 1). As hours passed, the radius of the search area lengthened. An accompanying item describe heightened security in Lima, Ohio, where Dillinger gang mates Harry Pierpont, Charles Makley, and Russell Clark awaited trial for murdering Sheriff Jess Sarber as they freed Dillinger the previous autumn ("Pals Expect Delivery" 3). Another item reports that, "in the belief that John Dillinger might attempt to reach New York City," patrolmen were on alert. "It is improbable that Dillinger could break through the well-organized police lines spread for him in adjoining states," the report reassured readers ("Watch Here" 3). On April 29, the *New York Herald-Tribune* promised followers of Dillinger that "for weeks the patient, implacable circle of Federal justice has been closing in on his mad gyrations, like a great fist" ("400 Trained").

The optimism that marks these passages demonstrates the success of the FBI public-relations campaign. For the first time, the coordination of a nationwide, multiagency manhunt made sense; the much-ballyhooed Urschel kidnapping arrests had helped to convince the public of the Bureau's forensic excellence, although that 1933 story had failed to develop any sense of manly contest between bandits and the Bureau's agents. Dillinger's story succeeded in staging such a duel. I would argue, however, that the impressive descriptions of the power brought to bear against Dillinger helped to foreclose any real threat he posed the populace. In this sense, these descriptions did not help the Bureau's main PR aim of vilifying Dillinger. They may have helped to popularize him; for all the proleptic tension the manhunt generated, Dillinger's apprehension would eventually spell the end of an awfully good story. Each day he stayed free generated more tension, more outlandishly long odds.

Before April 22, the press seemed to cheer the FBI dragnet. That changed with the debacle at the Little Bohemia roadhouse in Mercer, Wisconsin. FBI agents had gotten close enough to exchange gunfire with Dillinger once before. On March 31, they tracked him to an apartment in St. Paul, Minnesota, but Dillinger and his favorite girlfriend, Evelyn Frechette, escaped through the unguarded back door. About this escape, *Time* wrote that Dillinger "sprayed his way to freedom" with a machine gun. Through hyperbole, the writing glamorizes the violence of his lam at the same time that it represses the targets of those bullets.

Little Bohemia proved a much more embarrassing disaster. Under the cover of night, led by Chicago SAC Melvin Purvis, better than a dozen heavily armed federal officers approached the roadhouse where Dillinger and his gang had been staying. Mistaking a carload of Civilian Conservation Corps workers leaving the lodge for Dillinger, they opened fire. The CCC workers, who did not stop when hailed, were all badly injured. One died. Dillinger and his male companions escaped; several women who had been with the gang were arrested the next morning by shaken FBI officials, who had lost one of their own in a gun battle with Baby Face Nelson.

Although assistant Attorney General Joseph B. Keenan hit a confident, reassuring note in the next day's papers, the declaration suddenly sounded desperate: "I don't know where or when we will get him," he promised, "but we will get him. And you can say for me that I hope we will get him under such circumstances that the government won't have to stand the expense of a trial" ("Says 'We Will' " 2). Clouds of criticism quickly dimmed the Bureau's previous luster. Although editorials in the *Washington Post* and other papers pressed on for extended licensing of federal law officers, the line between local incompetence and federal efficiency no longer seemed as clear: "[Federal agents] can not afford to fail, for Dillinger at large is a national disgrace" ("Behind John Dillinger" 8). With much less reserve, the *Miami Herald* snarled, "Federal agents and deputies sprung a trap. . . . the gunmen made the law look foolish and escaped. With two dead, one killed by a slight mistake on part of officers; several wounded. Typical outcome" ("In Today's News" 6). Senators criticized Hoover, and his demotion was rumored (Toland 286). Hoover "had better catch Dillinger . . . tout de suite . . . or else . . . the verbal kicks in Congress . . . and in the department . . . may become one kick . . . out," wrote Karl M. Kahn in the conservative *Washington Times* (Kahn's ellipses).

A few criticisms struck at the Bureau's federalist rhetoric. The *New York Times* turned the tables on earlier criticism of locals, suggesting that federal agents "muffed" their "ready-made chance" by not enlisting the aid of Wisconsin woodsmen: "The natives—woodsmen and hunters who can draw a bead on a running deer and get him almost every time—are laughing loud, long and bitterly at what they call 'the bungle of the revenooers.' 'If they'd only let us help them, we'd a got that Dillinger,' they say. 'But those revenooers were high hat and didn't want any local talent' " ("Gibe at Raid" 2). Much in the passage—the alleged efficiency of marksmanship that contrasts the empty-handed federal hunters, the insistence upon "native" and "local" identity, and the clumsily rendered northwoods dialect—makes a direct assault upon the federals' position. The *Baltimore Sun* editorial page concurred: "From all accounts," it jeered, "there are so many men chasing the fellow that it is surprising there are not more casualties among the pursuers" ("Down the Spillway" 12). The clearly "regional" humorist Will Rogers administered the coup de grace, quipping, "Well, they had Dillinger surrounded and was already to shoot him when he come out, but another bunch of folks come out ahead, so they just shot them instead. Dillinger is going to accidentally get with some innocent bystanders some time, then he will get shot" (Toland 286).

The federals' mapping initiatives—to suture together the nation's many jurisdictions, to marshal and display the well-disciplined federal forces, to detect and apprehend the fleeing felon—failed utterly at Little Bohemia. Not only had the federals failed to capture Dillinger, they hadn't even identified the occupants of the ill-fated CCC vehicle. The gang had again scattered to the wind. An oft-repeated report that two dogs kept by the resort's proprietors had barked at the FBI agents' approach, alerting the bandits, did little to reassure the public of the Bureau's advanced technology and methods.

If the cartographic imperative to map and to certify best characterizes the Bureau's strategy in the early 1930s, a countervailing discursive practice that I will call Dillinger spotting arose in the months after Crown Point. Dillinger was given to making audacious public appearances. The day after escaping from Crown Point, he arranged a meeting with his flamboyant lawyer Louis Piquett on Wellington Avenue in Chicago. Later in the summer, he took in at least one Chicago Cubs game at Wrigley Field, sitting among the crowd and bumping into Piquett again, this time by chance. Dillinger raided the Warsaw, Indiana, police station for guns and bulletproof vests in April and was suspected of another assault on Bellwood, Indiana, police on May 1. But his encounters with civilians were never violent; any aggression seems stagy. " 'Don't follow me, you ———, or I'll shoot the hell out of you," he tells a Chicago gas station attendant, only after reassuring the man that he has no intent of robbing him ("Dillinger Seen on South Side" 1). Another paper's version of the attendant's story renders the confrontation as a wry brush with fame: " 'Don't you know me?' he asked me. And I said 'I don't know you, no.' 'Well, you'd better not,' he said as he went out the door. Then he turned around and said 'You can tell your friends I gave those Indiana coppers a good trimming' " ("Dillinger Is Being Trailed" 16).

In addition to these authentic sightings, a series of less verifiable Dillinger sightings made their impression on the news. By April 24, the

Miami Herald sounded as if it had heard enough: "Guns elsewhere. Big and little. Dillinger was reported in only two states yesterday. He is slowing up. Then one of the states chalked down error. Minneapolis arrested three men, claimed they were Dillinger gangsters, then denied that allegation. The latter is probably correct" ("In Today's News" 6). The *Herald*'s exhaustion was understandable. To say today that someone is omnipresent is a facetious comment upon the status of the individual in an era of self-referential media: an actress is omnipresent, a product is omnipresent. In the early summer of 1934, a steady stream of stories had John Dillinger being sighted across the nation. *Newsweek* in particular took a noticeable pleasure in tracing Dillinger rumors. "Dillinger has been reported from far-flung sections," it reports on March 24. "Bank robberies from South Dakota to South Carolina were blamed on him" ("Dillinger: Negro Has Story" 14). A week later, they report Dillinger "seen in Indianapolis. He was also reported in Fargo, N.D., and spotted in Elmira, N.Y. In Elmira, the man recognized as the gangster turned out to be a former bodyguard of President Roosevelt" ("Legal Briefs" 20). Apparently convinced that their farcical tone was appropriate, the next week *Newsweek* pressed on: "Meanwhile Chicago chuckled over the story of two automobiles, one with Indiana and one with Illinois plates, which spent hours chasing each other around the Windy City. When at last they met, out of each car bounded police, mutually convinced that the other machine contained Dillinger" ("Dillinger: The Killer" 10). There the story promptly ends, as if to concede that editorializing on the incompetence of local police would be superfluous.

The sightings kept marching in, and the place-names proliferate: on May 5, *Newsweek* notes that "Men who 'looked like' Dillinger gangsters robbed two banks" ("Crime: Congress Speeds Bills" 12). "Rumor had the ace bad man in various States," it crows on July 7. "He was reported riddled to death by officers' bullets in Waterloo, Iowa. He attended a Chicago ball game between the Cubs and Dodgers. In California he held up a filling station in the Santa Barbara National Forest" ("Crime: Dillinger and Company" 9). The *Baltimore Sun* called Dillinger "the most ubiquitous outlaw ever heard of" and conjectured that police were employing him "simply as a convenient excuse for failing to clear up their local hold-ups. . . . it is really unthinkable that a criminal whose portrait hangs in virtually every police station in the country can pass undetected from town to town and be suddenly identified only when in the process of robbing a bank with the aid of a sub-machine gun" ("Ubiquitous Outlaw" 8).

Clearly, Dillinger achieves a somewhat remarkable status as news-worthy object: unverified reports of his presence gain admission to this national newsmagazine almost as readily as do verified, detailed sight-ings. In a sense, Dillinger becomes less an *object* than a *topic* of news, generalized rather than individualized, charismatic albeit unlocatable. He becomes at the same time a menace and a hoax: according to *Newsweek*, when Kentucky Governor Ruby Laffoon received a letter signed "Dillinger Squad No. 13" and threatening his life if he did not pardon a murder convict, he merely strengthened guard around the state prison and "refused to have the Governor's Mansion guarded" ("All in a Week" 9). Another *Newsweek* item noted that in Flint, Michigan, "Five men and a woman held up a bank, relieving it of $30,000. Except for the woman, every member of the band was 'recognized' as John Dillinger" ("The News-Week at Home" 9).

Dillinger spotting grew giddy, even silly. Even the staid *Washington Post* editorial page fell in line with those for whom Dillinger had begun to explore a fantasy or to attack an inchoate dread: "He jumps to a steamship at sea and steals several thousands of dollars in gold. Quite a stunt, even for Dillinger. Next he attacks the most impregnable storage of wealth in the world, the United States Treasury. Nobody ever did that before! What a hero he will be with his pals! It's as daring as Dillinger, as simple as Simon" ("Two Crimes Solved?" 8). An oft-repeated story involved an innkeeper in Stratford-on-Avon who, hearing his four unknown customers using slang terms like "Chief" and "Okay," called the constables in, only to find that the four men were Rhodes scholars traveling to Oxford ("All Speak American" 22).

The dour *Literary Digest* did its best to savage the rumormongers, sneering that Dillinger "is supposed not only to be able to appear and disappear at will, but even to appear in several places simultaneously. One day he is said to be in Indiana, the next day in London. One day he is discovered in Michigan, the next day on the high seas. One day he is reported dead, the next alive" ("Not Beelzebub" 10). "His ultimate fate is as certain as if it were already settled," the *Digest* reassures. However, even the *Digest* made its joke on Dillinger's Beelzebubian shape shifting. Three weeks after his death, it published an illustration of an advertising solicitation that the magazine's parent company, Funk and Wagnalls, had sent to "John Dillinger, Crown Point, Ind." Stamped below the June 18 return postmark was "Moved, Left no address" ("Topics" 8).

I would argue that these frivolous representations of geographical uncertainty express less a concrete desire to see Dillinger than an aestheticization of Dillinger into a generalized political presence or meaning. People *followed* Dillinger because he was exciting. I would argue that they *cheered* for him, however, because he emblematized a resistance to the federal project of cataloging and mapping that grew increasingly to involve even the law-abiding American citizen. Thus it was his humiliation of federal agents at Little Bohemia that gave rise to the Dillinger-spotting craze—not the Crown Point escape, where the familiar locals were routed.

In Dillinger spotting, the press helped create a drama which rebuffed the ambitions of Hoover. Dillinger spotting proposed a reappropriation—or perhaps an unfocusing—of the Hooverian national map. Whereas the Hoover family's lifelong project had been to bring into resolution and concordance various partial representations of the nation, Dillinger spotting abjured clear-eyed cartography. A cult of curiosity, it invented shadows and bogeymen and established an alternative map of sightings or nonsightings. It reveled in fugitiveness, ceasing to care—as in the *Newsweek* stories about Dillinger—whether the concrete object was even present. Its doubles became newsworthy: *Time* printed a photograph of "Honest John Dillinger," a University of

Indiana student whose hair was red, as was the fugitive's latest dye job, who matched the outlaw in height and weight, and who was "reared at Martinsville, only 18 miles from Mooresville"; the resemblance is said to be "extremely embarrassing" to "Honest John." But his name and face appears where the names of victims of shootouts involving Dillinger do not. These "real" details have been distanced by the pseudo-history of the aestheticized criminal, who in his absence changes the terms of the newsworthy ("Bad Man at Large" 18).

In addition, the Bureau found its cartographic project—the establishment of a secure nation, its jurisdictions sutured into a pleasant whole—challenged by the reappearance of Dillinger maps in various forms. The capture in Tucson had been celebrated by the *Tribune* with a pair of maps—one showing the point of capture just north of the Mexican border, the other mapping key moments in Dillinger's presumably ended "career" against a map of the Midwest ("Dillinger Gangsters' Four Month Campaign" 28). But as Dillinger's rampage wore on, newspapers began to reinscribe it across maps of what was now supposedly Hoover's nation.

One map, that of pursuit, is established around the federal agents on the case: federal agents "just miss catching up" with Dillinger in St. Paul and at Little Bohemia; at Sault Sainte Marie, Michigan; in Chicago; near Fond du Lac, Wisconsin. This map is supplemented by the tracings and possible tracings of his gang: responsible for a number of robberies between March and July, it was suspected in many more—often incorrectly, which blurred the line between authoritative and inauthentic reportage and spurred a process of Jesse James–like mythologization. Graphic maps appeared in newspapers: one, in the *Times* on April 24, is captioned, "The area of the latest Dillinger outbreak." Yet the area it shows is a quarter of a million square miles across six states, three Great Lakes, and Canada; other than the three recent FBI close calls with Dillinger, it shows only state names and Minneapolis, Milwaukee, and Chicago between its broken lines that indicate borders. The rest is a forlorn blank ("Dillinger Escapes Posses," illustration, 2).

The insult to the Bureau was compounded when the federal government's failure to catch Dillinger became international news. London's *Telegraph* related the "lone wolf" Dillinger to the "man-eating tigers" who drove U.S. foreign trade policy. More alarmingly, Nazi newspaper *Zwoelf Uhr Blatt* advised tougher treatment of American criminals: sterilization ("Dillinger Excites" 3). The Berlin paper used Dillinger's rampage to reject American objections to Hitler, reasoning, "So long as protests come from over there against a country whose leaders make their decisions with a deep sense of responsibility that never errs on the side of unwarranted leniency for murders [*sic*] and the congenitally inferior, we and the whole world are concerned" ("Berlin Press" 2). Clearly, to receive German press suggestions on enforcing order did not amuse J. Edgar Hoover.

Another article, a brief item about Dillinger pausing to wrap a blanket around an elderly woman whose family's car he was commandeering—"Here you are, mother," he reportedly said—appeared in the *Los Angeles Times* under the headline "Dillinger Plays Raleigh for Moment in Flight" (2). The comparison to Sir Walter Raleigh immediately connotes gallantry, suavity. But in addition, it makes Dillinger an adventurer, an explorer, a writer of the American map; Raleigh made several voyages to the Americas and once manned an expedition to discover the fountain of youth. The item appears beneath a map of Dillinger's exploits, ranging from Ohio to Arizona; the line of his travels ends in a question mark.

The notorious *Time* article of May 7, 1934, contains perhaps the most inflammatory transformation of the Hooverian map. It stresses the failure of the FBI-coordinated interdictive effort, particularly its ineffectuality at guarding state lines: "From Crown Point in seven weeks Dillinger's bullet-strewn trail wound and rewound through half a dozen states" ("Bad Man" 18). The map traces Dillinger's exploits between March 3 and April 23. Superimposed across Michigan, flanked by twin machine guns, is the legend "Dillinger Land": "Game Starts Here," it promises, like a Parker Brothers board game that can be played at home. The dotted line loops enticingly through seven state jurisdictions; along the way, it juxtaposes such pleasantries and commonplaces as "Sunday dinner with father" and "hair-cut, food, gas" with "Robbed 1st National Bank of $52,344" and "Raids police station for ammunition." Somewhere in northern Minnesota, the dotted line ends in a spray of question marks and the caption, "Game Ends Where?" "Dillinger Land" ("Bad Man" 19). To the nationalistic energies of J. Edgar Hoover, the legend is an effrontery.

About Dillinger, *Time* wrote, "he would achieve a great unwritten odyssey: Through the Midwest with a Machine Gun" ("Bad Man" 19). The comparison to Ulysses ranks among the silliest attempted by reporters. Still, it begs the question: to which Penelope would Dillinger return? J. Edgar Hoover's insistence upon the inevitability of apprehension casts the prison as Dillinger's long-missed destination. John Dillinger Sr. and the citizens of Mooresville offered up their own forgiveness and loyalty in order to bring their prodigal son home. Evelyn Frechette and other sweethearts posed a third option: was it possible that, through plastic surgery and an alias, a reformed Dillinger could return to public life? If so, readers would never know it.

Even if silly, the comparison to Ulysses sniffed out a principle common to Homer and Dillinger: that the pleasure of the narrative hinged on forestalling its conclusion. Where Homer used a traveling point of view to watch both Penelope at her loom and Ulysses at his travels, the reporters found themselves largely stumped: they could not invent Dillinger's presence out of words. But the public did: by inventing and circulating the simulacrum of Dillinger, they celebrated Dillinger's absence and confused the question of his presence. When Dillinger was everywhere at once, his story was out of the hands of Hoover and the press. Persistent suggestions that Dillinger did not die at the Biograph, such as those in Nash's *Dillinger Dossier,* descend from the Dillinger-spotting craze.

At the Biograph, where Dillinger fell on July 22, crowds of hundreds appeared, many dipping handkerchiefs into the pool on the street to save swatches of the outlaw's blood. "Most Dangerous Man of Decade," the *Los Angeles Times* wrote of the gang leader with one murder arraignment to his credit ("Dillinger's Trail Long" 1). *Time* eulogized Dillinger as "a slight, dark-haired, harmless-looking little man in shirt-sleeves, wearing a white hat and gold-rimmed spectacles." While the article names Melvin Purvis as the coordinator of the ambush, the writer avoids awarding any heroism to the shooters: "A volley of lead cut him down in his tracks, one bullet through the head, one near the heart. Down the street two women were shot by mistake." Tonally, *Time* elegizes the star outlaw.

> They took all that was left of the most notorious killer and robber of 1934 to the Chicago morgue. There they laid his naked corpse out on a rubber slab and the Hearst papers also laid him out in gruesome front-page newspictures.* In Washington Attorney General Cummings heaved a mighty sigh of relief.
> At his Mooresville, Ind. farmhouse Dillinger's father took the news hard. Barefoot, clad in overalls, he stood in the doorway, tears streaming down his cheeks. "Is it really true?" he asked, bewildered. "Are you sure there is no mistake? I have prayed and prayed it would not happen. . . . I can hardly talk. . . . Johnny was not near as bad as he was painted." ("Death of Dillinger" 14).

The grim morgue paragraph depicts the press's processing of Dillinger: the last appearance of his body generates a paroxysm of reportorial representations, which are themselves then reported. (The asterisk after "newspictures" noted that "One edition of Hearst's *Chicago American* carried seven pictures of the corpse.") Thus did Dillinger's reputation increase exponentially during the short few months of his public heyday. These, the last two paragraphs of the news story, dramatize the importance of the fugitive outlaw's body to the sense of story closure. Where Attorney General Cummings, presumably privy to agents' reports from the death scene and the morgue, can breathe a final, relieved sigh, the bandit's father can only weep and question the news. Even as his speech tries to compose itself toward eulogy, its ellipses, like their readers, strain toward the story's continuation, or the next story's eruption.

Many factors, then, contributed to the mythologization of Dillinger and his durability as nemesis to J. Edgar Hoover. First, the backlash against Prohibition-era crime and the representational politics that restricted—or bowdlerized—the possibilities for fictional criminal characters caused a brief heyday for censors that spurred newspapers to jump on the Dillinger story. The press aestheticized him—both in Slotkin's terms, the recasting of true history into myth, and in the sense of creating narrative structures around him. Second, the hot pursuit of the Federal Bureau of Investigation made him, more or less explicitly, a pathbreaker. His escape coincided with Hoover's drive toward federal police ascendancy. In the press recoding of Dillinger as a local, we can see traces of opposition to the federal discourses of surveillance and scientific management, and the reassertion of local identity and competence. Third, Dillinger's persona—his calm, self-possessed manner and gentlemanly flourishes, his charisma and bravery, and his passing resemblances to Hoover's own Boy Scoutish G-men—made it difficult to vilify him as a menace to the American citizen. Instead, he and a sympathetic press made it appear that he threatened only banks and interfering policeman, neither of whom enjoyed much popularity among the American public. If the Robin Hood analogy, finally, was largely inappropriate, the sense of the Forest—and of the right of the guerrilla with leadership abilities to rule there—did ring true in Dillinger's career. He showed Americans that there still would be blank spots on the map, and Americans showed their pleasure in return by pretending to find him there.

4. "an infinity of bleak tomorrows"

The Closure of Fugitive Space in the Noir West

The triumph of the G-man was a manly triumph; the strict requirements placed upon Federal Bureau of Investigation agents in the 1930s imposed a model of vigorous, well-trained probity where before the public had perceived corruption and sloth. Even as the '30s FBI moved toward systematization, official and unofficial representations of its investigations highlighted the individual agent who, through hard work, a little luck,

> **Gangsters is foreigners. He's an American!**
>
> —Gramp Maple, *The Petrified Forest*

and the blessing of J. Edgar Hoover, could become a household name, as did Melvin Purvis before he sought publicity independent of the FBI's sanction and found himself frozen out by the director.

This chapter examines three outstanding films noir produced in the wake of the second great crime wave of Hoover's tenure. In *They Live by Night* (1948), *White Heat* (1949), and *Gun Crazy* (1949), a new style of policing the fugitive is put on display, including a range of new policing strategies that deepened vastly the connections between jurisdictions that Hoover's leadership forged during the years after Prohibition.

In remarking upon the similarity of representations of policing and fugitive tactics in these films, I acknowledge Philip Kemp's observation that the politics of "a group of films as amorphous as *film noir*" is problematic (81), in that noir itself has been variously defined as a non-genre, depending less upon period or topic than mood. In writing about the politics of noir with reference to the influence of the House Committee on Un-American Activities (HUAC), Kemp analyzes a set of recurring themes, including the power of money, class warfare, and self-interest without social conscience, to speculate upon what Jim Cook and Alan Lovell have called a "structured sensibility." Kemp writes, "If we reject the notion of some vast, clandestine network permeating every Hollywood studio, we seem to be faced with only one other option: that for nearly a decade one aspect of American filmmaking was pervaded by a set of political assumptions so widely held as to have become virtually undetectable both by those who expressed them and those who virulently opposed them" (82).

In comparing representational patterns in three otherwise unlinked films noir, I would proceed upon a similar argument: that Hooverian postwar discourses on crime were sufficiently widespread—and suitably congruent to other American fears and fascinations—that his ideas, not so much political as procedural, became "virtually undetectable." In these three films—with *The Petrified Forest* (1936) as a predecessor evincing significant contrasts—we see a repositioning of the officer within the law enforcement dragnet. But we see also a cartographic advance, an assertion of the police across the miles and into the lives of America, that was supplemented by, but by no means depended upon, the ideological ravages of HUAC.

Toward the grim end of Nicholas Ray's 1948 doomed-lovers melodrama *They Live by Night*, naive outlaw Bowie the Kid, played by the young Farley Granger, has an idea. He decides to approach the cynical huckster who, for twenty dollars (plus five for a ring and a tip to the two resident witnesses, old relations of the proprietor), has married him to his young, hard-bitten bride Keechie at a funeral home–like wedding stand (complete with neon sign) across from a Greyhound depot. Hoping that the same man who has sanctioned his elopement with Keechie can, through a different performative utterance, transform their nightmare world of flight into a rosy domestic bliss, Bowie asks the old man to get them to Mexico. But the old man refuses to attempt this transformation:

"I won't sell you hope when there ain't any."
"No chance?"
"None at all."
"No place for her and me?"
"I don't know of any, son."

Unnerved, Bowie decides to scram without Keechie, who sleeps, weak and sick from her pregnancy, at a nearby motel. But Mattie, the motel's shady proprietress, has already betrayed him to the police, offering up Bowie in exchange for her husband's freedom. The parole warden, sensing Mattie's anxiety at cutting such a deal, reassures her that her guilt is wasted: the horizons of Bowie's lam are contracting fast, and there's no chance of his living a straight life. "Killing, maybe. It's the only way he can live. Perhaps that's our fault," he muses. Indeed, when Bowie returns to the motel for one last moment with Keechie, a cadre of armed men wait in the dark trees, and Bowie dies in the sudden glare of a floodlight as he is reaching for his gun.

The two pronouncements—the wedding seller's and the parole warden's—interrupt what has, outwardly at least, been a dreamy lam for the couple. Their swing through the Southern states has revealed a seeming play land of motels and tourist camps, used-car lots, coffee stands, and nightclubs wherein the expectation of transiency makes the fugitive criminal into just another face on the highway. The criminal underworld, so hierarchically organized in the schema of Cooper and Hoover, here is uneven, rhizomatic in Gilles Deleuze's sense, uneasily pitched in whatever spaces are available and necessary, itself a deterritorialization of the legal economy. Edward Anderson's 1937 novel *Thieves Like Us*, upon which *They Live by Night* is based, anticipates Deleuze in calling its criminal hideouts, where "not even possum hunters ever came," Holes: "T-Dub said the best way to leave a Hole was early in the evening when the traffic was heaviest. Stay off the main highways as much as you could and follow timbered country. Keep a couple of five-gallon cans filled with gasoline and circle cities like Dallas and Fort Worth where the Laws had them scout cars and radios" (234).

Functionally, in *They Live by Night*, the underworld combines extraordinary resilience and cellular independence; criminal relationships have sturdiness and value (T-Dub and Chickamaw, the two crooks with whom Bowie has broken from jail, speak of their investment in him), but to cut off the head of the hierarchy merely sends subordinates in new directions, motivated by self-preservation toward independence and further crimes. And Bowie's gang finds port not only with criminals who run apparently legitimate businesses but also amongst shady businessmen who are all too happy not to ask questions when someone wants to deal quickly and in cash.

As hunted fugitives, Bowie and Keechie fear being recognized. For a short time, as obvious newlyweds—Ray's film has been called the most romantic work in film noir, and Cathy O'Donnell plays Keechie with a smoldering languor—the two opportune themselves of a delicious irony: rather than fugitives, they are taken for honeymooners. They *want* to be left alone; they *want* the most remote cabin. But when they break their nocturnal discipline and risk acting like honeymooners, the card-house charade comes crashing down. They find themselves outsiders, left to bitterly disparage riding, golf, dancing, and other social activities, in part because Bowie's years of incarceration and Keechie's hard girlhood tending a service station have not acculturated them to socialized leisure and in part because they fear being caught. Set into relief against the sociability of a Southern resort, where the soloist serenades them knowingly, "You get burned when you play with fire," these feelings of paranoia and exclusion press the couple to beat a hasty exit when a drunk staggers into their table; they cannot afford to cause even the slightest scene.

They Live by Night paints a dark, hopeless picture of the lam in postwar Texas, but the pressure of the police seems displaced, sublimated. A tough guy who wins the draw on Bowie in the nightclub men's room has identified him but merely demands he beat it out of town; such a demand from a policeman would be an anachronism, a return to isolated jurisdictions. This tough guy seems to be merely a local businessman, protective of the area's reputation and worried that Bowie might scare crowds off.

Instead, in the 1948 film, Bowie's paranoia seems to emanate from his recognition that crime has set him apart, irremediably defined him in absolute opposition to the law-abiding citizen, and inverted his relationship to society—a tension captured in the title *They Live by Night*.

"You got to look and act like other people," one of his older jailbreak partners instructs him. Bowie's problem is that he *yearns* to be like other people: a pretty wife, a convertible car, a straight life. In a sense, he becomes the honeymooner that others recognize; it is this self-misrecognition—and the whiff of hubris it entails—that derails his lam and brings his downfall. The film enforces an essential difference separating criminals from the law abiding, their present and future inexorably chained to the crimes of their past. Alain Silver and Linda Brookover cite Bowie's hope that accumulating enough stolen cash to hire a "Tulsa lawyer" to overturn his one conviction as evidence that he is simply "too naive to survive" (265); in the absolutist environment, crimes cannot be purged other than by submission to law.

Ironically, the defining differences between criminals and the lawful in *They Live by Night* are denied, in title and total, by *Thieves Like Us*, published 11 years earlier. Anderson offers a much more morally ambiguous Dust Bowl tale in which "them capitalist fellows," the bankers Bowie robs, are widely seen as just as crooked as the gangsters: recognizing Chicamaw, an old one-legged man says, "I just wish you had got this bank here 'fore it busted and took my wad. I'd rather for a poor boy like you to have it than them goddamned bankers. Both of them bankers are out of prison now and still living swell on what they stole from me and about four or five hundred more folks here" (284–85).

The novel's jailbreakers find the lines between lawlessness and legitimacy much more traversable. The phrase "thieves like us" recurs frequently as a disparagement of professionals, and T-Dub rues his life by saying, "A kid can't see things. I should have made a lawyer or run a store or run for office and robbed people with my brain instead of a gun" (280). Clearly one explanation for the texts' divergence is genre: Anderson's terse, pulpy novel brooks no production-code bowdlerization. His tragic couple never marry, save in a lie Bowie tells Keechie, and her pregnancy takes them by surprise, whereas the film tidies up Anderson's sexual loose ends.

But the film's revision of Anderson's story is shaped as well by changing discourses surrounding crime. *They Live by Night* imagines the lam as psychic torture and the criminal as visibly indistinguishable from other Americans, animated by classic bourgeois motivations but trapped into living a nightmare existence on the flip side of the American everyday. Such a vision is consonant with many representations of crime in the years following World War II. Early in 1946, as the war machine ground down, crime reclaimed its place in the lead pages of the nation's press; the FBI's bulletin of crime statistics ("compiled with the FBI with the cooperation of law-enforcement officers throughout the nation," explained J. Edgar Hoover) calculated a 12.4 percent increase in crime over 1944 figures. Hoover published a blitz of articles in American magazines on the Bureau's findings, seizing the opportunity to redefine crime and set priorities for crime fighting in the postwar era. In one such article, a *New York Times Magazine* piece, Hoover called the statistical increase a "mounting crisis," calling for "something positive and drastic" to be done, including "a general tightening of our attitude toward the criminal who has established the fact that he is completely untrustworthy" (Hoover, "Crime Wave" 26–27).

In "crime wave" coverage of those postwar years one can find evidence of shifting conceptions of the American criminal. The ethnic overtones of crime discourse had shifted since the last great American crime scare, in the 1920s, when immigrant groups from Southern and Eastern Europe bore the brunt of prejudicial assumptions. Though public association of certain ethnic groups with organized crime remained strong, the series of articles Hoover published or stocked with statistics and ideas makes no mention of the Mafia or of organized crime. Hoover's repression of this threat until the late 1950s—for reasons which Richard Gid Powers characterizes as bureaucratic, including a desire to maintain control of *any* national operation against crime (*Secrecy and Power* 332–36)—influenced the notion of the criminal that emerged from the postwar crime scare. This postwar criminal was not alien to the United States; with a few exceptions, such as Vance

Packard's 1946 reinterpretation of FBI crime figures, eugenicist correlations of ethnicity and conduct took a back seat to causal factors of psychology, environment, and personal responsibility. In a national sense, criminals, including the communist, were naturalized.

Packard's *American Magazine* piece, "Hot Spots of Crime," draws on human geography to elucidate FBI statistics, pointing out skyrocketing crime figures in the booming Far West and correlating hot weather and murder rates. An accompanying map of the nation color codes states by their crime rates and shows in cartoon relief two criminals at their work: a white safecracker in Nevada and a black man shooting another in the Deep South, in keeping with the article's assertion of a disproportionately high crime rate among Southern blacks.

But a second illustration, derived from Earnest A. Hooton's 1939 study *Crime and the Man*, profiles three felon types with an uneasy mix of statistical analysis and eugenic and phrenological speculation:

FORGER: Usually an older man, tall, with thinning hair. Often of Teutonic ancestry, he is well educated, as criminals go. Operates in all parts of U.S., but favors Texas

ROBBER: Typical holdup specialist has wavy hair, round chin, pug-ugly nose; is tall, hard-bitten, usually under twenty-five. Most active in fall and winter; and prefers the Far West

MURDERER: Average killer has high forehead, wide jaw, sparse hair, and a tall, chunky body. Usually older, estranged from wife, quite ignorant. Appears most often in the South. (Packard 35)

Above each paragraph appears an artist's rendering of a typical perpetrator; each is a white male, ethnically indeterminate. Only the forger's identification as "Teutonic" informs an otherwise undetailed whiteness in these three profiles. Thus Packard's article, while invoking the discourses that historically had ethnicized public conceptions of crime, ultimately endorses a simpler, all-American model, with white vs. black the only operant racial distinction.

Elsewhere, old notions of the criminal figure were under attack. A 1947 two-page spread in *Life* seemed explicitly aimed at debunking such stereotypes: below a field of twenty-eight mug shots, including several women, the magazine contended,

> One of the most fallacious notions anywhere is the belief that there is such a thing as a "criminal look." Every day newspaper readers can be heard muttering, "He certainly looks like a crook," when they come across a suspect's picture. This, however, is a highly overrated method of criminal identification. To prove it *Life* invites its readers to separate the innocent from the guilty among the twenty-eight faces shown here. Of these people, half have been convicted of crimes ranging from kidnaping to wilful homicide. The other fourteen, like the majority of respectable Americans, have never been publicly accused of anything more heinous than overtime parking. They are members of an organization called the Mystery Writers of America, Inc. ("Speaking of Pictures" 21)

We might critique the game the article proposes; it assumes that "the criminal look" might be refuted objectively, while in fact one need merely follow the invitation to "turn the page" and "find out which are the mystery writers and which are the criminals" in order to begin establishing inductively a new "criminal look." And the opposition of "criminals" versus "honest citizens" echoes Bowie the Kid's paranoia, suggesting that, regardless of looks, the essentialist categories function mutually exclusive of each other. But the article's intent, though it steers conspicuously around picturing African-Americans or questioning stereotypes about blacks and crime, at least seems apt today.

The impulse to destabilize "the criminal look" and reaffirm essentialist categories of criminality were two trends influencing discussions of crime in 1946. First, the FBI's 1945 crime reports made much of an increase in juvenile delinquency. According to the reporters, 21 percent of those arrested in 1945 were minors, and the two most frequently reported ages of arrestees were seventeen and eighteen. "Fifteen per cent of the murderers, 36 per cent of the robbers, 51 per cent of the burglars, 34 per cent of the thieves, 26 per cent of the arsonists, 62 per cent of the car thieves, and 30 per cent of the rapists are under 21 years old," Hoover reported ("The Crime Wave" 26). If it had not been abundantly clear before, such figures reminded Americans that crime was a *native* as well as domestic problem.

Secondly, by 1946 J. Edgar Hoover had wheeled the cannons of his rhetoric to fire upon the real or imagined Communist threat, which he labeled "our Achilles' heel" in a speech before the American Legion on September 30. The Communist Party's "boring from within" strategy, as Hoover characterized it, had created a host of sympathizers. "The Communists themselves boast that for every Party member there are ten others to do the Party's work. These include their satellites, their fellow-travelers and their so-called progressive and phony liberal allies," Hoover declared ("Our 'Achilles' Heel" 10).

Important in Hoover's conception of communism—and integral to the widespread and often abusive surveillance and harassment campaigns that followed—was the imputation of communist influence within accepted American political groups: progressives, liberals. As crime had in Hoover's metaphors of the 1930s, communism situated and spread itself across a spatially rendered society, "boring from within" like termites and by other means: "The Communist influence has projected itself into some newspapers, magazines, books, radio and the screen. Some churches, schools, colleges and even fraternal orders have been penetrated, not with the approval of the rank and file but in spite of them. . . . Eternal vigilance will continue to keep your ranks free of shifty, double-crossing Communist destructionists" (10). Thus the identification of communists was simultaneously urgent and problematic; they were no longer outsiders but, "shifty," could be within the ranks, working from the inside out, creating "satellites." The spatial metaphors of the 1930s no longer sufficed to describe American crime; criminals now could occupy the gravitational center.

With these twin concerns affecting the priorities of policing, at least as Hoover conceived and preached them—he labeled juvenile delinquency and the "inroads" made by Communists the "two main fronts" on which "our enemies are massing their forces"—representation of the criminal lost some of its jingoism and its concern with the urbane gangster figure. Many popular representations of the criminal concentrated instead on the grimness of criminal life, apparently seeking to discourage rather than to exclude. A 1950 *Coronet* article titled "Wanted: America's Most Dangerous Criminals" began,

> Hunted from town to town, from furnished room to furnished room, these nine men live the shadow life of the fugitive from justice. Armed desperadoes, ready to kill in order to keep their dubious freedom, they live in hiding, useless and deadly members of society.
> Ultimately they will all be caught. Some of them, resisting arrest, will be killed by F.B.I. men who, even now, are closing relentlessly around them. Time is running out on these hoodlums. The blazing '30s are gone forever. A force of 4,000 highly trained "G-men" are utilizing every device of criminology to draw the net tight around their quarry. (115)

The article profiles the notorious Willie Sutton, a three-time prison escapee, and eight other men who were among the first to appear on the FBI's Ten Most Wanted Fugitives list, which debuted earlier that year (Newton and Newton 3). The short capsule biographies assert the dismal life of the fugitive and the certainty of his capture. Far from glamorous, these fugitives are vicious: Frederick "the Angel" Tenuto "brutally overpowered" Philadelphia prison guards, and Morris Guralnick, "arrested for stabbing a girl," then "resisted furiously, biting off the finger of a policeman." They are disfigured: Glen Roy Wright coughs constantly and bears multiple scars, whereas Guralnick has a broken nose and missing teeth. They are family destroyers: Thomas James Holden killed his wife and her brothers, and Morley Vernon King, who speaks four languages and appears well groomed in a collar and tie in his mug shot, strangled his wife and left her under the back porch of a hotel.

Crucially, the article posits the dead end that so terrorized Bowie the Kid, whose nickname evokes a Western outlaw tradition that is as illusory as the "Tulsa lawyer" who would be Bowie's savior. Over two decades, the FBI vision of the criminal underworld changed; the "career," whereby one progressed through an organization toward a crime-boss role, diminished, replaced by a hopeless stagnation and dismal recidivism. About Henry Randolph Mitchell, *Coronet* writes, "Federal agents believe his acts of larceny, forgery, and robbery will follow an endless pattern until his time runs out." Thomas Kling, sticking up a tavern two years after his release from prison, was "back at the only trade he knew." Guralnick's "only known occupation is that of popcorn vendor in burlesque houses." And the feverish determinism of the article's opening paragraphs, in which the FBI's favorite clichés come fast and furious to haunt the hunted man, finds its grim satisfaction in the confident assertion, "There is only one space that remains to be filled in this file on William Sutton: *date of capture* ("Wanted: America's Most Dangerous Criminals" 115–17).

This grimness is amplified in a stark 1952 *Coronet* photo essay depicting "The Price of Crime." Sixteen pages of black-and-white photographs hint at "the infinity of bleak tomorrows" and "human agony" that stretch out before American criminals as well as their families. Rather than the battered hoodlums of the Most Wanted list, the evocative prose describes a sympathetic, human perpetrator, the made-one-mistake type. To these softer cases, the article warns of the dehumanization and shame of the justice process: "Shorn of human dignity, defaced in the eyes of strangers," a thief "squirms like a trapped animal in the iron grip of captivity. And, like an animal's, his struggles are futile, hopeless." That hopelessness *is* an essential component of criminality, argues *Coronet*; jailhouse levity hides "warped, disordered thought-patterns. . . . justice in the end wins out. These are the men and women, who, despite a show of forced mirth or bravado, are held prisoner by their own memories." The essayist even attempts a theological detour: "For the criminal, the penalty of law is only a beginning. His retribution is infinite." And the horror extends to the criminal's family as well as the victim ("The Price of Crime" 99–114).

A 1950 *Newsweek* item titled "Manhunt" offers a dispatch from the hellish fugitive frontier: William Raymond Nesbit, named on the FBI's most-wanted list, was recognized by a pair of schoolboys as a "hermit" who'd been "living in a cave along the nearby Mississippi River bluffs." After seeing Nesbit's picture in the *St. Paul Dispatch*, the boys smoked him out of his dugout by stuffing snow into a stovepipe chimney and got a good look at him. They notified police, and the police effected a capture of the meek fugitive: "There wasn't any fight, or anything," reported fourteen-year-old James Lewis. To complete "the dream of all junior G-men," the two boys were flown to Washington to shake J. Edgar Hoover's hand ("Manhunt" 53). The climate of the lam was turning cloudy and cold.

> GABBY: *Alan, what's the first thing you see when you get to France?*
> SQUIER: *Customs officers.*
> —The Petrified Forest

The 1935 Robert Sherwood play *The Petrified Forest* and the 1936 film that followed break thematic ground for the grim flight films of the late 1940s. Set in autumn 1934 at the Black Rock Bar-B-Q, a gas station and greasy spoon in the middle of the Arizona nowhere, the play evoked John Dillinger, dead less than six months at the play's January 1935 New York premiere: "His image was fresh in everyone's mind, which added an eerie realism to the play," write A. M. Sperber and Eric Lax (46). Two touches specifically evoke the well-publicized details of Dillinger's lam: the gang's use of bystanders as human shields and the phrase "hick cops," which later becomes part of an important distinction: "Hicks or G's?" asks gangster Jackie as an armed car appears outside the restaurant's window.

Humphrey Bogart played the role of gang leader Duke Mantee in stage and screen versions. It became the role that launched Bogart's career, writes biographer Joe Hyams: "Bogart made 29 gangster films in a row for Warner's in the three years between *The Petrified Forest* and *High Sierra*. He was a jailbird in nine of these pictures and electrocuted or hanged in eight" (56–57). In Duke, Bogart played a weary, fatalistic gangster, doomed even in his character note in Sherwood's play, which, consciously or not, evokes Dillinger, both in description and in its note of elegy: "well-built but stoop-shouldered, with a vaguely thoughtful, saturnine face. He is about thirty-five and, if he hadn't elected to take up banditry, might have been a fine left fielder. There is, about him, one quality of resemblance to Alan Squier; he too is unmistakably condemned" (37).

Initially, *The Petrified Forest* lambasts the nationalist impulses of the New Deal. A disillusioned lineman critiques the Postal Telegraph's extension into the empty spaces of the desert (a power pole and lines are visible in the film's first external shot of the isolated roadhouse), even as he is its agent. Like radical regionalists of the period such as Lewis Mumford, the play's lineman endorses redistribution of property; in Russia, he says,

They're opening up new territory—and for the benefit of all, not so's a few land grabbers can step in and take the profits after somebody else has done the real work. . . . Those engineers in Russia are building something new! That's where they've got it on us. We ain't building—we're *repairing*. Just like you and me. What do we do—day after day? We climb up poles, and fix the wires, so that some broker in New York can telegraph in a split second to some guy in Los Angeles to tell him he's ruined. (8)

The filmic lineman's radicalism is toned down, but he adds, "the republic's in bad need of saving."

War vet Jason Maple, the roadhouse's proprietor, defends America but does little to dispel the sense of regional malaise—"the American West at a breaking-point," as Rudolf Erben has put it (312). Maple complains that he is underemployed, yet his aspiration is to own a Los Angeles auto tourist camp—essentially a lateral relocation into a metropolis. Young Gabby Maple, played by Bette Davis, is an ambivalent regionalist; she paints the desert but dreams of fleeing to the Old World to join her divorced mother in France. And chatterbox Gramp Maple is stuck in the Old West, regaling every new arrival with tales of Billy the Kid.

The hired man, Boze, might be the young successor to Gramp's desert-rat figure, but Boze's egotism and energies are wasted in the new, disgruntled West. (In the play, even his boasts to Gabby betray disenfranchisement: "If I'd been with Princeton or Minnesota or any of those big clubs, I'd have been All-American" [14].) Still wearing his "Molby Tech" game jersey ("Never heard of it," Duke snaps), Boze broods over stolen glory. Without a team, Boze lacks a systemic place, and whereas his old hoboing spirit and heroic potential might have succeeded in the Old West, in the hinterlands that modernity merely exploits, he is wasted, like an extra part detached from the machine.

The arrival of the aristocratic Chisholms, passing through from Dayton, Ohio, on their way to California, underlines the station's status in modernity. Its role is to stock interchangeable supplies and services for transient customers. The Chisholms announce themselves brusquely by asking after the restrooms and demanding "Gas and oil, please"—a lack of social nicety which locates Gabby below the officious Joseph, the Chisholms' black chauffeur.

Into this setting, where a family manages to subsist, not unlike George Wilson in *The Great Gatsby*, on the mechanical appetites of people hurrying somewhere else, come Alan Squier, a failed writer hoboing across the country, and Duke Mantee with his gang. Both are romantics: Squier sees the vicissitudes of the Depression as "Nature hitting back. . . . She's taking the world away from the intellectuals and giving it back to the apes," and perceives Gabby as a budding artist whom he can free by sacrificing himself for insurance money. Duke waits doggedly for a reunion with the woman who rides in the second car. In his stubborn refusal to leave, Duke displays a dark fatalism. "I've spent most of my time since I grew up in jail," he says, "It looks like I'll spend the rest of my life dead." Resisting the pleas of Slim, his black henchman, who repeatedly asserts that "we got to lam out of here," he holds court in the dining room of the Black Rock, mediating the discussions between various characters with his pistol and growing grimmer as the hours pass. "Be seeing you soon," he tells the dying Squier as he exits.

Windblown and scant of customers, the Black Rock seems the ideal place for the fugitives' rendezvous. Yet the gangsters are routed, and the film's dismal politics recouped, by the power of news and entertainment media to distribute themselves even into the hinterlands. Exposition of *The Petrified Forest*'s exterior story—the movement of the outlaws and their pursuers through the Southwest—flows into the film principally through a pair of props: a copy of the *Denver Post* and the Maples' radio. Seizing his paper, Gramp Maple shows the banner headline, "Oklahoma City Massacre: 6 Killed, 2 Fatally Wounded," to everyone he can. A large photo identifies Mantee.

The radio provides up-to-the-minute news, and its reports turn up the pressure on Duke and his gang. Turned on at his request to keep the gathered hostages pacified—along with open bottles of liquor on the tables—at first it plays soft, sticky music. But soon it also brings bulletins of "the greatest manhunt in human history," trumpeting, "Mantee and his gang are headed for the border. The greatest border patrol in history has been established from the Gulf of Mexico to the Pacific Ocean." The bulletin details recent sightings of both cars, as well as the second car's Dillinger-like raid on a Texas police arsenal, and reports that patrols are sealing off the outlaws' anticipated escape route, south to the Mexican border.

Though the timorous Mr. Chisholm prays that "someday the government will take measures to protect the lives and property of its citizens," the radio makes it apparent that the Mantee manhunt has benefited from federal involvement. Without mentioning the FBI by name, the radio's details conform to the federal policing role publicly sought by Hoover: leadership and coordination of diverse local forces, including Jason Maple's Black Horse vigilante meeting. The film, which avails itself of exterior scenes that would be impractical onstage, underscores the point further by having a U.S. Mail carrier bring Gramp the news that Mantee is expected in the area. Aided by radio, the patchwork manhunt imposes an effective dragnet, and the news that the second car of fugitives has been apprehended a hundred miles away travels quickly: "There's posses all around here," the vigilantes tell Duke. "You got the whole mighty strength of this nation after you now, buddy."

However, in keeping with regionalist impulses, the radio also reasserts the dignity and identity of the rural Southwest—albeit an identity that is constructed out of the same Wild West stereotypes that make Gramp Maple an engaging curio—by endowing the local police forces with renewed energy and potency: "You know how the officers of the law are in this red-blooded frontier region: they shoot first and ask questions afterward."

In one particularly evocative sequence in the film, the radio is imbricated into the very change of scene. Halfway into the film, as Squier departs the Black Rock, having hitched a ride with the Chisholms, the big car's radio brings a manhunt bulletin. With the description of Duke's getaway car, the scene switches away from the environs of the Black Rock for the first time since the opening credits; the camera verifies each detail of the radio description as it is voiced: the car's license plate, its bent fender, bullet-perforated rear window, extra gas cans. Only then does the view draw back and reveal the foundering car and, in their first appearance, the bickering gangsters. In this extraordinary transitional construction the radio's expository power is cemented, and for a moment the filmic viewer assumes the position of the vigilante, apprehending the criminal's presence through mechanized signifiers. Prompted by broadcast bulletins, the camera deputizes us.

In its pairing of crime with social critique and its moral ambiguity, including a fugitive (as Raymond Durgnat puts it) "sufficiently sympathetic for the audience to be caught between, on the one hand, pity, identification, and regret, and, on the other, moral condemnation and conformist fatalism" (7), *The Petrified Forest* anticipates the conventions of film noir, which commenced, Jon Tuska argues, in 1940–41 (xxi). My concern is not to argue the film's inclusion within the canon of noir, but to highlight the film's concerns with American geography and the dissemination of crime news. Like *They Live by Night*, *The Petrified Forest* envisions a landscape in which the criminal wilderness is being mowed down.

The successes of anticrime rhetoric, however, could not drown out the enabling effects of improved transportation upon criminals. Even after years of curtailed wartime production, by 1944 the Department of

Commerce counted thirty million registered autos in the United States. Faster and more plentiful automobiles spurred the development of roads and associated conveniences designed to accommodate and comfort the transient motorist. Even in 1944, as war still raged on two fronts, Congress appropriated $1.5 billion to launch the Federal Aid Highway Act, which the administrator of the Federal Works Agency promised would effect a great network between cities and the "thinly built-up wedges of land" that exist between the main roads fanning out between cities. The interstate highway system, according to Major General Philip B. Fleming, was at its heart a great democratic project, capable of spreading the benefits of modernity throughout poorer rural and urban districts, though his vision plays a horrendous shell game of displacement, rather than relief, with the poor:

When it is possible, express highways will slice through the undeveloped wedges of land, and the circumferential roads will cut across these forlorn districts and tie them to the main traffic arteries. Cities will thus be given an opportunity for a more even development of their outlying areas. Another part of the plan will provide a means of remedying some of the so-called "blighted" neighborhoods in downtown sections.

These slum or semislum areas can be converted into desirable residential districts through wise city planning. By the wholesale demolition of outdated buildings, the laying out of new streets and parks and playgrounds, and the erection of modern apartment houses, they can be transformed into handsome neighborhoods which are sure to appeal to thousands of citizens who would like to live near their jobs in the adjacent business district. (Fleming 94)

High-speed highways promised ease, but the carefully engineered flows of the highways also made for an increasingly anonymous transient space. There would be "no hot-dog stands fronting immediately on the main highways, and no filling stations," reported Fleming (93). Speeds had climbed: "the average driver hits an average speed of 47 miles per hour when he gets on a good road," claimed Fleming; new highways, he said, would be "designed for speeds of 75 miles per hour" (94). And by the 1930s, the social activity of auto gypsying, which Warren

Belasco links to the "strenuous life" espoused by Theodore Roosevelt, had died down, succeeded by increasingly commercialized auto camps, cabins, and the ubiquitous motel, with its registry and its parking at the door (107–21).

What was good for the goose was good for the gander; criminal use of improved transportation made such technological development "a two-edged sword," wrote police communications scholar V. A. Leonard, one that necessitated a leap forward in police technologies and practices.

Fast automobiles left conveniently unlocked at the curb by careless or trusting motorists or purchased outright with an illicit income have solved his transportation problems. Networks of improved highways favor his safe retreat unless the police are able to close every avenue of escape without delay. Given five minutes, the fugitive is three to five miles away from the scene of his crime. Under the protecting cover of darkness he can be completely lost by the following morning. (Leonard, *Police Organization* 270)

In order to counter the anonymity and speed of automotive flight, police turned to the possibilities of coordination and cooperation between multiple officers or even disparate jurisdictions—not in detective work and long-term apprehension, the sort of work the FBI excelled in, but in redefining the possibilities of crime prevention and hot pursuit. Most important among the innovations of the 1940s was the proliferation and improvement in privately operated police radio. The Public Safety page of the magazine *The American City* routinely trumpeted new milestones in safety service communications throughout the 1940s, including testimonials from police chiefs and other officials. In 1943, Gary, Indiana, police chief Millard T. Matovina announced that his department's new FM radio system, made by General Electric, overcame the "dead spots" in the department's jurisdiction that the previous AM system could not reach. "There is comparative freedom from static and noise, and car-to-car conversations have been carried on over 25 miles, with 10 miles as a normal operating range. Conversations have taken place between Gary and downtown Chicago 25 miles away. This increased car-to-car range has been helpful in chases and blockades," Matovina reported (15).

The possibility and desirability of police-operated radio had been addressed in a paper given to the convention of the International Association of Chiefs of Police as early as 1920, and 1921 saw experimental broadcasts in Detroit, led by Police Chief William Rutledge and transmitted by a station that after 1922 bore the call sign KOP (Burton 37–38). The number of radio stations operated by local police grew from twenty-nine in 1930 to sixty-two (plus two operated by state police forces) in 1931 (Burton 49). Newspaper editor turned radio commentator H. V. Kaltenborn told the attorney general's 1934 crime conference, "No city has ever discontinued the use of police radio" and reported that the mere broadcast of crime bulletins over Minnesota station WCCO had "increased our police efficiency 50 percent" (112–13).

But the 1940s saw technology improved with less expensive, frequency-modulated systems becoming widely available, and the "dead spots" in the nation's police communications networks began to shrink and fade away. By 1950, writes V. A. Leonard, "the use of radio communication was universal in the American police services, and radio installations were to be found even in the smallest departments" (*Police Communications* 14). A Wilmington, North Carolina, FM system installed in 1942 allowed two-way communication between a complex web of municipal units representing diverse forces, including:

> vehicles of the Fire, Police, and Water Departments, and the County. Connected to the system are the Fire Chief's car, and the city's fireboat which now the Chief can direct from the land. The water department's emergency truck which has a receiving set permitting emergencies to be handled expeditiously. Two of the county government's patrol cars are equipped with receiving and transmitting sets but not with car-to-car transmitters. Broadcasts to these cars come from the city police-control room. (Rippy 15)

J. Fred Rippy Jr. notes that the FM system's installation had so far cost $4,300, whereas the transmitter alone of the AM system had cost $5,000 some years previously.

From police radio came a range of benefits. The urban patrol car was envisioned as a tool to aid the foot patrolman on his beat: "It is really motorized foot patrol," reasoned a 1945 *American City* item on Milwaukee's purchase of thirty-five patrol cars. "The officer rides from one potential crime area, leaves the car, inspects potential crime hazards on foot, and then rides to the next area. In this way the patrolman can protect a larger area than entirely afoot" ("More Patrol Cars" 11).

But the ability to dispatch cars remotely allowed a much more profound change, a force decentralization, "by virtue of which the police beat"—not the station house—"is the basic unit of operation in the modern police department," writes Leonard (*Police Organization* 278). Dispersed forces and improved relays between telephone receiving and radio dispatch, combined with improvements in roads and patrol cars, drastically cut response time. The ability of police cars to speak and listen to each other and to coordinate response on the fly, so to speak, sacrificed central authority for a far more responsive network, the efficiency of which could be rendered into terms that aped the simplicity of Newtonian physics:

Through the agency of communication, maneuverability and speed of movement, effective mobilization is possible at a moment's notice. Whether the emergency be the investigation of a reported suspicious character in an outlying neighborhood or response to a major bank alarm, the results are the same, the rapid and intelligent movement of the required strength to the scene of action. Thus, through the simple formula—mass times rapidity of action—the striking power of a numerically inferior body of men is amplified up to a point where they may perform the tasks assigned to them adequately. (Leonard, *Police Organization* 279)

"The Police Department now would feel that it had lost 50 per cent effectiveness should the radio be removed," the city manager of Watertown, New York, asserted after two years with an emergency-services radio system (Wood 15).

An April 17, 1946, *Los Angeles Examiner* editorial reprinted in *The American City* alluded to the logical extension of local police radio networks: their coordination into a regional networked system that could function in concert with or independent of federal authorities.

> Azusa is the latest town to join the foothill community chain which embraces Pasadena, Covina and other localities.
>
> This is good for Los Angeles also, for now the patrolling range of the police will extend to cover scattered and isolated regions until now regarded as comparatively safe by elusive criminals.
>
> The day should not be far off when every square foot of Southern California will be within reach, and within the action of efficient police equipped with radio. ("A Vital Network" 17)

Coordinating local police and police organization through radio to enable on-the-fly pursuit illustrated a land shift in policing. While police networks obeyed Hooverian imperatives of coordination and the suturing together of jurisdictions, they also served to further decentralize elements of command and control and, further, to deprofessionalize them. The technology of police radio created by everyday practice a second, more efficient organizational structure whereby police administrators were substantially removed as the hubs of information and minute-by-minute command. Police radio stations could be manned and operated by dispatchers no more skilled than a telephone operator or secretary.

Thus the fetish of law enforcement, its object of disproportionate attachment, shifted between the mid-'30s and the late 1940s, as the balance of this chapter will argue. No longer was the character and potency of the G-man the focus of crime dramas. The task of apprehending the criminal fell instead to rank-and-file policemen working within an increasingly multilayered and technically sophisticated network of law enforcement. Bravery, integrity, and the scientists of the Bureau were the G-man's weapons, whereas the filmic policeman of the late '40s knew how to run the machine.

Two fugitive films of 1949 juxtapose a hopeless lam against a new, decentered police force. *White Heat*, a Raoul Walsh film, starred Jimmy Cagney, who had been the menacing star of *Public Enemy* (1931) before switching sides—a coup that, as much as any, expressed the end of the gangster-film vogue—to star in 1935's *G-Men*. Back in the gangster fold, Cagney's portrayal of Cody Jarrett is a riveting, memorable performance—"Middle-aged, a little bit paunchy, but as keen as a veteran mountain-lion," wrote Bosley Crowther in the *New York Times* ("A Native's Return" 1). But *White Heat* is remarkable for its balanced narrative, which splits time between a minutely characterized Jarrett gang and the efforts of Treasury agents to build a case against Cody for committing the train robbery that opens the film. Their technologies of surveillance tail Cody through a dark, variegated modern landscape, a battle that has been analyzed by James F. Maxfield and Frank Krutnik, among other critics.

From that opening mail-train robbery sequence, *White Heat* depicts the staggering pace of modern crime. Set on the California state line, the sequence opens with rapid cuts between four views: the exterior of a train in mountainous territory, a car speeding along a twisting road, and interior shots of gangsters inside the car as well as inside the train. The robbery is a complex and multiphase operation: a conductor is knocked unconscious and a rebellious brakeman shot before the train stops; Cody leaps from a bridge overpass to the top of the train; a mail car is dynamited with a man inside; Cody shoots the engineer and fireman; one of Cody's men is caught in the steam from the engine's blow-off valve and burnt badly. As in *Petrified Forest*, a radio news bulletin, set a week later, provides exposition and effects a geographical transition—as if evoking remote distance with the broadcast medium as signifier—to a wintry hideaway where Cody's gang has holed up and the same announcer's voice is emanating from a radio set. "Now we're supposed to be in Arizona," a gangster smirks; a "cold-blooded" robbery there has been attributed to the Jarrett gang.

The film's landscapes reflect a warren of hideout sites that are connected automotively: from the mountain cabin, which the gang abandons under cover of an approaching storm ("A storm keeps everybody busy," Cody explains), they flee to an auto court with a sign prominently displayed on camera: "Milbanke Motels—All over Los Angeles." At another point, Cody evades a high-speed pursuit through Los Angeles by ducking into a drive-in theater and sitting like a moviegoer with his wife and mother as the police sirens scream past.

Like *They Live by Night*, *White Heat* depicts a dismal lam. While Cody and his gang can lay low within the anonymous spaces of automobile culture, the hideouts are tenuous and uncomfortable—"I been cold for a week, Cody," protests his mercenary wife, Verna. "Not even a fire. Who's gonna see a little bit of smoke a hundred miles from nowhere?" And paranoia ravages Cody and the gang—"Stay on dirt roads all the way," Cody instructs a second driver leaving the mountain hangout. But there are just as many threats within his gang, including a mutinous lieutenant and the slatternly Verna, whose screenplay character note reads, "Verna's philosophy is simple: What's in it for Verna?" (*White Heat* 66). Worse, Cody is tormented by psychosomatic headaches that strike him at moments of stress—"Like having a red-hot buzzsaw inside my head," he says. And stress runs rampant for the fugitives: every member of the gang is a wanted man, and Cody's underlings are eager to spend the hot money from the train robbery. With their identities so widely distributed by newspaper and radio, the gang has as many reasons to fear civilians as it does policemen and Treasury agents (dubbed here "T-men," as if Hoover's formidable G-men might replicate themselves across the entire alphabet). "What's the use of having money when you've got to start running every time someone sees your shadow?" asks Verna. Triage on the lam is severe: Cody orders the steam-burnt gangster's execution rather than trust him to keep his mouth shut under a doctor's care.

Also like *They Live by Night*, *White Heat* draws absolute delineations between the criminals and the law abiding; the gray areas irrupting in this space during Prohibition and visible in the hard-times chronicle *Thieves Like Us* have been closed by the hard-line moralism of postwar crime rhetoric. Such clear distinctions are useful in order to streamline the role of character Hank Fallon, a Treasury agent who specializes in infiltrating prisons to gather information from convicts. When Cody surrenders on a minor rap in Illinois that would provide an alibi for the federal offense of robbing the train, Fallon becomes Vic Pardo, a small-time hood who is sentenced immediately after Cody and follows him to the jail cell. Yet Fallon, whose prison-infiltration rap sheet— "Eight sentences in five years!"—might, if environmental-influence criminologists had a say, at least indicate some hardening, betrays no signs of moral compromise. Patrick McGilligan argues that Fallon's inability to empathize with Cody "removes from the story what might have been another level of conflict and emotion" (*White Heat* 31).

Without losing his jailbird credibility, Fallon acts as Cody's prison angel: Fallon espouses the warden's rules, saves Cody's life when an enemy tries to kill him, and nurses Cody through a headache attack, as Cody's mother used to do. (Fallon starts a fistfight to avoid being identified by Bo Creel, a convict he once sent to prison, but it's the would-be murderer whom he slugs, and later he's congratulated for it by his three cell mates.) Even in escaping the jail, Fallon stays clearly within the moral right. When Cody intimates his desire to break out, Fallon, in Vic Pardo character, seizes Cody's trust by improvising a plan:

CODY : I figured we cut in Tommy Ryley.
VIC : Ya cut in one and before ya know it it's ten. What do ya want Ryley for?
CODY : He's got a gun stashed.
VIC : Don't need a gun. (126–27)

Eschewing violence and keeping the number of convicts involved to a minimum, Fallon's proposed plan contrasts the modus operandi of the modern police to Cody's blast-it-out method:

CODY : Without artillery? Can't be done.
VIC : No? I'm pretty handy around electricity, remember? Well, I figured a way to fix the generators. Know what that means?
CODY (slowly; admiringly) : Yeah, I got a faint idea.
VIC : The generators control everything. Searchlights. Gun turrets. Main gate. Who needs artillery? (127)

Though the news of Ma Jarrett's death sends Cody into a helpless rage and puts guns and force back into an impromptu breakout, the undercover agent continues to function as a control valve: "This don't look so hot, Cody," he pleads. "My way there wouldn't have been any shooting" (143).

While Fallon's moral fiber remains unbent by his stints in the prison, his success at subterfuges large and small suggests that the police have assessed and incorporated the criminal's ability to appear "normal" in any social setting and to improvise opportunistic escapes when necessary. Fallon's Vic Pardo disguise deceives the canny Cody until the penultimate scene of the film, when Fallon is recognized and denounced by Bo Creel. But several times, Fallon devises useful subterfuges in order to communicate from the lam with Evans, his Treasury Department supervisor. He leaves a message on a gas-station washroom mirror and then complains, within earshot of the gang, that the attendant needs to clean the room; caught sneaking out on the eve of the payroll robbery that closes the film, he excuses it as a need to see his wife. And when Verna complains about her malfunctioning radio, Fallon promises to fix it but instead uses its components to fashion an oscillator which will emit a radio signal that Evans and his men can pick up. Caught by Cody attaching the oscillator to the back axle of the gang's truck, Fallon claims to be attaching a drag chain, a verisimilitudinous detail that once again impresses Cody: "That's usin' your head," he barks.

Fallon's contrivance of an oscillator, the triumph of police ingenuity, communications, and coordination, becomes the piper which draws a host of police forces to the film's climactic setting, the surreal Hortonsphere tanks and pipes of a modern chemical plant. James F. Maxfield has analyzed this scene as a "clash between the Old and the New," the Trojan-horse subterfuge of the gang and the technical surveillance of the Treasury agents, pointing out that the modernity of the setting is where the "nineteenth-century" Cody loses control (68–70). Though it is here that Cody's madness and malice bubble over and

Fallon kills him with a high-powered rifle, it is the procedural work—the various FCC auto patrolmen as they report receiving signals and the pair of nameless policemen who triangulate the transmitter's position—that the film lingers over. Here and in two earlier scenes—a spectrograph and fingerprint analysis in Evans's office that ties Cody's gang to the hideout, and a demonstration of the ABC method of automotive tracking and pursuit, in which three unmarked patrol cars weave a perimeter around a subject car—the generally fast-paced film devolves into a pedantic demonstration lecture on procedure. This fetishization of technologically enabled police coordination, writes McGilligan, "may have been exciting at the time, but nowadays it is the most dated aspect of the film." Whereas the film drew heat from critics for Cagney's memorably brutal portrayal of Cody Jarrett and its graphic violence—Bosley Crowther's first review called it "a cruelly vicious film. . . . its impact upon the emotions of the unstable or impressionable is incalculable" ("The Screen in Review" 7)—*White Heat* seems equally committed to making a spectacle out of police machinery: the spectrograph photographs of dirt samples from the train robbery site are displayed within the frame like the telling faces of lovers, and the teletype machine rattles like a machine gun in the office of the T-man whose organization reigns triumphant in the end.

> *Twenty or 30 sheriff's guards and 60 armed men were supposed to close in on them. Again, I thought that was ordinary stuff. . . . I decided to do it by letting the audience again supply the details. By having the couple in the swamp, completely enveloped in fog. They're aroused by hearing a splash in the water. Then a splash from another direction. . . . We also saved a tremendous amount of money by not showing all those men in cars.*
> —Gun Crazy director Joseph H. Lewis

Where were the frontiers beyond which the fugitive could evade the nation's police in the rapidly coalescing national landscape of the late 1940s? The automobile expanded the possibilities of blending into another locale; it also brought the burden of additional distinguishing characteristics—make, model, license plate number—and a range of countering strategies from the police. In a nation seized by the possibility of designating and outing communists in our midst, trying to "look and act like other people" became problematic; it failed to account for the devaluation of "the criminal look" as a stereotype. The criminal was registered, internally by an emergent moral absolutism regarding lawlessness, and externally, by the nearly instantaneous disseminating power of the Hooverian net.

The mountain cabin where the Jarrett gang holes up after the mail train robbery proposes a seemingly unmapped territory, one that persists even after the telegraph and the highway have come to *The Petrified Forest*—though Cody denies Verna her fire, to guard against telltale smoke. The fugitive wilderness has figured in other lam tales, including the hellish subterranean hollows of Jim Thompson's *The Getaway* (1958) and the idyllic homestead of Terence Malick's 1973 film *Badlands*. These holes in the fabric of the American map fit fugitives' purpose—the holes posit the persistence of the undetectable. But to seek a wilderness refuge entails a more or less total removal from the social sphere. The fugitive wilderness must inevitably evoke or call into question its polar opposite across the lawful-criminal divide, the normative American home and its various constituents: family, property, job, community, relationships, place.

The story of two lovers who meet in a carnival shooting contest and turn to crime, the 1949 film *Gun Crazy* imagines a law enforcement dragnet which is the culmination of Hooverian aspirations. To cross the border to Mexico is the only hope of escape, and even the wilderness has the federal government's stamp on it. In its conclusion, it imagines a near-ideal distillation of panoptic law enforcement, wherein the *policeman* fades into anonymity, replaced by an effective, technical, nationwide *policing*.

Gun Crazy was based on a 1940 *Saturday Evening Post* story of the same name by MacKinlay Kantor, who later won the Pulitzer Prize for *Andersonville*. Set in the Midwest in the summer of 1934, "the days of frequent and daring bank robberies throughout that region" (367), Kantor's story is yet another thinly disguised Dillinger story with a pinch of Bonnie Parker and Clyde Barrow thrown in. A generally conservative writer whose office wall featured a poster that read in bold letters "Fuck Communism," Kantor seems attuned and sympathetic to the Hoover line on crime and its representation. As outlaw character Nelly Tare knocks over Great Plains banks, the narration by Nelly's boyhood friend, reporter Dave Allister, echoes the flashy style of mid-'30s FBI narratives: "Federal men didn't enter the picture until the next January, when Nelly kidnapped a bank cashier in Hiawatha, Kansas, and carried him nearly to Lincoln, Nebraska, as a shield from avenging bullets. That little state line strung out across the prairie made all the difference in the world. The so-called Lindbergh Law had come into existence, and Nice Nelly Tare became a Public Enemy on an elaborate scale" (367).

Kantor's story is revisionist history, a wishful rendering of the 1934 Dillinger lam in which the FBI pursues without slipups and the locals are receptive to what is this time a combined state, county, and federal manhunt: "Nelly had to be somewhere inside that area. There couldn't be any mistake. Practically every farmhouse had a radio by 1934, and all broadcasts were interrupted to give farmers the news. A plane went whining south and west, flying low and retailing by short wave the description and position of every suspicious-looking vehicle in the region" (370). As the story was published, locals Dave and Clyde track Nelly down and tackle him, gambling on their memory of his long-standing squeamishness about blood and death. Kantor explained later that this gentle denouement was written in response to *Saturday Evening Post* editor Wesley W. Stout's refusal to publish it as it was originally written. "I think he was wrong," Kantor insisted; his original ending features a much bloodier end in which the manhunt's officers get their kill, gunning down Nelly as Clyde and Dave look on. The story's original conclusion, then, provides a catharsis in which Nelly "vanished in darkness" as the bullets hit him: "He wore an expression of baffled perplexity, as if he thought it strange that he who had loved guns so dearly his whole life long, should at last be slain by them." The triumph of law is unequivocal; the climax of the federally coordinated manhunt includes a sexually suggestive reification of masculine violence's relation to law and authority.

After Kantor penned his story, eight years passed before he wrote the first screenplay for the film. But the vast changes between the film and that story originate in Dalton Trumbo's rewrite of Kantor's screenplay under the name of Millard Kaufman. Perhaps the best-known of the Hollywood Ten, Trumbo was at that time blacklisted for his membership (from 1943 to 1948, he claimed) in the Communist Party. During his thirteen-year blacklisting, under various pseudonyms, he wrote or co-wrote *Spartacus*, *Exodus*, *Papillon*, and *The Brave One*, for which he (as "Robert Rich") earned the 1957 best screenplay Academy Award. However, the award was not presented to Trumbo until 1975 (Nordheimer 22), and the Writers Guild of America, which determines the credits for screenwriters, restored credit for *Gun Crazy* and several other films to Trumbo only years after his death (Robb 25).

Trumbo's substantial recrafting of the film earned him solo writing credit: in a "fugitive, high-speed state of mind," writes Jim Kitses, Trumbo reduced a screenplay of over 180 pages to 116, slashing Kantor's exposition of Bart's childhood problems (23).

Kitses aligns the two writers by citing them as "positive-negative mirror images, both righteous patriots and ambitious artists who had risen from humble origins" (22). But I would argue that Trumbo's writing the film essentially *as* a fugitive spelled a reconsideration of the dynamics of the manhunt. In Trumbo's rewrite, the orgasmic triumph of the police over the feminized, brutish outlaw is recast into a paranoia tale told from the brink of the Cold War, a drama that stages contests between family-bound and transient lifestyles and that sets the fugitive adrift in a nation ruled by surveillance and the relay of policing information.

Gun Crazy thematizes the rejection of community and the horrors of homelessness. The film contrasts transience and the relatively homebound, family-oriented lifestyles exemplified by Ruby, older sister of renamed outlaw Bart Tare, and to a lesser extent Bart's two friends, sheriff Clyde and journalist Dave. As it endorses the lifestyle of house-wife Ruby, the film also distinguishes two different strains of transient lifestyle: carnival and criminal. At first, the carnival seems like the more exotic of the two. The traveling carnival that brings Annie Laurie Starr's sharpshooting act to Bart's hometown of Cashville is owned and emceed by the slick and corrupt Packet (who negotiates with a mammoth cigar in his mouth); it presents such exotic sights as tum-blers, flame swallowers, and belly dancers.

Clearly, the citizens of Cashville view these outsiders ambivalently. The crowds include plenty of well-behaved men and women, and in fact it is policeman Clyde who mentions the carnival to Dave and Bart, suggesting, "Let's go down there tonight and have some fun like we used to." But the carnival scenes are conspicuously devoid of children. And the citizens' distrust surfaces at the shooting match between Bart and Laurie, when the crowd demands that Packet guarantee his wager on his star. Bluey-Bluey, the troupe's portly clown, echoes the crowd's assessment of the operation, boasting to Bart, "We have the crookedest little carnival layout west of the Mississippi. Why, we got more ways of making suckers than we got suckers."

The crowning glory of the carnival is its spectacular display of the white woman, Laurie, "the darling of London, England." Indeed, she *is* white: played incandescently by Peggy Cummins, pale-skinned, blonde-haired, she wears a cowboy getup in her shooting exhibitions. (Kitses notes that Kantor originally wrote Laurie's introduction to include the phrase "the power which won the West"—an ambiguous phrase but easily connotative of the triumph of whiteness over darker-skinned Native Americans.) Hooked by Laurie, Bart joins the carnival but soon tangles with Packet, who has romanced Laurie in the past and still black-mails her with his knowledge of a killing she committed in St. Louis. Bart ends the dispute by firing a bullet past Packet's head; the lovebirds flee in Laurie's car. Thus freed from the town-to-town march of carnival transiency, Bart and Laurie seem to have escaped toward domestic stability. They visit a justice of the peace and, a moment later, they are picking out a ring in a jewelry store window.

However, traces of carnival tawdriness persist in the pair's ideas about how to get along in the modern West. Rather than emulating sister Ruby and her husband Ira's middle-class familial aspirations, Bart and Laurie aim for a big score. The roadside establishment where they say their late-night vows (unlike *They Live by Night*, these consecrating moments never appear onscreen) looks more like a carnival attraction than a chapel. "The Desert Justice: Get Married," huge signs blare; "See Thos. L. Glenn: Married Safe and Sure." Neon signs for cocktails, a café and a motel glow in the background, apparently on the same building. A subsequent montage presents wholesome moments at what appears to be Yellowstone National Park, but the honeymoon grinds to a halt under the neon of Las Vegas. They hock the ring at a pawnshop, married, jobless, and broke. "What a fool I was to think we could buck Las Vegas," Laurie fumes. In the economy of the carnival, they have been transformed from the sucker makers to the suckers.

If marriage is one signifier of stability or settlement, it is inadequate without home or work, the film suggests. A binary rhetoric between work and crime becomes a trope in the film. Although Bart imagines a steady job demonstrating guns for Remington "or one of those outfits," he apparently does nothing to land employment of any kind, and Laurie's avarice bursts its container. Scorning a forty-dollar-a-week job, it is she who proposes making a living through holdups. "I want things, lots of things, big things. . . . I want a guy with spirit and guts," she urges Bart. When he refuses, offering to hock his guns instead, she threatens to leave. The next scene shows Laurie's triumph: a gumball-machine globe next to a hotel "Traveler's Aid" window shattering and Bart standing aghast, gun in hand, as a counterman empties the cash box onto the countertop.

The following montage of holdups—liquor store, tavern, gas station—sees them into the second transient lifestyle. In addition to the rapidly changing settings and the speedy getaways, the couple's tactic of switching costumes—clothing, automobiles—contrasts with the staid, homebound Ruby. A three-part sequence surrounding the Hampton robbery demonstrates the potential of disguises: first, Laurie poses as a coquettish hitchhiker in order to steal a Cadillac from a presumptuous middle-aged Chicago businessman. Then, driving the Cadillac to the Building and Loan, Bart and Laurie wear their carnival cowboy getups—Laurie tells an inquisitive policeman that she is with the Cheyenne rodeo, moments before she belts him across the face. Minutes later, they abandon the Cadillac and speed away in a nondescript sedan. As they approach a police blockade—"Pull up easy," Laurie orders Bart—they have again transformed themselves, this time into a bookish couple with dour eyeglasses. With polite smiles, they tell the police that they are from Hampton.

However, at each step the film makes clear that the pleasure and utility of disguise also has psychic costs. The roadblock forces them to dissemble flawlessly. More importantly, the transition into criminality forces a domestic transiency that grows into a haunting concern. Never again during this middle sequence of the film does the notion of a home arise. Though they are able to quickly fit in—"Well, drive carefully," the policeman admonishes them, waving them through the roadblock—their transiency becomes much more profound and painful than during their carnival period.

In addition, Laurie's wildness begins to threaten the marriage. Initially the film minimizes the couple's criminal threat: "How can anybody get hurt if we don't hurt them?" Laurie demands. Crime saves the marriage; there is no more talk of her leaving, though Laurie's growing predilection for violence shocks Bart. She threatens to shoot pursuers; after a robbery of the Rangers & Growers office, her widened eyes and purring voice as she watches for pursuing cars suggests that the dangers of robbery (rather than Bart, perhaps) excite her erotically.

As Laurie grows more depraved, the pleasure of *her* pleasure is supplanted by a Sisyphean vision of homelessness and destitution. The film communicates its tonal shift via the domestic strife and the horror gathering on Bart's face. Realizing that the lam has not proven economically viable—"It's cost us everything we've gotten to keep going so far"—Laurie accepts a deal: they will quit after one last job.

That final heist, a payroll robbery at an Armour packing house in Albuquerque, is a gamble with the promise of domestic stability as its stakes. To prepare, the two take jobs at the plant and settle down into a workday routine. However, the film foreshadows their domestic failure; the criminals don't seem to have the knack of holding down straight jobs or occupying a matrimonial home, even over a short term. Laurie incurs her boss's wrath for wearing pants to the office, while Bart cannot resist boasting dangerously that his wife and he will "get a lot of money out of this place." The film undercuts any suggestion of domesticity in Bart and Laurie's Albuquerque home; as they sketch the robbery out across the front page of the *Albuquerque Star*, the two crouch on the floor, like children or people hiding. Even the camera angle emphasizes their isolation; it peers at them from the ceiling, a sight line that disavows any human vantage point. And the prerobbery Albuquerque sequence omits any hint of their socialization into the community. Only one of the many faces appearing in the substantial robbery scene at Armour receives any characterization and that a hostile one: it is Miss Sifert, Laurie's shrewish supervisor, who scolds Laurie for wearing trousers and is later rewarded with a bullet after she pulls the office burglar alarm.

Scenes after the successful robbery promise to relieve the fugitives' tense isolation but ultimately compound it. Laurie and Bart manage to return to the carnival atmosphere for one last night of pleasure before they cross the border into the Mexican unknown. They ride the Pasadena roller coaster and the carousel, pleasuring in the rough-handling rides, but the scenes differ from those at the film's beginning, where Bart mingled with crowds of people. Here Bart and Laurie make no contact with other fairgoers; they laugh but struggle to evade a garrulous vendor who promises to guess Laurie's weight. If his come-on seems invasive to a lady, it is doubly so to one on the run from the law, threatening to expose vital, undisguised information to a world of listening passersby.

A dance hall scene follows, much like the one in *They Live by Night*, about which Jim Kitses suggests that the pair's moving onto the dance floor with other couples "signals their attempt to cross back into the daylight world of mainstream America . . . to no longer live a Janus life" (82). But like Bowie and Keechie, Bart and Laurie find an absolutist divide between the criminal life they've chosen and the straight life they desire, the fatal difference that has poisoned their attempts to pose as wage earners and keep a home. Their attempt, of course, is interrupted by the arrival of inquiring policemen, whom Bart and Laurie witness examining the bill they used to pay their way into the dance hall. The couple cuts back across the dance floor against the flow, maintaining dance posture as a sort of pathetic disguise, trying to "look and act like other people," but as Laurie's fur coat flies off, Bart pulls her onward. The coat, like the Cadillac, is property, a symbol of affluence; for fugitives, the film suggests, such things are tenuous, to be cast off like lizards' tails whenever the fugitives' identity may be revealed.

Nor can they reclaim their familial place. "Didn't it ever occur to you that once we started, we could never ask anybody for help, no matter if we were dying, for the rest of our lives? That we're all alone, and always will be?", Bart agonizes in the Montana blizzard scene. Too late, he sees the power of the reasserted lines between lawful and unlawful citizens, lines that now contest the bonds of blood. Chased out of Pasadena, the two hop a freight car and show up at Ruby's house in Cashville, but her cold reception confirms Bart's fears. "Why did you have to come here?" she demands. Bart answers, "It's because there's no place else to go."

The remainder of this sequence—the chilly distance between Bart and his sister's family, Laurie and Ruby, and Bart and the duo of Dave and Clyde, who come to importune Bart to give himself up peacefully, though he greets them with his gun unholstered—stage a triumph for Hooverian absolutism. It argues the impossibility, in the new postwar landscape, of a fugitive's return to familial intimacy, like Dillinger's comfortable return to his father's farm in Mooresville for Sunday dinner.

Though the police who eventually triumph in *Gun Crazy* play nearly no part in its developing narrative, the fetishistic attention to police communications establishes their presence and sophistication, as in a series of relatively instant cuts from the duo's getaways to police officers or police radio or teletype. In the midst of several robbery sequences, the scene cuts to anonymous officers taking information by telephone or dispatching their license number over police radio. One such dispatch scene leads to a shot of swarms of police cars and motorcycles pouring out of a garage. The Armour robbery, furthermore, invokes the FBI jurisdiction, and a federal teletype machine narrates details of the widening manhunt in close-up. The teletype's letters rattle off with agonizing slowness, allowed a duration that violates the film's otherwise frantic pace. As in *White Heat*'s slower scenes, the suspense is a fascination purely with the technology itself.

Gun Crazy also depicts a sunny press-police relationship, emblematized by the rapport between Bart's two childhood buddies, sheriff Clyde and newsman Dave. Curiously, the pair work as a team throughout the film, appearing only in tandem or as one telephones the other, and ultimately they stand together as witnesses to Bart's death. Their pairing at the film's final moments implies a symmetry of checks and balances: the press will report the shooting fairly and accurately, with a sympathy to the police's perspective, while the police will give the press access—"Got some news for me? I sure could use it," Dave implores Clyde. A scene from the *Cashville News* office illustrates the partnership at work; as the couple's latest misdeeds clatter across the wire-service teletype, Dave calls out to his editor, "Joe, hold the front page." Sheriff Clyde looks on over Dave's shoulder, his presence at the city desk incongruous unless the press plays a part in his policing and communication strategies.

This potential for police-press symbiosis is borne out in the series of bold headlines that punctuate the film's crime scenes. Frequently following closely upon the shots of the various, anonymous police dispatchers, these headline shots similarly feature different, fictitious newspapers, arising as abrupt scene transitions. The universality of the police-press cooperation is suggested by the odd fact that none of these "headline" papers displays the name of a city on its banner; it is as if the technologies of communication and dissemination have at last made locality superfluous, the nation an unvariegated whole. I would argue that the newspaper headlines are particularly sympathetic to Hooverian notions of the fearsome cross-country dragnet and its possibilities. The first such headline, "Hold up Pair Crash State Line Barrier!" specifically evokes Hoover and Cooper's model of the interstate criminal, the jurisdiction jumper. A second headline has Packet implicating Laurie in the long-ago St. Louis homicide, next to photos of the pair in their cowboy getups: thus, over space and time, via coordination and communications, the details mount. "Dragnet Covers State," a later headline blares, and, moments later, the cavalry is called out: "FBI Enters Hunt for Payroll Bandits."

Furthermore, the fictitious newspapers' very names suggest their ability to survey and surveil localities (the *Star Dispatch*, the *Daily Eagle*, and the *Evening Standard*) or to disseminate information over great distances (the *Daily Bugle*, the *Daily Globe*, the *Post News*). Though plausible and even familiar, these newspaper names denote elevated or otherwise privileged vantage points, the surveillance utility of which Foucault discusses in *Discipline and Punish* (200–209). The information disseminated through the daily news and appended to the news, weather, and sports enhances the possibility of eyewitness sightings, of every citizen as detective. It increases the multiplicity of vantage points; it opens the nation to the apprehending eye.

One of the most impressive accomplishments of the collaboration between police and press appears only in the background of a momentary shot. Arriving in Los Angeles, Bart steps from the car to purchase a New Mexico newspaper from a streetside newsstand. He plucks a newspaper from a partition in a vast wall of newspapers; to his left and right, as high as an adult can reach and down to knee level, one sees other partitions, alphabetized and labeled to represent the states of the Union. This Los Angeles newspaper stand presents the accumulation and classification of an entire nation's local news into a single setting, one that any citizen may browse. From his Albuquerque paper (also the *Star*, the sole paper identified by place of publication), Bart reads about the Armour robbery, about the funerals of the two people shot by Laurie.

As a consequence of the coordination of localities, remaining a fugitive within the borders of the nation seems akin to remaining under a searchlight. Their Armour heist plan anticipates an escape to Mexico, where they can get "a nice ranch and settle down." They pass through the California state customs inspection, and Bart reassures Laurie a bit pettishly, "Just take it easy. Hundreds of cars go through here every day." This contrasts the relief Bart exhibits when he tells Laurie he has secured their passage over the Mexican border. Whereas for Kantor in 1940, the irony of the "little state line strung out across the prairie" was its unleashing of the FBI, by 1949, in Trumbo's screenplay, the California state line poses only another brush with an inquiring official. The powers of pan-American police surveillance are such that the only border that retains meaning to the fugitive is the national border. "I'm afraid of the shore patrol," Bart confesses.

In Trumbo's imagined panoptic community, the policeman's role changes. I would argue that the lam of Bart and Laurie is brought to a close without the emergence of any characters among these refigured policemen, even though the film represents many such officers.

I make this assertion despite the presence of Clyde, Bart's lifelong friend, who can be said to have tracked Bart down in Cashville and later in the swamp at Madera National Park where the final shootout takes place. Whereas the story's other policemen work as an organization of anonymous trackers and pursuers, Clyde apprehends Bart in a curiously passive fashion, his motivation one of friendship to Bart and his sister, Ruby. And whereas the police organization operates on eyewitness tips and communiqués, Clyde acts in a somewhat Holmesian fashion, on hunches and old community-based knowledge. He is a specifically local policeman; Bart's outlawry provokes no reaction or communication from him, other than interaction with Dave and a chat over coffee at Ruby's house, until Bart actually returns to Cashville. Then he and Dave take an unimposing *Cashville News* wood-paneled wagon to visit Bart at Ruby's, leaving Clyde's gun behind at the *News* office. After Bart flees Ruby's, Clyde does avail himself of telephone communication, but, improbably, at his last stand against Bart—the swamp shootout—he approaches Bart and Laurie with only Dave at his side.

Setting Clyde aside for a moment, then, the remainder of the film's cops make a curious team. One might call them relatively absent from the film, although they are there, and numerous. More precisely, I would say that the police identify themselves by their *lack of* identity. The dispatchers dispatch—but anonymously, appearing once and dis-appearing. Their uniforms feature no legible badges, indications of rank or jurisdiction, or other distinguishing features. Neither the black microphones into which they speak nor the desks or walls in the mar-gins of the film frame supply information as to their identities or local-ities. They speak to officers, apparently, but ones whom we do not see. Cars and motorcycles pour out of police garages but again without any differentiation as to individual officers, even the sort of anonymous but recognizable establishment of character types that we see in filmic bat-tle scenes, for example. No, *Gun Crazy*'s patrolmen are faceless figures behind windscreens and windshields. Only one police car ever chal-lenges Bart and Laurie, their lone pursuer after the Hampton robbery, and Bart (because of his fear of shooting living things) cannot shoot the driver, as Laurie commands. With a deep breath, he steels himself and shoots out the cruiser's tire, causing it to spin out at the road's edge. Bart's deliberation and grim reaction to seeing the cruiser spin suggest that the police cars have become more emblematic of authority than the very men who drive them. "Did you get him?" Laurie barks, intoxi-cated by speed and danger. "Yes," a weary Bart responds.

Other than Clyde, two policemen make an impression. The first is Clyde's father, also sheriff of Cashville, who apprehends Bart after he steals the gun from the hardware store. Yet the manner of the capture, in which Bart trips into the rainy gutter and the gun skitters across the street to the sheriff's feet, shows Sheriff Boston benefiting from instinct and timing (and the would-be thief's ineptitude) more than any assertion or use of policing power. (A kindly specter, he testifies on Bart's behalf at his trial.) The second is the nosy beat cop who approaches Laurie as Bart is robbing the Hampton Building and Loan. But this policeman, too, behaves noninterventionally; though he whisks Laurie's gun from her hip holster, he merely looks the gun over, compliments it and, eyeing her cowgirl getup, asks her what "outfit" she's with. "The Cheyenne rodeo," she replies, and the policeman apologizes for not knowing the rodeo was coming through town; alas, he could have escorted them through. Even this pally officer works to extend the police's information networks.

Whereas the three films I have discussed previously envision an interventionist police force, in *Gun Crazy* the role of intervening seems to subside relative to a surveillance and communication function that, in addition to developing technologically, has diversified into private and corporate domains. We see plenty of watchmen: at Armour, at the California state line, at the gates to Madera National Park. If policing has diminished, *security* has tightened. What's more, the film's soundtrack features a cacophony of sirens: alarms at the banks and at Armour as well as a chorus of police sirens. Even the hounds that howl in the distance during the couple's struggle on foot through the Madera mountains figure as alarms of a sort: devices that both warn of danger or illegality and that harbinger the investigation and pursuit to follow.

Clyde's parting words to Bart at Ruby's imply that the sheriff understands his role apart from but in support of the nationalized machinery of hue and cry that will eventually bear down on Bart and Laurie: "You know you haven't a chance of beating the law out of here. The moment you go, we'll have to turn in the alarm. There won't be a road or even a path you can get through." "Be seeing you," Dave adds ominously.

The conclusion of *Gun Crazy* stages the triumph of a panoptic style of policing over the outlaws, who run wildly toward Cashville, then drive into the San Lorenzo Mountains to escape pursuit. But that pursuit is *not really there*—in other words, they run wildly without apparent pursuers. A road crew forces them into a sudden turnoff that runs up into the mountains, breaking through a Madera National Park sign that warns, "Stop for Rangers." They pass a "road closed" sign, and a bad bump stalls Ruby's car. When it will not restart, they flee on foot—the wild setting suddenly permeated by the sounds of multiplying sirens.

This sequence imagines the lam as the antithesis of the gracious social living Bart and Laurie strive for by joining the dance hall crowd. Laurie protests that she is exhausted, but Bart orders her onward: "Just a little farther. Then we can rest." They fall face first into muddy water and must hurry onward, then are hunted by dogs. Toward night, they wade into a flat swamp and rest on a patch of dry ground, surrounded by low plants.

It is on this patch of land, surrounded by water, that the film's final shootout takes place. The scene is apparently wilderness: crickets chirp, frogs croak. Yet the setting is a (fictitious) national park; this wilderness exists under the direct administration of the federal government. Bart and Laurie awaken to the sound of splashing in the dark. "Bart, we're in real trouble this time," says Laurie. Her eyes dart this way and that—as if, in this wilderness, any sound is now emblematic of their faceless pursuers. A dense mist obscures their vision of the pursuers who have finally arrived.

It is Dave and Clyde, of course—the pair who, earlier, at Ruby's, beseech Bart, "Don't force us to turn this into a manhunt." A curious remark: why is this not already a manhunt? By so saying, Dave and Clyde insinuate a distinction between organizational surveillance—not unmanly, but relatively manless—and a putatively "manly" hunt, one marked by heroism and violence. Their remark acknowledges that the old techniques of the volley of gunfire are still at the police's disposal.

***

By the end of the 1940s, improvements in funding, equipment, coordination, and practice had made American police a much more viable force against the mobile fugitive. Police telecommunications brought even small towns and remote sheriff's offices into contact with other departments and the federal hub, and mobile radio networked individual patrol units with central dispatch and each other, enabling decentralized command. Thus Hoover's mapping and surveying project—the filling of the nation's unpatrolled spaces, the reinforcement of connections between already plotted points—drew close to its goal of a national policing map, an achievement that, once reached, would serve only to feed future coordination and reinforcement, just as the "technologically and physically dynamic" longitudinal net of the USCGS inspired continual recalibration.

The unmanned manhunt was, of course, a fiction; the machinery of pursuit still relied upon police commanders and officers to operate it purposefully and effectively. Yet as a fiction, it held great sway in news and entertainment representations of the lam through the late 1940s and early 1950s. Jim Thompson's 1958 novel *The Getaway*, twice translated to film, is set within the arid, hellish space of Hoover's bugged frontier:

> Flight is many things. Something clean and swift, like a bird skimming across the sky. Or something filthy and crawling; a series of crablike movements through figurative and literal slime, a process of creeping ahead, jumping sideways, running backward. It is sleeping in fields and river bottoms. It is bellying for miles along an irrigation ditch. It is back roads, spur railroad lines, the tailgate of a wildcat truck, a stolen car and a dead couple in lovers' lane. It is food pilfered from freight cars, garments taken from clotheslines; robbery and murder, sweat and blood. The complex made simple by the alchemy of necessity. (122)

The flight of Doc and Carol McCoy finds them naked and fly covered on a hill of manure, going stir-crazy in underwater caves, and ultimately trapped in a horrifying community of fugitives in the mountains across the crucial Mexican border. If shooting the marshal ended the threat of apprehension once, as in *High Noon*, the dawn of a less confrontational, more surveillance-oriented police force meant that it became impossible to kill one's way out of a jam, at least for long. The unmanned manhunt reflected the paranoia of the McCarthy era and presaged the 1955 Walter Wanger thriller *Invasion of the Body Snatchers*, where the plodding, affectless pursuit of zombies turns the living into terrified and excruciatingly visible aliens within their own town.

Thus Laurie's cry at the end of *Gun Crazy*—"I'll kill you! I'll kill you!"—sums up her doomed tactics throughout the film. A product of the old-fangled carnival school of illegality, with its low stakes and frequent relocations, she fails to understand that a murderous lam cannot sustain itself against contemporary policing's pancontinental gaze. As Dave and Clyde wade into the swamp, sounding a Hooverian warning—"You haven't got a chance. There are too many guns around this swamp"—Laurie's eyes widen ferally and she stands, bracing to shoot. As she cries "I'll kill you," waiting for the pursuers to come into view, Bart realizes the futility of her gesture, and, failing to distract her by shouting her name, he shoots her. She becomes his first and only human victim. Reacting to the gunfire, Dave or Clyde (the agency is unclear) fires six shots, and the film ends thus, with the apprehending officer and the assisting reporter examining and then turning away from the dead bodies.

"Are you all right, Sheriff?" calls another anonymous voice through the brush. "Yeah. Yeah, we're all right," Clyde responds, to no one—or to everyone, rather. In *Gun Crazy*'s end, having broken the bonds of community benevolence that characterized his father's career as sheriff, Clyde responds as a subject of a policing force that succeeds by not showing its face.

5. "i might as well be in the penitentiary as in his hands"

Wright, Ellison, and the Black Fugitive

Initially *Invisible Man* may seem a strange inclusion in this project, which has focused on the changes in the lam wrought by the advent of federal policing. Despite the recurrence of "running and dodging" in the passages above—a phrase and a pattern I will say more about later—Ralph Ellison's 1952 novel is not explicitly about a criminal's flight. While he engages in violence, including arson and a mugging, its narrator neither defines himself as nor draws police attention as a criminal. Ellison himself proved particularly resistant to romanticization of criminals as black leaders. In a 1977 interview, he mourned, "During the Sixties, this myth of the redeemed criminal had a tremendous influence on our young people, when criminals guilty of every crime from con games, to rape, to murder, exploited it by declaring themselves political activists and Black leaders. . . . it appeared that for many Afro-Americans all that was required for such a role was a history of criminality (the sleazier the better), a capacity for irresponsible rhetoric, and the passionate assertion of the mystique of 'Blackness' " ("The Essential Ellison" 366).

In *Canaan Bound: The African-American Great Migration Novel*, Lawrence R. Rodgers locates *Invisible Man* as the "culmination" of the migration genre (9). For Rodgers, migration is a "central subject of black literature and folklore"; "the African removal, escape from bondage, the journey to a promised land, and the challenge of recovering southern memory amid its constant erosion" are merely episodic moments in what has proved to be a centuries-long diasporic movement for African-American

> Dizzily, he drew back. This was the end. There were no more roofs over which to run and dodge.
> —Richard Wright, *Native Son*

> They would surely catch him. The mere thought of dodging and running again from the police made him tense. No, he would stay and plot how to elude them.
> —Wright, "The Man Who Lived Underground"

> For they were outside, in the dark with Sambo, the dancing paper doll; taking it on the lambo with my fallen brother, Tod Clifton (Tod, Tod) running and dodging the forces of history instead of making a dominating stand.
> —Ralph Ellison, *Invisible Man*

culture (3). The search for a "nonmarginal place in which to reside and prosper" links the migrant worker of the 1920s and 1930s to the fugitive slave. Numerous conventions persist from antebellum slave narratives to post-Emancipation migration stories: the dream of a North without racial bias or barriers, this dream's disappearance, and the fugitive/migrant's frustrated transition into more or less successfully coping with his or her new situation (98–99).

Ostensibly, the end of formal slavery and the black migrant's historical transition from fugitive slave to free emigrant spelled an end to "running and dodging"; as Ellison's veteran says of the narrator, "He's going free, in the broad daylight and alone. I can remember when young fellows like him had first to commit a crime, or be accused of one, before they tried such a thing. Instead of leaving in the light of morning, they went in the dark of night. And no bus was fast enough" (154–55).

However, Ellison and other authors also undertake a project in cultural geography, tracing the obstacles and interrogations remaining for migrant blacks in the twentieth century. While Ellison's novel is not in the Hooverian sense a lam novel, it makes a trope of the lam. Though Ellison minimized the influence of slave narratives upon the form of *Invisible Man*, in the "general story" of "Afro-American experience" that he credits with inspiring the novel's narrative pattern, we can unearth the traces of a fugitive subjectivity that dates to an antebellum socioracial climate and practice. I mean that these traces show up in the novel's narration, in the narrator's associations, impulses, and reactions: criminality and flight are never far away from the narrator's mind, even if the setting or activity are entirely legal.

This chapter makes several arguments. First, I discuss the problematization of space and mobility that was an enduring product of the plantation system and the various laws and practices that encouraged apprehension of fugitive slaves. Houston A. Baker Jr. argues that *Native Son* and *Invisible Man* are linked by a concern with the status of African-American space. "For place to be recognized by one as actually

PLACE, as a personally valued locale, one must set and maintain the boundaries," Baker writes. "If one, however, is constituted and maintained by and within boundaries set by a dominating authority, then one is not a setter of place but a prisoner of another's desire. Under the displacing impress of authority even what one calls and, perhaps, feels is one's *own place* is, from the perspective of human agency, *placeless*" (201). The occupant of such a determined space would live "maximally secured by another, a prisoner of interlocking, institutional arrangements of power," Baker continues (201).

The all-important notion of a black American's "place"—or lack of it—finds a contemporary apotheosis in Richard Wright's fiction, I argue, and Ellison's novel makes black homelessness a condition that penetrates even the most law abiding spaces a black American might occupy. I trace a historical narrative that posits the establishment of such "institutional arrangements of power," showing how they were maintained, how they inform African-American subjectivity in the antebellum South, and suggesting that their continuation, even in the ostensibly self-chosen space of the industrial North, is evident in these two works.

Finally, I discuss the tropes of criminality and flight in Ellison's novel—motifs that persist, permeating the narrator's experience, even as he tries to keep to the high road.

The American landscape, whose conquest and crossing mean so much to national identity and narrative, has never functioned as fully as home and refuge to African-Americans. In white American fiction and myth, socioeconomic movement has frequently been conceived, achieved and manifested in geographical movement, whether that movement be from East to West or from farm to city. In 1840, an anonymous article in the *Merchants' Magazine and Commercial Review* remarked upon the economic "promise" of land elsewhere: "The poor man at the east, with a large family, laboring, for example, upon the ungenerous soil of New England, finding that here is a country westward, where labor is dear and broad acres yielding an abundance of the necessaries of life are cheap, is induced to migrate with his household goods and all his effects, to this 'land of promise' " (Still 263). The linkage of "land" with "promise" implies a freedom to emigrate: to leave, to move, and to arrive across the American continent. In *The Rites of Assent: Transformations in the Symbolic Construction of America,* Sacvan Bercovitch discusses the rhetorics through which the "errand" of Puritan migration to and through America was empowered and justified by religious history and prophecy for the benefit of numerous white groups and communities (30–49). As this "promise" was staged and restaged—in varying conditions and to various results—in numerous of the twentieth century's most important novels—*O Pioneers! The Grapes of Wrath, The Great Gatsby*—the *possibility* of moving remains, for white characters, a constant of American identity. Even in narratives where an economic motive is less evident—*Walden, On the Road*—this operant privilege remains a theme, discussed in terms of "freedom" or Transcendental "experience."

Frequently African-American literature does not evince the same comfort with and conquest of the continent. Its ambivalence about mobility within a "land of promise" roots in nineteenth-century slave narratives. On one hand, the possibility of escaping slavery by fleeing the South presented the most dramatic illustration possible of the principle of salvation through mobility. The literature of the Great Migration similarly advertises economic and social deliverance in the North. Other African-American texts, such as Zora Neale Hurston's *Their Eyes Were Watching God* and Alice Walker's *The Color Purple,* have recast American patterns of emigration as a means of escaping oppressive relations within the family or marital structure.

Yet the possibilities for African-American mobility have always been troubled. Before Emancipation, the condition of slavery translated into a disenfranchised relation to travel and emigration for most African-Americans. Slavery sustained itself in great part by blocking, through legal and cultural practice, the ability of slaves to travel to the free North.

Early state criminal statutes designated patrols and punishment for slave runaways; the earliest such act, a 1704 South Carolina statute, required an armed militia that, at times of alarm, would seize all slaves found off their master's plantation without a pass or permit (Osgood 385). Later federal laws sanctioned removal of escaped slaves from Northern states without trial or interference. The Constitution itself featured a fugitive clause (Article IV, Section 2) that bound persons "held to service or labor in one State" to that labor, even after escaping to another state. The 1793 Fugitive Slave Law made escaped slaves residing in free states susceptible to arrest and reenslavement without a jury trial; the only testimony necessary for the slave's conviction and deportation was the avowal of ownership from the master. The 1850 Fugitive Slave Law approved by Millard Fillmore provided that "the claimant" of any fugitive slave (or the claimant's attorney) "may pursue and reclaim such fugitive person" or "remove such fugitive person back to the State or Territory from whence he or she may have escaped," using "such reasonable force or restraint as may be necessary under the circumstances of the case." The 1850 act also strengthened prohibitions on interfering with the process of retrieval and mandated that "in no trial or hearing under this act shall the testimony of such alleged fugitive be admitted in evidence."

For runaway slaves, then, federal laws providing for their interstate pursuit and extradition existed nearly a century before they came to exist for other types of criminals. That these laws were not enforced by the government but instead left to the agencies of slave owners and their hired proxies may well have lowered the incidence of fugitive apprehension and arrest. However, it left that process of apprehension and arrest in the private sector, where brutal revenge might be taken in ways that circumvented the limits on police practice. "The greatest failure of the criminal law of slavery was the slim protection it afforded blacks against white violence," writes Daniel J. Flanigan (iii).

The law's prescription of master's justice, rather than punishment by official agency, helped to shape and justify a cultural practice of regular inquisitions made upon black Southerners by whites. Slaveholders' notions of property rights—constantly reiterated in defenses against abolitionists and in court cases involving crimes committed by or upon blacks—asked the acquiescence and participation of poorer whites in a racial topography that raised the status of the poorest whites by allowing them to share in the stewardship of black slaves. Aiding this was the Southern planter's cultivation of an "extraordinary and positive unity of passion and purpose" with poorer whites, described by W. J. Cash in *The Mind of the South*, based on regional pride and opposition to Yankee intervention, as well as racist tenets: if the poorer white Southerner "had no worth-while interest at stake in slavery, if his real interest ran the other way about, he did nevertheless have that, to him, dear treasure of his superiority as a white man, which had been conferred on him by slavery; and so was as determined to keep the black man in chains" (66).

This general proposal was reinforced episodically by rewards offered to those who apprehended runaway slaves. Gilbert Osofsky writes, "To collect the reward on a fugitive or perhaps claim the person of a slave whose master could not be located must have been enticing bait for the poor whites who patrolled the Southern countryside. A good catch not only seemed a fulfillment of one's communal responsibility but it might also mean instant wealth" (19).

Slaves were well aware of the danger of running away. Seth Concklin, writing in 1851, despaired, "Searching the country opposite Paducah, I find that the whole country fifty miles round is inhabited only by Christian wolves. It is customary, when a strange negro is seen, for any white man to seize the negro and convey such negro through and out of the State of Illinois to Paducah, Ky., and lodge such stranger in Paducah jail, and there claim such reward as may be offered by the master" (Still 27). Sanctioned by law, encouraged by bounty incentives and racist motivations, the duty (and, for many, the pleasure) of interrogation became a fixture in the lives of white Southerners. Such interrogation was not only the prerogative of the "armed patrols" observed in 1860 by Frederick Law Olmsted, who described them as "invested with more arbitrary and cruel power than any police in Europe"; an anecdote of Olmsted's indicates that the "security of the whites" depended as much upon

the constant, habitual, and instinctive surveillance and authority of all white people over all black. I have seen a gentleman, with no commission or special authority, oblige negroes to show their passports, simply because he did not recognize them as belonging to any of his neighbors. I have seen a girl, twelve years old, in a district where, in ten miles, the slave population was fifty to one of the free, stop an old man on the public road, demand to know where he was going, and by what authority, order him to face about and return to his plantation. . . . The man quailed like a sparrow, and she instantly resumed the manner of a lovely child with me. (444–45)

Although, as Flanigan points out, the regulation of slave movement was not especially effective (37), the anecdote of the young white girl interrogating the old black man evokes Michel Foucault's model of juridical discipline, particularly his discussion of the effects of what he calls the carceral system of policing and its extension into the realm of the everyday. "Operating at every level of the social body and by mingling ceaselessly the art of rectifying and the right to punish," Foucault writes, disciplinary policing "lowers the level from which it becomes natural and acceptable to be punished" (*Discipline* 303). William Craft testifies to slave policing's inversion of designations of lawfulness:

The lowest villain in the country, should he be a white man, has the legal power to arrest, and question, in the most inquisitorial and insulting manner, any coloured person, male or female, that he may find at large, particularly at night and on Sundays, without a written pass, signed by the master or some one in authority; or stamped free papers, certifying that the person is the rightful owner of himself. If the coloured person refuses to answer questions put to him, he may be beaten, and his defending himself against this attack makes him an outlaw. (36–37)

Delegation of such power to the whole of white Southern society created a surveillance entity that appeared everywhere and could ask anything at any time, often from apparently benign social positions. And the effacement of distinctions between police and nonpolice made trusting "any man, white or colored," difficult for runaways. Even black citizens in the border regions between North and South could sometimes be bribed or threatened into turning in fugitives, and because people could be punished for giving assistance, many who would have helped slaves were afraid to. In 1854, Charles Gilbert escaped from Richmond to Old Point Comfort, Virginia, but while he waited for a boat, "he was apprised of the fact that the hunters and watch dogs of Slavery were eagerly watching for him. Even his nearest relatives, through fear of consequences had to hide their faces as it were from him. None dare offer him a night's lodging, scarcely a cup of water, lest such an act might be discovered by the hunters, whose fiendish hearts would have found pleasure in meting out the most dire punishments to those guilty of thus violating the laws of Slavery" (Still 236). Gilbert hid for four weeks below a hotel rather than expose his kin to danger or risk making new acquaintances.

However, I would point out that Southern white surveillance practices functioned to problematize transit for *all* black citizens, even nonescapees. "In Georgia (and I believe in all the slave States,) every coloured person's complexion is *prima facie* evidence of his being a slave," writes Craft (36). On everyday business, Southern blacks were compelled to present credentials proving that they were free, or, if slaves, that they had leave to be away from home (Gara 46). Thus the phrase "knowing one's place" had a double resonance for the black Southerner: one's economic and social place, one's proper physical place. Frequently nuisance ordinances were enacted in order to prescribe or prohibit certain "places" to African-Americans, writes Theodore Brantner Williams, who describes two such ordinances. An 1813 Charleston law prohibited "negroes from swearing, smoking or walking with a cane on the streets. . . . No negro dances were to be held without the consent of the city wardens nor were negroes to assemble at any military parade" (40). Thirty years later, an Augusta, Georgia, ordinance forbade free

Negroes "to ride or drive about the city save on business" or to carry sticks, smoke, attend military parades, or sell certain products (41). Osofsky argues that "in the deepest sense the entire South was a prison house, and all white men, solely because of their skin color, were prison keepers" (19).

For all African-Americans in the mid-nineteenth-century South, this investigatory gaze varied in intensity between various types of spaces. Open roadway space, for example, connotes capture and betrayal in numerous fugitive slave narratives. "I had long since made up my mind that I would not trust myself in the hands of any man, white or colored," wrote William Wells Brown, who viewed the woods as his only safe hiding place during his flight north into Ohio. "After dark, I emerged from the woods into a narrow path, which led me into the main travelled road" (216). Similarly, Henry Bibb wrote, "I always dreaded to pass through a prairie, and on coming to one which was about six miles in width, I was careful to look in every direction to see whether there was any person in sight before I entered it; but I could see no one" (145). "My object was neither to be seen on the road nor to approach the town by daylight," agrees James W. C. Pennington in his *The Fugitive Blacksmith* (217). Pennington is accosted on a Maryland road by, it turns out, a friendly white man who nonetheless demonstrates his power of inquiry:

He drew up his horses, and addressed me in a very kind tone, when the following dialogue took place between us.

"Are you travelling any distance, my friend?"

"I am on my way to Philadelphia."

"Are you free?"

"Yes, sir."

"I suppose, then, you are provided with free papers?"

"No, sir. I have no papers."

"Well, my friend, you should not travel on this road: you will be taken up before you have gone three miles. There are men living on this road who are constantly on the look-out for your people; and it is seldom that one escapes them who attempts to pass by day." (219)

Sure enough, a page later he is taken "near the mile stone" by a rather disembodied presence—he is passing a tavern, "as quietly and as rapidly as possible, when from the lot just opposite the house, or signpost, I heard a coarse stern voice cry, 'Halloo!'" (220).

Pennington's anecdote is eerily reminiscent of Louis Althusser's model of ideological interpellation. The "coarse stern voice" reveals no immediate source or speaker; initially, at least, Pennington seems to be apprehended more by a spatial and economic *position*—the milepost—than any policing effort or entity. Of course, this dispersal and privatization of policing power conflates the two functions of ideologization and repression. The era of slavery conjured an ideology that prohibited or problematized movement; the surveillance and regulation of space was crucial to that production of black Southern subjects.

This spatial division into proper and improper regions, both policed by multiple sets of eyes, again evokes Foucault, who says simply, "Discipline proceeds from the distribution of individuals in space" (141). To argue that the Old South was penitentiary-like for its black inmates has various implications. Foucault's model of discipline is ultimately *productive* in the sense that it disseminates policing from central, elevated loci (in his narrative, the king and his express proxies) to multiple, mobile, and subtle agents—even into the subject himself.

It is true that some black Southerners managed to resist and subvert the aims of this discipline, as John Hope Franklin and Loren Schweninger document in *Runaway Slaves: Rebels on the Plantation*. They malingered or played hooky. They stole, conspired, assaulted, or killed their masters. They escaped the South completely, upending its claim upon them as property and as subjects. The successful escape of Ellen and William Craft, who impersonated a white man and his servant, respectively, as they voyaged north, and Harriet Beecher Stowe's episode of Eliza passing for white to escape a slave catcher in *Uncle Tom's Cabin*, offer anecdotal evidence of the slipperiness and performativity of racial designations, and the exploration of racial passing in William Wells Brown's *Clotel; or, The President's Daughter* (1853), Frances E. Harper's

Iola Leroy (1892), James Weldon Johnson's *The Autobiography of an Ex-Colored Man* (1912), and Nella Larsen's *Passing* (1929) are but four of the many texts that document a continuing fascination with the prospect of eluding racial surveillance by disguising or concealing one's blackness. Like Richard Wright, Nella Larsen also sought refuge in the less polarized racial landscape of Europe. Such maneuvers were not accessible to all African-Americans, however, nor did passing constitute a viable politics of resistance to systemic American racism. Most passing novels, points out Juda Bennett, involve a return to blackness, though, as in the case of Larsen's Clare Kendry, at a high personal cost (51–54).

My point is that the Old South cross-racial surveillance produced a subject for whom being in one's place—in a behavioral but also a specifically geographical sense—and breaking the law became binarily opposed options. In the phrase that gives title to this chapter, "I might as well be in the penitentiary as in his hands" (Still 295), Pete Matthews proposes such a set of alternatives: one's place, or the risk of a specifically *legal* punishment.

The Panopticon, remarks Foucault, induces "a state of conscious and permanent visibility that assures the automatic functioning of power" (201). The gaze of white people became a sort of ground-level Panopticon for black Southerners, I would argue, from which "innocence"—being sanctioned in their travel by their owners or freedman status—did not exempt them. The carceral project, Foucault explains, shifts policing interest from the specific offense to "the departure from the norm, the anomaly" (299). That interest trained its sights upon the "departure" of the black subject on the move. That its anomalization of black mobility endured long after Emancipation—and extended far north of the Mason-Dixon line—is evident in the *Chicago Tribune*'s remark upon John Dillinger's Crown Point escape with black murderer Herbert Youngblood: "Youngblood, being a Negro, would facilitate identification of Dillinger and practically made impossible the latter's freedom in the open if the two continued to travel together" ("Seek

Dillinger Gang Hideout" 1). The proof is in the pudding: the much-sought Dillinger managed to elude detection, even in Chicago, where the manhunt was heaviest, whereas the unknown Youngblood was shot dead in Michigan within a week.

Biography itself justifies the frequent critical pairing of Ralph Ellison and Richard Wright; Ellison was best man at Wright's wedding to Dhimah Rose Meadman in 1939 and acknowledged Wright as a friend, inspiration, and source. Both authors inherited the promise and problems inherent in black migration and flight during and after the Great Migration. The possibility of black economic salvation in the North was bedeviled by industrial exploitation and Northern racism. Particularly, though, the interlinkage of space, race, and criminality concern Wright and Ellison. In a number of stories and novels, Wright depicts black fugitives on the run; I will discuss *Native Son* and a novella that follows shortly after and improvises upon its themes, 1944's "The Man Who Lived Underground." *Native Son*, in particular, Ellison has hailed as a thematic predecessor: in "Remembering Richard Wright" he tells of reading "most of *Native Son* as it came off the typewriter, and I didn't know what to think of it except that it was wonderful" (*Collected Essays* 670). Ellison's *Invisible Man* does not explicitly depict criminal flight, but the novel combines the motifs of *running* and of *vision*, plotting a landscape in which, I will argue, the fugitive is omnipresent.

Native Son (1940) is set in 1930s Chicago, late in the Great Migration, but in its vision of the city we see the detritus of plantation-era surveillance and geography. Although Wright's Thomas family are themselves migrants, Wright proposes a framework of black immobility, for explicit economic discrimination keeps the Thomases trapped in the worst part of the city. Sam Bluefarb calls Bigger's predicament a "labyrinth": "if he would escape from the labyrinth of his city and society, he must first escape from the labyrinth of his own mind" (145). However, I would argue that the disassociation of city and mind is not as simple as Bluefarb makes it. Bigger Thomas has internalized a map on which space is racialized. Crossing its demarcating lines in order to get a job that pays him with wages and respect also, paradoxically, activates in Bigger a carceralized subjectivity marked by guilt and claustrophobia.

For Bigger, the very definitions of criminal behavior depend upon racial difference. He is a small-time hood as the novel opens, having already committed several robberies with his gang, but he knows that to rob whites or white-owned businesses is to bring the attention of the police. Besides the police, the threat of detection and capture radiates from a diffuse range of entities, all of them white. The most explicit and threatening is state attorney Buckley, introduced via a campaign poster in the book's opening pages. Though Bigger knows that Buckley profits from political graft, the accusatory gaze works only one way:

> [Bigger] looked at the poster: the white face was fleshy but stern; one hand was uplifted and its index finger pointed straight out into the street at each passer-by. The poster showed one of those faces that looked straight at you when you looked at it and all the while you were walking and turning your head to look at it it kept looking unblinkingly back at you until you got so far from it you had to take your eyes away, and then it stopped, like a movie blackout. Above the top of the poster were tall red letters: YOU CAN'T WIN! (12–13)

The poster locates the white-run judicial system at a panoptic center, able to perceive at any angle. Buckley's slogan, presumably directed at the criminals it is Buckley's job to prosecute, also sums up Bigger's perceptions of the black man's prospects in the industrial North.

Policing doesn't stop with the police, however. Wright also involves a huge number of white men in the policing effort: the search party of "eight thousand men, white men, with guns and gas, [who] were out there in the night looking" for Bigger (297). Calling Bigger a "nigger" and "boy" and appraising a "brown gal" in a nearby apartment as "a peach" (301), they evoke the Southern lynch mob even before they capture him above the rising street noise, "a flood of strange joy" (309): "Lynch'im!" and "Kill that black ape!" they cry (314). Like antebellum lynch mobs, the

Chicago searchers freeze the fugitive's relations to the black community as well; a newspaper reports that several black men are beaten, hundreds are rounded up for investigation, and hundreds more are dismissed from jobs because of hysteria over Bigger's flight (282–83). Not surprisingly, Bigger reflects that a group of black men reading papers in a doorway were "hating him for having brought this attack upon them" (285).

Additionally, the white press operates as a substantial and versatile policing mechanism. Reporters manage to break the Dalton family's will to silence after Mary's disappearance. To Bigger, they seem "harder than Britten, but in a more impersonal way, a way that maybe was more dangerous than Britten's . . . like men out for keen sport" (228). The snooping reporters hurry Bigger into cleaning the furnace improperly and then, remarking upon his clumsiness, discover Mary's partly incinerated bones. During the period of Bigger's lam, in fact, the press stands in for the police; as the various police forces unravel the crime and conduct the manhunt, multiple daily editions blare the latest news into the novel's text, giving the very real sense that it is *they,* not official police, who are the investigators. Kenneth Kinnamon has demonstrated that the scathing racism of Wright's fabricated *Chicago Tribune* stories conforms closely to the paper's practices in the 1930s; the article Bigger reads in his cell in Book Three was adapted from an actual *Tribune* story (16–17).

Other surveilling or pursuing agents depart from the human, as if the cultural dragnet under which Southern blacks lived before Emancipation had been reinstituted and extended. Kate, the Daltons' cat, is also white. Wright mentions its whiteness twice in the paragraph in which the cat spies Bigger stuffing Mary's body into the incinerator; its eyes are "two green burning pools—pools of accusation and guilt" (105). Later, Kate leaps onto Bigger's shoulder while the reporters snap photographs. Even the "few white clouds" that drift above him as he smokes outside with Gus are like reconnaissance balloons, overhanging the gang's contemplation of robbing a white store (15). The snowstorm that effectively locks Bigger into Chicago and against which his capture is made is again and again discussed in terms of whiteness, "a white curtain" (187), "falling as though it had fallen from the beginning of time and would always fall until the end of the world" (211). And the telltale bones among the Daltons' incinerator ashes are, of course, white (253).

Like a slave in antebellum geography, Bigger is intimidated—moved to specifically criminal guilt—by most interactions with whites. Meeting Henry Dalton for the first time, the phrase "I'd like to talk with you a little," moves Bigger to think, "Goddammit! He knew what was coming. He would be asked about that time he had been accused of stealing auto tires and had been sent to the reform school. He felt guilty, condemned" (55). Mrs. Dalton, too, moves him to fear; in Mary's bedroom, she becomes an "awesome white blur" (98).

This blurring of the surveillance entity is important. The efficacy of the disciplinary mechanism depends to some degree upon its hiddenness or diffusion, and the subject's inability to discern its inattention. The "state of conscious and permanent visibility" desired in the subject of panopticism cannot flourish in the tangible *absence* of surveillance (Foucault, *Discipline* 200–203). Similarly, Wright delocalizes the entities that surveil Bigger, that prod his sense of guilt. Yet he maintains their identification with whiteness. Beyond the police, press, and mob, the entire white population becomes a source of paranoia, a *naturalized*, pervasive entity: "To Bigger and his kind white people were not really people; they were a sort of great natural force, like a stormy sky looming overhead, or like a deep swirling river stretching suddenly at one's feet in the dark. . . . whether [black folks] feared it or not, each and every day of their lives they lived with it; even when words did not sound its name, they acknowledged its reality" (129). Accordingly, as Bigger realizes that Mary is dead, his first thought is of a diffuse, white accusatory presence: "The reality of the room fell from him; the vast city of white people that sprawled outside took its place" (100).

Like plantation-era geography, the geography of *Native Son* is heavily racialized, and for Bigger, crossing its demarcating lines activates a sort of carceralized subjectivity marked by specifically criminal guilt. Bigger and his family live in a "Black Belt" apartment owned by the white Dalton family; the Dalton-Thomas relationship suggests a distant master–slave quarter dyad. In this neighborhood, Bigger moves easily, "relaxed, his mind pleasantly vacant of purpose" (15), even though the official police presence there seems much heavier than on Drexel Boulevard, where the Daltons live. While on his own turf, Bigger understands that "white policemen never really searched diligently for Negroes who committed crimes against other Negroes" (14). The black community has its own policing eye, but in the Ernie's Kitchen Shack scene, it functions principally to enforce racial divisions. When Bigger finds himself at Ernie's in the presence of Mary and Jan, he "felt ensnared in a tangle of deep shadows" (82), guilty and nervous about his appearance even though it is the whites who have brought him there. Though it is the white couple who are the anomaly, Bigger reacts as if trained to the inquisitor's gaze: "the waitress and several people at other tables were staring at him," he decides, "They knew him and he knew that they were wondering as he would have wondered if he had been in their places" (83).

Greater Chicago menaces Bigger, however. Even before he kills Mary Dalton, the "quiet and spacious white neighborhood" of the Daltons appears to him "a world of white secrets carefully guarded." He finds the Dalton home surrounded by "a high, black picket fence," but it is he who feels "constricted inside" (49). Prophetically, he understands the implications of his presence on the street in specifically criminal terms: "Suppose a police saw him wandering in a white neighborhood like this? It would be thought that he was trying to rob or rape somebody" (49).

Being out of place in racial terms, even if he is *in place* according to his newfound job with the Daltons, stirs criminal associations or acts in Bigger. It is (mis)placement, more than any conscious wish or malice when Mrs. Dalton catches him with Mary in Mary's bedroom, that spurs Bigger's most significant act. Mrs. Dalton is blind, and Wright paints her as indistinct, only an "awesome white blur" (98), yet Bigger smothers Mary, not to conceal their drunken grappling but "for fear of bumping into something in the dark and betraying his presence" (97).

In Wright's hopeless racial geography, the prospects of the fugitive are rather dim. The opening scenes in the Thomas apartment initiate a pattern of denial: first Bigger and Buddy trap the black rat within their room by blocking off its exit hole (2–5). Then Bigger laments not being allowed to fly—"It's like living in jail," he despairs. "Half the time I feel like I'm on the outside of the world peeping in through a knot-hole in the fence" (20). The movie theater titillates with the promise of escape, but Bigger knows that if Jack were to approach Mary Dalton in Florida, he'd "be hanging from a tree like a bunch of bananas" (34).

Bigger's euphoria at having killed and turned blame upon a white man at first produces an illusory self-assurance: "Because he could go now, run off if he wanted to and leave it all behind, he felt a certain sense of power, a power born of a latent capacity to live" (188). In fleeting moments, he envisions the crime as a self-defining act, "an anchor weighing him safely in time" (119) and opening "avenues of escape" (130) or "avenues of action" (218). "Anchor," of course, carries also the forensic sense of responsibility, of guiltiness. Thus it is the crime itself—rather than, as he first envisions, his everyday life—that becomes that which he need escape. His nightmares are terrible, guilt stricken: again and again he has visions of Mary's severed head or other horrors. The nightmares belie his euphoria; the "certain sense of power" cannot undercut the "organic" sense in which he is still subject to his own sprawling, disindividuated guilt, now given "anchor" by a tangible and inescapable crime. The black fugitive, Bigger suggests, cannot outrun his own history, nor by ducking the police can he duck his own subjection to the sense of being (abnormally, racially) policed.

When Mary's bones are discovered, Bigger is not immediately identified as the killer: "They would be looking for the murderer," he realizes (253), and, catching a moment where the men are looking *away* from him, he sneaks out. "He had to get out of this white neighborhood," he thinks (255). His reflections on beginning to run down Drexel Boulevard make the lam the natural endpoint of his existence in a racially divided Chicago: "It was all over. He had to save himself. But it was familiar, this running away. All his life he had been knowing that sooner or later something like this could come to him. And now, here it was. He had always felt outside of this white world, and now it was true. It made things simple" (255). "Simple"—as if running from the police simply made express an implied relation between himself and whites, and *whiteness*, that which had been the principal force in the formation of Bigger as subject.

Bigger flees into the Black Belt under "a gauzelike curtain of snow" (255), for the white blizzard has blocked routes out of the city. This blizzard becomes a literal and symbolic cordon pinning Bigger in Chicago; as all roads are blocked, Bigger finds himself in a world of white. The newspapers track the progress of the manhunt as it closes down upon Bigger's South Side neighborhood:

> He looked at the paper and saw a black-and-white map of the South Side, around the borders of which was a shaded portion an inch deep. Under the map ran a line of small print:
>
> > Shaded portion shows area already covered by police and vigilantes in search for Negro rapist and murderer. White portion shows area yet to be searched.
>
> He was trapped. He would have to get out of this building. But where could he go? Empty buildings would serve only as long as he stayed within the white portion of the map, and the white portion was shrinking rapidly. (284)

A fictitious *Chicago Tribune* story interprets Bigger's crime as a justification for continued and more extensive segregation policies. "Crime such as the Bigger Thomas murders could be lessened by segregating all Negroes in parks, playgrounds, cafés, theatres, and street cars. Residential segregation is imperative. Such measures tend to keep them as much as possible out of direct contact with white women and lessen their attacks against them" (324).

The "Flight" chapter ends with Bigger's apprehension amid sirens and searchlights—the harbingers of the arrival of the police. Notably, he is not taken by the organizational policeman, modeled on the federal agent, who had already become the bane of white fugitives. Wright has Bigger trapped by the barely disguised lynch mob, men with faces like "white pasteboard," atop a snowy roof as the crowd in the street makes a noise like "a flood of strange joy" (305, 309). The presence of police, we are left to assume, prevents the lynching. But the job of the police, of course, is to lock him in a jail cell—the institutional end point of the spatial control of the black man.

I will repeat a phrase: "White people were not really people," thought Bigger, "they were a sort of great natural force, like a stormy sky looming overhead, or like a deep swirling river stretching suddenly at one's feet in the dark" (129). In the blizzard of *Native Son*, Wright pairs white people with the "stormy sky looming overhead." In his 1944 novella "The Man Who Lived Underground," Wright conjures the dangerous river, which runs through the sewer into which Fred Daniels flees and into which he disappears at the story's end. "The Man Who Lived Underground," though it is also a text about defeat, finds Wright's protagonist pioneering a black fugitive space that is much less defeatist than that of *Native Son*—as if the exhausted possibilities of Bigger's landscape had begun to exhaust and defeat Wright. The space Fred Daniels finds has personal as well as political power.

The landscape of "Underground" shares with *Native Son* the hallmarks of a surveillance state: like Bigger, Daniels flees from sirens and sees himself execrated in the newspaper headlines. Whereas Bigger's pursuers seem to include the whole of white Chicago society, Daniels's nemesis is more localized. Policemen have beaten and interrogated him as a murder suspect. Though these three policemen—with their Anglo-Irish surnames Lawson, Murphy, and Johnson—represent the only real investigative agents within the story, Daniels's reactions betray a systemic paranoia that overspills his relationship to the police. " 'I've got to hide,' he told himself," is the first line of the story. "They're looking for me all over," he adds (518). Even after the manhunt fades away and he is exploring the dark subterranean layers of the city, Daniels tends to metaphorize challenges as if he were a panoptic subject: "It seemed that he was playing a game with an unseen person whose intelligence outstripped his" (527).

Daniels enters the sewer with the assumption that the possibilities for escape above ground have been exhausted or are hopeless—"Yes, he had to hide, but where?" he frets (518). The sewer presents its own hazards—currents, down curves, explosive gases, diseases. At first, he wants to leave, but "an irrational impulse held him rooted" (520). The irrationality of remaining below ground builds as he (like Bigger) kills a huge rat and encounters a dead baby. Yet Daniels, "confoundingly alone," is "lured by the darkness and silence . . . curious, afraid" (521).

Yet in this dismal setting, Wright explores the possibilities of subterranean flight. Many of Bigger Thomas's failed moves toward self-definition (religion, writing, violence, crime) reappear as opportunities that Fred Daniels, in his underground experience, has the free time and space to contemplate. The difference seems to be in Daniels's perspective. Even as Bigger believes that his bedroom affords him a privileged opportunity to occupy the position of *watcher* rather than *watched*— he listens in undetected on the affairs of the Dalton household—he never achieves the blurred, diffuse, *lost* quality of the panoptic eye. In the Dalton home, Bigger's place is always charted, and at the crucial moment where he needs to escape detection, he himself does the work of registering his presence, of establishing "an anchor": by smothering Mary in her bedroom as her mother approaches.

Daniels, on the other hand, finds a forgotten place. According to Michel Fabre, Wright conceived the story after reading a *True Detective* account of a string of commercial robberies that puzzled Los Angeles detectives from 1931 to 1933, when a policeman caught a robber who'd made a life in city basements (93–94). Because Daniels's pursuers (we learn later) are called off by the arrest of another suspect, his tenure there is uninterrupted. Yet Daniels, not knowing this, stays vigilant against capture. The spatial innovation of living underground—of making *new* space of a no-space—seems to alleviate his paranoid position as black subject of a racial panopticism.

Indeed, Daniels is able, at least for while, to approximate the subject position of the accusatory gaze. He soon adapts to the lost, uncharted subterranean spaces, becoming, like the dead baby he encounters during his first moments underground, a lost object himself—"freed from his past," suggests Fabre (100). As Daniels digs passages that allow him to enter the basements of buildings and to steal what he needs for survival, the sense of irrationality shifts. When an opportunity to reenter the street at twilight provokes his longing, "sober judgment urged him to remain" underground (536–37). Shortly before he returns to the surface, he fights "an irrational compulsion to act" (552).

The cinema scene suggests a moment in which Daniels releases himself from the uneasy position he has occupied above ground. Passing a glowing red exit sign, Daniels encounters an otherworldly sight, "a black curtain that fluttered uncertainly. He parted the folds and looked into a convex depth that gleamed with clusters of shimmering lights. Sprawling below him was a stretch of human faces, tilted upwards, chanting, whistling, screaming, laughing" (527). Realizing that the moviegoers, "shouting and yelling at the animated shadows of themselves," are only simulating a subject position by which they are the viewers, not the viewed, he attempts "to touch them" but realizes that he cannot. "These people were children, sleeping in their living," he mourns. But the encounter that follows suggests the profound change in Daniels. As he leaves the "reserved section," where he clearly does not belong, he meets a sort of policeman, a man whose job is policing space: a theater guard, "a white man in trim blue uniform." "So used had he become to being underground," writes Wright, "that he thought that he could walk past the man, as though he were a ghost. But the man stopped. And he stopped" (528). For once, Daniels does not flinch in the face of surveillance—in this case, his actual discovery out of *place*. Daniels accepts directions to the washroom from the guard, and then he stands and watches "the man turn and walk up the steps and go out of sight. Then he laughed. What a funny fellow!" (528).

Additional episodes show Daniels adjusting to the watcher position that has been made possible by his flight to the underground. Like *Native Son*'s Buckley, Daniels becomes able to watch a furtive theft with a condemnatory eye, even though he plans the same theft himself: "The hands trembled; again the right hand slipped a packet of bills up the left sleeve. He's stealing, he said to himself. He grew indignant, as if the money belonged to him. Though *he* had planned to steal the money, he despised and pitied the man. He felt that his stealing the money and the man's stealing were two entirely alien things" (541). Later, when his subterranean access allows him to pilfer from the safe, he has a hidden viewpoint on the watchman's interrogation by two policemen and the watchman's subsequent suicide (556–58). He listens to a boy being beaten for another theft he has committed (555). He watches business transactions and worship services. He manages a somewhat Dadaist subversion of aboveground values, using hundred-dollar bills as wallpaper and kicking diamonds across his floor.

Critics have discussed Daniels's eventual reemergence from underground and return to the police station—where at once he declares himself "guilty" and pleads to show off the underground to the officers who have beaten him earlier—as a messianic gesture. Edward Margolies sees Daniels realizing "that the nether world in which he dwells is the real world of the human heart—and that the surface world which hums above him in the streets of the city is senseless and meaningless—a kind of unreality which men project to hide from themselves the awful blackness of their souls." Thus he ascends to the street to proclaim that he, like all men, is guilty "by virtue of his being human" (88). Yet Margolies's metaphysical reading lets slip the social dynamics that enable a figure like Buckley to profit by graft while still occupying the position of accuser, of prosecutor. It neglects the possibility that soulful "awful blackness" is neither universal nor inherent. It is, I am arguing, cultivated and trained.

Daniels's subterranean kingdom collapses after he is shocked by the sight of the watchman killing himself. Although he had earlier mused that "he could send a bullet into that man's brain and time would be over for him" (546), when the watchman raises the gun to his head, Daniels yells, "Don't!" (558). It is his first willful communication to others since he has gone underground, and it startles the watchman, who fires anyway. The suicide neatly wraps up the burglary, Daniels's most felonious underground act: "Our hunch was right," says the first policeman, "He was guilty, all right." "Well, this ends the case," replies another (558).

But Daniels, who has stolen the money that leads to the watchman's interrogation, cannot bring himself to the coolly disaffected criminality of a Buckley. Shocked into reflection—"he stood for what seemed to him a thousand years"—he returns to fugitive black guilt in the scenes that follow. The language in the paragraph that follows the shooting stresses Daniels's agency in bringing about the watchman's death—he "crawled back through the holes he had made." "A fever burned in his bones," Wright writes. "He had to act, yet he was afraid. His eyes stared in the darkness as though propped open by invisible hands" (558). "Invisible hands": again, the source of the black man's terror is inchoate, internalized, pervasive.

The remainder of the story represents Daniels's return to the specular end of the interrogatory gaze. His first move is to attempt to offer up the knowledge he has gained as fugitive—of himself, of others, of the unmapped underground—to others: the watchers, the police. Wright renders Daniels, during his return to the surface, as a docile body: childishly uncertain and submissive yet disciplined and efficient—"When he moved again his actions were informed with precision" (559). He offers first at a church but cannot find the words or the listeners in order to conduct his transaction. The churchgoers evict him for his dirtiness and incoherence, but his inability to take the role of confessor agonizes him; he panics, and the scene grows strange to him: "a deluge of song swept over him" (560). "He felt that he was falling and he grew frantic" (561). A last exchange at the church door jolts Daniels back to a disciplinary "reality":

> "But, Mister, let me tell. . . ."
> "Get away from this door, or I'll call the police!"
> He stared, his trembling smile fading in a sense of wonderment.
> "The police," he repeated vacantly. (562)

"Smiling again now," Daniels goes to a police station and asks for the policemen who have arrested him before, in order to announce that he is "guilty" (565). Reduced again to the status of disciplinary subject, Daniels offers his fugitive knowledge up to the policemen: "He grew frantic to make them believe, his voice tumbled on eagerly. 'I saw a dead baby and a dead man' " (568). For Daniels, the blue-uniformed policemen return him swiftly to a reality that, if disadvantageous, seems at least familiar and real: "how simple it was," he marvels when he "remembered the names of all of them: Lawson, Murphy, and Johnson" (566).

The policemen's cruel response comprises Wright's gloomy comment on the inadmissibility of the outsider's knowledge in the American 1940s. It is telling that Wright himself became a fugitive of sorts: he traveled to France two years after the story was published in Edwin Seaver's anthology *Cross Section*, establishing residency there in 1947 and writing *The Outsider* and other books in Paris. For both Bigger Thomas and Fred Daniels, as fugitives, achieve a knowledge of themselves and of their racial position that has emancipatory potential, yet neither finds opportunities or listeners for the dispersal of that knowledge. The policemen of "The Man Who Lived Underground" begrudgingly acknowledge the possibility of the fugitive's knowledge, after calling him "nuts," drunk, a "fool," "crazy." But they privilege the aboveground world over the possibilities of the subterranean and, furthermore, move to strike the fugitive knowledge of the underground, burning first Daniels's "confession"—the one document that ties him to specific legal processes—and then shooting him before they slam the manhole cover down on his world. "You've got to shoot his kind. They'd wreck things," Officer Lawson says grimly as Daniels falls into the raging sewer (576). At the close of the story, the policeman acknowledges the enormous potential of the black fugitive's self-exemption from white surveillance and takes a stand against it.

Fred Daniels's communicative disenfranchisement before the policemen resembles Bigger Thomas's inability to speak other than "listlessly" in the presence of his interrogators, which Laura E. Tanner reads as evidence of a "master language," involving even the novel's narrator, to which Bigger is not entitled (140–41). Valerie Smith counters by arguing that for Bigger, coming to terms with and relating his own story affords him new authority over his life (439–46). In Ralph Ellison's rejoinders to the fugitive confines mapped by Wright, narration itself at first bears the mark of policing but becomes a laboratory for the remapping of the specular subject's world.

Ellison's novel followed *Native Son* by 12 years, but the interim was a transformative period for African-Americans, principally because of World War II. The war involved African-Americans militarily, building a corps of black veterans and demonstrating their patriotism even despite the discrimination they faced during and after their service. It engulfed them domestically as well, where their involvement in war production triggered renewed migration from the South into industrial cities and solidified and broadened a nascent black middle class. The entry into the war "marked the beginning of the end of Negro ethnic group insularity; an entirely new phase of American Negro life was underway," writes Harold Cruse. "Until 1940, the word 'integration' had not appeared, even in the language of the NAACP; the war inspired the first articles in *Crisis*, NAACP's official publication, demanding the "integration of the armed forces" (208–9). The Office of War Information attempted through its Bureau of Motion Pictures to instill a "protofeminist outlook, progressive racial views, and pro-labor sentiments" into popular wartime entertainments, though Clayton R. Koppes notes that only "occasional gestures" resulted (25–32). And Jackie Robinson's breaking of the Major League Baseball color barrier in 1947 provided valuable symbolic confirmation of integration and damning evidence of continuing segregationist sentiment.

The twelve-year interim proposed an intellectual divide as well; the 1940s, says Bill Mullen, were "an apocalyptic turning point in the formation of a radical black politics" (5). In 1941, a year of embarrassments, the American Communist Party, as Wilson Record puts it, "had gotten itself out on a limb, isolated from the main trunk of American liberalism" by opposing American involvement in the war (208). Hitler's June 22, 1941, violation of his nonaggression pact with Stalin mortified American communists, among them Richard Wright, who had spoken out in support of the "This is not the Negro's war" party line. The economic boom of the war and the disenchantment of radicals like Wright weakened the communist influence in black intellectual life, and no postwar black radical philosophy successfully challenged or countered the party's "militant dogmatism" (Cruse 225). Thus Ellison addressed the lam from a substantially different position vis-à-vis black radical politics and the nation's racial geography.

The epigraphs to this chapter arrived at different times and in different ways. Ellison's consideration of "running and dodging the forces of history" occurred to me as a central passage from the earliest stages of this project, rife with suggestion as to the meanings and potentialities of fugitiveness. I noticed only very much later the earlier linking of those two verbs, *to run* and *to dodge*, in the Wright pieces. Very neatly, however, these three passages bespeak their respective texts' treatment of fugitive strategies. "This was the end," Wright writes in *Native Son*, "There were no more roofs over which to run and dodge" (308). To call the last rooftop "the end," however, while prophetically accurate, is geographically absurd: Bigger has reached nothing more significant than the end of the block, the point at which his rooftop flight runs up against the stop-or-jump dilemma (as in *Thelma and Louise* or *The Fugitive*). Bigger cannot see beyond this block, however, beyond the limits of the "Black Belt"; his mental labyrinth controls the novel's vision of the city of Chicago.

Fred Daniels, who decides to "stay and plot how to elude" the police, operates in a cultural geography no less prejudiced than Bigger Thomas's. Daniels's brief reprieve from the cross-racial interrogatory gaze comes when he *finds a place* where he is unmistakably unseen, unmonitored, unchased. "The mere thought of dodging and running *again* from the police made him tense," he decides (523); clearly his anticipation of tension already acknowledges a cessation of running. *The Outsider* (1953) shows Wright contemplating escaping the gaze by remaining hidden in plain view: Cross Damon seizes the opportunity to change opportunities and try a new life. Like Daniels, Damon eventually is defeated in his quest to remake his individual relation to the world through flight. The repetition of plots influenced by racial and economic oppression, suggests Valerie Smith, "bespeaks a world devoid of options, where one's words and actions are closely scrutinized, and where one feels that the future has been scripted by some 'other' " (434).

Ellison does Wright's "running and dodging" in different voices. In broadening the pursuit from police and policers to "the forces of history," Ellison's narrator proposes a much more explicit realization of how the police have long been augmented—and, especially for African-Americans, far exceeded—by a policing function and practice rooted in social relations and history. Ellison himself bespoke the fecundity of African-American history, its imbrication by other stories, literary and oral: "We tell ourselves our individual stories so as to become aware of our *general* story. I wouldn't have had to read a single slave narrative in order to create the narrative pattern of *Invisible Man.* It emerges from experience and from my own sense of literary form, out of my sense of experience as shaped by history and my familiarity with literature" (Davis and Gates xix).

Bernard W. Bell, in his *The Afro-American Novel and Its Tradition,* credits Ellison (along with James Baldwin) with rediscovering the folkloric heritage of myth, legend, and ritual that reanimates African-American fiction after the naturalist aesthetic of Richard Wright (192). Incorporating the *"general* story," then, gave Ellison's nimble narrator access to historical *figures* for the problems of the individual. Hence the novel offers Brer Rabbit, Jack-the-Bear, Marcus Garvey, Booker T. Washington, Uncle Tom, and the lexicon of such characters as Peetie Wheatstraw and Mary Rambo.

Where Wright defines a cultural box and explores his characters' failed attempts to find its outside or to remain there, *Invisible Man*'s landscape is, as Ellison suggested on more than one occasion, influenced by the Oklahoma City of his boyhood, where he strove to become a "Renaissance man." In the introduction to *Shadow and Act*, he characterizes the city thus:

Ours was a chaotic community, still characterized by frontier attitudes and by that strange mixture of the naive and sophisticated, the benign and malignant, which makes the American past so puzzling and its present so confusing; that mixture which often affords the minds of the young who grow up in the far provinces such wide and unstructured latitude, and which encourages the individual's imagination—up to the moment "reality" closes in on him—to range widely and sometimes even to soar. (*Collected Essays* 51)

The ambiguous relation between intellectual "latitude"—tellingly, Ellison's metaphors for freedom describe space, movement—and the grimly containing "reality" is the central conflict of the novel, of course, as the narrator's aspirations toward personal growth and autonomy are consistently blocked by social and institutional limits. Ellison's narrator has a strong dose of the Oklahoman in him: he aspires to growth and mobility, repressing the extent to which, for black Americans, these wishes are already overwritten by a tradition of *running* and *dodging*. The motions of flight function more subtly and pervasively in the complex, duplicitous landscape of Ellison's novel: indeed, the grandfather's dream admonition to "Keep This Nigger-Boy Running" is the slow-arriving punch line to each of the narrator's endeavors. In *Invisible Man*, the tradition of fugitiveness functions as an inescapable undercurrent to the African-American everyday.

First of all, if *Invisible Man* is not by Hooverian standards a fugitive tale, it is full of images of the fugitive in what is, in this study, the classic sense—individuals running from the police. The particular running that is *fugitive* is a seminal image for the narrator: as he awakes in the hospital after the Liberty Paints explosion, he thinks,

> You know, doc, the same fall day I first saw the hounds chasing black men in stripes and chains my grandmother sat with me and sang with twinkling eyes:
> "Godamighty made a monkey
> Godamighty made a whale
> And Godamighty made a 'gator
> With hickeys all over his tail . . ." (234)

These black men are fugitives from the law: stripes and chains indicate prison clothing rather than the looser, plainer clothing supplied to slaves. In absorbing this image while on his grandmother's lap—and, furthermore, by juxtaposing it with a folk-Genesis rhyme—Invisible Man casts the black fugitive as an antediluvian figure. His relation to that figure is not shadowed by dread; the mild image of "hounds chasing" fades quickly under the grandmother's "twinkling eyes." Thus the fugitive is made a commonplace, a tradition. The two details seem to work contrapuntally, establishing obverse images of a black American's place (one's family: comfort; elsewhere: flight).

In a dream at the close of chapter 1, the grandfather leads the narrator to the gilt-lettered document which reads, "To Whom It May Concern: Keep This Nigger-Boy Running" (33). Throughout much of the novel, the idealistic narrator represses the degree to which this running fills his life as a motif and a condition. Possessed of a sense of personal and spatial freedom, Invisible Man looks at the promises of education, the Great Migration, the industrial workplace and the Brotherhood as open doors, their highest rewards attainable. A corollary symptom of the narrator's idealism is his resistance or repression of the African-American traditions of flight and fugitiveness, criminal or otherwise, even insofar as they are commonplaces within the novelistic communities he inhabits. Wright's black box functions in *Invisible Man*, but the narrator refuses to confront the transactions of surveillance and discipline until late in the book.

Invisible Man's relationship with Brother Tarp illustrates his repression of flight, of the historical problematization of black movement. In Brother Tarp, Invisible Man (IM) meets a living specimen of the Southern black fugitive; after nearly twenty years on the chain gang, Tarp broke step and fled to the North. Although the narrator here acknowledges that the fugitive is not an aberrant figure in black life—"I couldn't see it in his face or hear it in his speech, yet I knew he was neither lying nor trying to shock me," he admits (387)—he again represses the potential horror of flight (and the possibility that it, on some level, speaks for him) by using the shield of family. A momentary delusion leads the narrator to misrecognize Tarp as his own grandfather (384). In the afterglow of this comfortable moment, IM intimates his doubts about his place in the Brotherhood (384–85) and accepts Tarp's filed shackle link like a son accepting from his father a grandfather's watch, "not because he wanted the old-fashioned timepiece for itself, but because of the overtones of unstated seriousness and solemnity of the paternal gesture which at once joined him with his ancestors, marked a high point of his present, and promised a concreteness to his nebulous and chaotic future" (389–90).

Perhaps lulled again by the soft tones of Tarp's story—"I made friends with them dogs and I waited" (388)—the narrator concludes that it is the "seriousness and solemnity" of the presentation that "join[s] him with his ancestors." Yet the ancestral aspect of the encounter is already overlaid by its hallucinatory nature. This insistence upon a familial relation downplays the subversive elements in his grandfather's deathbed speech. IM's failure to recognize the irony in his grandfather's speech and dream gift reappear in his unquestioning acceptance of Brother Tarp's filed shackle link, despite its insinuation of his *own* passive acceptance of the Brotherhood's racist and chain-gang-like discipline.

The bus ride after the Golden Day debacle provides another example of the narrator's avoidance of the fugitive tradition, even as he goes north in "disgrace." Wincing to see the veteran and Crenshaw at the back of the otherwise empty bus, Invisible Man thinks, "I wanted to remember nothing connected with Trueblood or the Golden Day" (151). His desire not to be seen at this moment recalls the fugitive slaves' fear of being spotted, but the vet soon alleviates IM's dread. His speech proclaiming the end of the era of fugitive slaves lifts the specter of flight from the narrator's journey, blessing it instead with the promises of the Great Migration. "Think of what this means for the young fellow," the vet proclaims. "He's going free, in the broad daylight and alone. I can remember when young fellows like him had first to commit a crime, or be accused of one, before they tried such a thing. Instead of leaving in the light of morning, they went in the dark of night. And no bus was fast enough—isn't that so, Crenshaw?" (154–55).

Like the narrator, Crenshaw stages an outsized resistance to the vet's insinuation of history—the tradition of slave movement—into the characters' travel north. "I ain't had that experience," he says, "I went North of my own free will." "There's always an element of crime in freedom," the veteran insists, reiterating the inescapability of the black traveler's fugitive past (155). Again, the narrator misses the hint: with "a sigh of relief" (156), he accepts the more idealistic version of things, and he plans to be polite, polished, and sanitized upon inspection by New York's "big men" without any hint of the irony his grandfather located in deference to whites (157).

As the veteran has promised, Invisible Man arrives in a Northern landscape that has been transformed by the Great Migration; he fits in without an echo of the northbound-fugitive stigma he so fears. (Still, various people recognize him as a Southerner: Peetie Wheatstraw (172–77), the yam seller (262–66), and the lady who upbraids him for using her trash can (327–29). IM grows furious, however, when a white counterman recognizes him as a breakfast-time "pork chop man," with its Southern overtones.) Above the Mason-Dixon line, fugitives abound, as do police and their surrogates. The candy bar thieves running along the platform after Tod Clifton's shooting are trailed by "a man right behind" (443). Clifton himself sweeps up his dolls and hurries down the street, taking Sambo "on the lambo" when a policeman approaches (433). Similarly, the warning "Here come some more cops!" impels the narrator to flee the scene of his own impassioned interference with the eviction (284). At this Wrightian moment, when the sight of a "man hurrying after" moves IM from "swift caution" to "puffing, bustling effort," the narrator's careful mask of indifference to fugitive politics slips: he wonders "why he didn't yell 'Halt!' or shout, or shoot" (285), "Why had he been so silent, and why was there only one? Yes, and why hadn't they sent a patrol car to pick me up?" (287). The obverse sides of black place appear again: "If only it were like at home where I knew someone in *all* the houses, knew them by sight and name, by blood and by background, by shame and pride, and by religion," he mourns (285–86).

Although Invisible Man abjures the position of fugitive, while he is placed in this mode of fear, of flight—never having imagined that his open-air speech would incite a riot—he moves like one of Wright's characters, hyperconscious of his surroundings and affecting a non-chalance "copied from characters I had seen in the movies" (286). These avoidance tactics come to him as if from instinct, from repressed memory. It seems as if Ellison, too, when it comes to depicting *running* and *dodging*, draws upon Wright's imagery, as IM arouses "a flight of frantic white birds, suddenly as large as buzzards." IM longed "to look stupid, utterly incapable of thought and speech, and tried to shuffle my feet over the walk," assuming the exaggerated deference Bigger Thomas uses as a hedge against interrogation (286).

What the narrator's misadventures teach him (or *should*) is the inescapability of prejudicial organizational schemes dictating his *place* in the world. That place is always, to echo Baker again, "maximally secured," even in the sleazy bacchanalia of the battle royal, even in the politically subversive Brotherhood, even in the ostensibly nurturing environment of the college. IM's remembrance of the college, framed by narration that calls attention to the memory as a reconstruction, details his efforts to slip away from campus into the undeveloped land surrounding. Even this reverie is undergirded by a struggle over matters of control, of discipline and security. His idle walk away from the college campus offers "the forbidden road" and the illicit pleasures of the "gay student nurses," but even at this relatively innocent age, the character cannot miss perceiving "the black powerhouse with its engines droning earth-shaking rhythms," "the insane asylum," and "the ants moving nervously in single file" (34–35). The reverie soon dissolves into a Sunday-morning review, where the young students, "drilled four-abreast," "our uniforms pressed, shoes shined, minds laced up," present themselves, "eyes blind like those of robots to visitors and officials on the low, whitewashed reviewing stand" (36).

The students present a stark contrast to the self-assured rabbits playing "in the hedges and along the road," "so tame through never having been hunted" (35). This last detail betrays the degree to which the narrator already represses the disciplinary aspects of social structure; these "natural" animals are not rendered as "wild" or "free" but, strangely, "tame," made docile, integrated (at their risk) into the human social landscape. Here "tame" comprises the narrator's romantic assessment of a species of whom he can be the surveyor, interrogator, hunter. For a moment, we glimpse the narrator at an ambiguous point in a concentrically arranged set of disciplinary relations, a panoptic middle. It is as if, subconsciously, he must assert his vision, the visibility of someone else, no matter where on the food chain.

Elsewhere, however, the narrator is excruciatingly conscious of questions of his own visibility, his own appearance. On the bus, heading north, he plans his appearance and behavior in great detail (157). Upon arriving on Wall Street, he is startled to see black couriers and looks around for "policemen or detectives with drawn guns following," but he quickly buries the thought: "Of course no one would be that foolish" (165). In this setting, however, IM cannot entirely avoid a paranoia that is simultaneously diffused and official, much like many slaves' fear of the open or Bigger's fear of appearing on Drexel Boulevard: "This was Wall Street. Perhaps it was guarded, as I had been told post offices were guarded, by men who looked down at you through peep-holes in the ceiling and walls, watching you constantly, silently waiting for a wrong move. Perhaps even now an eye had picked me up and watched my every movement. Maybe the face of that clock set in the gray building across the street hid a pair of searching eyes" (165).

Here IM voices the implicit contiguity of official surveillance (the police) and diffused surveillance (social policing) for himself and other black travelers. The watchers are governmental (post offices) and faceless (men, "a pair of searching eyes"). They *look down* upon you. And although their vigilance awaits "a wrong move"—suggestive of lawbreaking or some clear-cut deviant act—IM also has the sense that the eyes are focused not upon the multiracial crowd but specifically upon him. In the next sentence, even the architecture seems to wear a badge: "I hurried to my address and was challenged by the sheer height of the white stone" (165). Little wonder, then, that the appearance of actual police—for example, in chapter 16, just before IM's first speech before the gathered Brotherhood—provokes violent imagery and the sense that the narrator is being followed. "One of the horses violently tossed its head and I saw the gauntleted fist yanked down," he remem-bers; "the stomping of hooves followed me to the door. Perhaps this was something for Brother Jack to know" (337).

Because of his idealism and optimism, running and dodging becomes a matter for study before it becomes praxis for the narrator. The passage describing the zoot-suiters "running and dodging the forces of history" suggests the progress of IM's thought on the matter. It revolves slowly. When Clifton is first intrigued by Ras the Exhorter's words and murmurs, "I suppose sometimes a man *has* to plunge out-side history," IM "didn't answer" (377); his disillusionment has not yet led him to perceive "history's" role in his own frustrations. A page later, he admits to Brother Tarp that he knows "not much" about Frederick Douglass; he contemplates the portrait of the fugitive orator and author with a misguided "sudden piety, remembering and refusing to hear the echoes of my grandfather's voice" (378–79).

Clifton's disappearance and death moves the narrator from his ignorance and repression of fugitive history and strategies to active study of them. Returning to the Harlem office, he notices that Tarp's "gift of Douglass' portrait was gone" (428). His organizational efforts to find Tarp and Clifton bear no fruit; only after he is shut out of the Brotherhood's strategy meeting and he leaves "in a rage," shopping for shoes while thinking "when they do decide to call me they'll have to find me," does he find Clifton (429). That fit of anger finds the narrator idly toying with the notion of disappearing, of being unaccounted for; his shoes remind him of childhood *running* races: "that light-footed, speedy, floating sensation" (430). He plays at fugitiveness without understanding it.

The Sambo-doll episode, however, jolts IM; it makes it utterly clear how little he understands about Clifton's "outside of history." Moments after he snaps back to attention, reminding himself to "get back to the district in case you're called," the Sambo-doll episode begins, chaotic and, for IM, frequently inscrutable. First an Italian vendor "looked at [IM] knowingly," marking him as the known quantity, the black man controlled by social and spatial organization. Then he hears Clifton's voice, spieling "words whose meanings I couldn't catch" (430). (Notably, a policeman approaches here, exerting pressure on the entire affair.) The strangeness of the street scene continues: Invisible Man is "puzzled"; he cannot seem to recognize or name the doll (431); he feels the call of his proper place, "the district," yet he is held captive, it seems—captive in absence, without leave—by the inanimate, boneless bouncing" (a somewhat paradoxical, if not impossible, description) "of the grinning doll" (432).

Clifton's spiel counterposes the doll to the systemic organization of IM's life, particularly in terms of disciplinary adherence to space, to place. Twice Clifton stresses Sambo's defiance of public law: "There's no license for little Sambo, the joy spreader. You can't tax joy" (433). But instead of a carnivalesque resistance, an unfettered public joyousness, the doll Sambo introduces an appeal that is furtive and yet still charismatic. "Who else wants little Sambo before we take it on the lambo?" asks Clifton, incorporating the doll's flouting of public regulation—licensing, tax—into his sales pitch but acknowledging simultaneously the incursions of that regulation. Clifton makes the criminal heroic, in other words, without obliterating the triumph of the police. The "lambo" becomes a means of surviving without triumph, a means of skirting the edges of the gaze of surveillance. Making that evasion a part of his spiel—"Follow little Sambo around the corner, ladies and gentlemen" (434)—suggests the possibilities of such fluidity, such defiance of the notion of an *individual's* fixed space even as systemic spatial regulation is affirmed. Clifton does not live long enough to live out this possibility or to testify to it (in, we can imagine, an interrogation conducted not by white policemen but by the novel's narrator). Cutting against the grain of the condition of African-American PLACE-lessness by renouncing the ambition to a fixable place, Clifton reshapes his world individually, at the cost of his belonging to the Brotherhood or his sharing the conditions of the black community.

It becomes IM's mission over the remainder of the novel to study this individual notion of PLACE—neither placement nor displacement, but a sort of *unplacement*, the abjuration of fixed address. Recoiling from the shooting, he seeks solace in the subway, "seeing nothing, my mind plunging." At first, he questions Clifton's thesis only in naive terms, each question pointing him back toward organizational structures within which he has begun to recognize his own disadvantage: "history," "the only organization offering him a chance to 'define' himself" (438). His musings upon history provoke a series of important revelations, however. First comes the narrator's abandonment of a panoptic view of history—"All things, it is said, are duly recorded"—for a more skeptical view in which "only those events that the recorder regards as important that are put down, those lies his keepers keep their power by" (439).

This self-emendation moves IM into an unprecedented critical relation to power and history. In the pages that conclude the novel's

Chapter 20, the narrator discusses place and placelessness as a representational concern. He wonders,

> What did they ever think of us transitory ones? Ones such as I had been before I found Brotherhood—birds of passage who were too obscure for learned classification, too silent for the most sensitive recorders of sound; of natures too ambiguous for the most ambiguous words, and too distant from the centers of historical decision to sign or even to applaud the signers of historical documents? We who write no novels, histories or other books. What about us, I thought. (439)

Invisible Man's queries are themselves ambiguous, naive in a sense and subversive, "dangerous." Addressed to "the historians today," they plead plaintively for a democratization of history, one we might locate today in the rising status of folk or oral history or the privileging of multicultural perspectives. For his referent, "we," one might take African-Americans, or more plausibly, the voiceless poor. However, the language of the paragraph suggests neither, for certainly blacks had written books and the poor had been extensively classified then, as have they now. IM's references to the representational strategies brought to bear upon these "transitory ones"—"learned classification," "sensitive recorders of sound," "ambiguous words," "historical documents"— suggest not simply history making but surveillance, cataloging, the inventorying and arranging work upon which the disciplinary policing depends. The "we" to whom he refers is those too obscure, silent, ambiguous, and distant for these sensitive and powerful mechanisms— "transitory" (439), "transitional" (441), "men out of time" (441).

The subway passage marks a movement on IM's part from fearing others perceiving him to analyzing practices of perception. The subway scene that opens his stay in New York articulates the shift: on that earlier ride, he is "crushed" against a white woman, feeling "the rubbery softness of her flesh against the length of [his] body." Quite sensibly— for a Southern black male of the era—"expecting her to scream," he tries to signal his helplessness, but, to his surprise, when he takes "a furtive glance around no one was paying [him] the slightest attention" (158). Even so, he privileges the interrogatory gaze of others against his own answering glance, choosing to walk the rest of the way and recovering from the experience by "staring at [his] own reflection in the glass" of a shop window, as if retraining himself to look investigatively at no one else and simultaneously to be looked at (158).

Chapter 20's subway scene locates Invisible Man in a strangely ambivalent space, on one hand near the people he calls "we" but simultaneously taking the position of the police, classifying, recording, documenting, wondering, "What about those fellows waiting still and silent there on the platform, so still and silent that they clash with the crowd in their very immobility; standing noisy in their very silence; harsh as a cry of terror in their quietness?" (440)

Meditating (at last) on the possibilities of hiding in plain sight, making purloined letters out of each of the subjects before him, Invisible Man both applauds and forecloses the possibilities of such "silence," of living unseen within the city's gaze. His own intense description augments that gaze, makes a study of those to whom he attributes a fierce desire for silence:

What about those three boys, coming now along the platform, tall and slender, walking stiffly with swinging shoulders in their well-pressed, too-hot-for-summer suits, their collars high and tight about their necks, their identical hats of black cheap felt set upon the crowns of their heads with a severe formality above their hard conked hair? It was as though I'd never seen their like before: Walking slowly, their shoulders swaying, their legs swinging from their hips in trousers that ballooned upward from cuffs fitting snug about their ankles; their coats long and hip-tight with shoulders far too broad to be those of natural western men. (440)

Remarking that they seem distorted "in the interest of a design," the narrator remarks, "Well, what design and whose?" In mystifying the fashion and physical details that bind these three boys together, he imputes a collectivity to this underworld that later he will reject in his own. Getting up to tail them through the crowd, he speculates upon their meaning: "They were men out of time—unless they found Brotherhood" (441). But then he is overtaken by the converse of his own reading, and, in a Yeatsian moment, he trembles as he conceives their inscrutability as messianic potential: "What if history was not a reasonable citizen, but a madman full of paranoid guile and these boys his agents, his big surprise! His own revenge? For they were outside, in the dark with Sambo, the dancing paper doll; taking it on the lambo with my fallen brother, Tod Clifton (Tod, Tod) running and dodging the forces of history instead of making a dominating stand" (441).

The notion of an "outside" here is, of course, limited by its own romanticism, inflected with the narrator's grief over the loss of his beloved friend and his hysteria over the Brotherhood's failure to retain and transform Tod. "They were outside the groove of history," he notes, and then adds responsibly, "it was my job to get them in, all of them" (443). In so saying, the narrator speaks ominously of his own power as a partly blinded subject of power: he *does* have the power to adapt "history," to broaden it, to notice and conscribe these hitherto unnoticed individuals. He is using the power as he follows them. "What was I in relation to the boys," he wonders; "Perhaps an accident, like Douglass" (442). Perhaps so, in terms of oratory and fame; the analogy, fully considered, ought to crystallize to the narrator how fully *flight* has been a component of his experiences so far. It does not.

Grieving, the narrator aestheticizes the boys' gestures as inscrutable communications. The boys make "a rhythmical tapping" with their shoes (440); they communicate "ironically with their eyes" (442); as they glimpse *their* reflections in the subway car's window, they betray none of the narrator's earlier self-conscious panic but snap their brims unaccountably (442). As they leave the train, again their "heavy heel plates" click out "remote, cryptic messages in the brief silence of the train's stop" (443). On one level this reads as a displacement of the narrator's erotic fascination with Tod Clifton, handsomer and blacker than himself. On another, though, it bespeaks a desire or fantasy: namely, that the characters exemplify a black recourse to an unpoliced, unpoliceable language. The narrator has experienced the policing of his own speech in the battle royal chapter and on multiple occasions among the Brotherhood.

To complement its fugitive beginning—Tod's "plunge from history," his flight from the unofficial policing of the Brotherhood and the official police who ultimately kill him—and its passing invocation of Frederick Douglass (442), the subway scene ends with a third image of criminal flight, the young candy-bar thieves fleeing the Five and Ten. Invisible Man's reaction to this sight betrays his nascent appreciation of the potential of the fugitive to destabilize the cultural and spatial binds in which black men find themselves: he "killed an impulse," he says, to trip the pursuer. "Forgotten names sang through my head like forgotten scenes in dreams," he rhapsodizes (443); the phrase suggests a therapeutic return to the childhood scenes that mark the beginning of his repression of the black fugitive tradition, the grandmother's rhyme and his dream of his grandfather.

Simultaneously, the phrase marks the ambiguous place of the narrator with respect to the possibilities of ahistorical, undisplaced living. In studying the young men—and, furthermore, functioning as narrator—he makes the disguised, the lost, and the forgotten more present, enumerable, locatable. After the woman trips the man pursuing the candy thieves, the narrator feels pressured by guilt. Why guilt at this moment, after he has romanticized the possibilities of inscrutability located in the three subway passengers and linked to Tod's own explicitly criminal flight?

I would argue that IM's ambivalence here rearticulates how he has functioned as an *organizer*, as an adjunct to the police. Indeed, even at the moment when he romanticizes the possibility of being "outside the groove of history," the narrator functions as an agent of the sort of policing motions that chart, annex, and regulate that outside. Such annexation maintains "the outside" as a falsehood, like the Brotherhood, which despite its rhetorics of change and opposition is policed by conservatives like Brother Jack, Tobitt, and Wrestrum. By spotting the youngsters and following them, by vowing to "get them in" to the Brotherhood's "history" (443), and by describing them—issuing, for better or worse, an all-points bulletin—the narrator works like Wright's newspapers. He is an auxiliary detective, perhaps less voracious than the press but no less descriptive or investigative.

Yet, by scene's end, the narrator does not follow through on his ambition to "get them in, all of them"—the boys, "other men dressed like the boys, and . . . girls in dark exotic-colored stockings, their costumes surreal variations of downtown styles" (443). Although he catalogs the crowd on 125th Street, finding his policing eye as previously he had when describing the "tame" rabbits, he does so with a mixture of weariness and euphoria: "They'd been there all along, but somehow I'd missed them. I'd missed them even when my work had been most successful," he realizes (443). The scene functions as a concession of sorts: the organizer, although defeated and guilt-stricken, feels his mind flowing at the possibilities of the underground.

The next two chapters spell his final break with the Brotherhood's organizational schemes, and in chapter 23, chased by Ras's men, he experiments with Rinehart's glasses and hat, becoming privy to the unmapped world of the con man, "both rind and heart." "His world was possibility and he knew it. He was years ahead of me and I was a fool. I must have been crazy and blind. The world in which he lived was without boundaries. A vast seething, hot world of fluidity, and Rine the rascal was at home. Perhaps *only* Rine the rascal was at home in it" (498). "Home"—the word resonates like a new organ pipe, for the narrator's oft-renewed *homelessness* is an issue he seems reluctant to address. His familial home is but a shadow in the novel; he is chased from the college, from his first job at Liberty Paints, from the Men's House, from office to office while in the Brotherhood. He finds no steady friend or lover, and he leaves the one home he loved—Mary Rambo's house—under a cloud of guilt. His first explicit announcement about his "den" is that "The point now is that I found a home—or a hole in the ground, as you will" (6)

The narrator's final position in the novel is multiply ambiguous, as Thomas Schaub points out: in a "border area" between a black area and a white building, dependent upon both his individual ingenuity and the public power with which he can tinker and from whom he can steal (131). To call this "home," I would argue, is Ellison's complex means of bringing issues of space and flight to rest. If the den is a home, its virtue is that, unlike the Thomas apartment deep in Chicago's Black Belt, it is not "already maximally secured," as Baker puts it. Baker speaks of "a new, operational law of personality . . . of placeless PLACE" (207).

Ellison's description of IM's den stresses its individual comfort: "I live rent-free in a building rented strictly to whites, in a section of the basement that was shut off and forgotten during the nineteenth century, which I discovered when I was trying to escape in the night from Ras the Destroyer. . . . My hole is warm and full of light. Yes, *full* of light" (5–6). Simultaneously, the passage defends the apartment's anonymity, disconnection, and lack of address. That the home is cryptic and cryptlike, I would argue, sparing the narrator from the inquisitions of the white policing gaze, is as important to the narrator's rebirth underground as his claim to "invisibility." Resisting surveillance yet claiming a place emancipates him from the traditions he endeavored so long to ignore. And his resistance of surveillance foils the "annexation" of this outer space by the agencies of mapping and policing: the light and power company, the landlords of the building, the police (or worse) who inevitably might enforce the racist rental policies of the building. Like Fred Daniels, Invisible Man finds an alternative space which frees him. Unlike Daniels, IM manages to occupy that space as a *home,* to disassociate it from the condition of being on the lam even though he continues to commit criminal acts. He can be said to be on the lam—for crimes real and imagined, recent and ancient, and from structures and entities that are present and manifold; they range from private, personal enmities (with Ras, with agents of the Brotherhood) and faceless racial hazing (the bat-wielding racists who chased him underground initially) to corporate (Monopolated Light and Power, who only know that "according to the master meter . . . a hell of a lot of free current is disappearing somewhere into the jungle of Harlem," 5) to the conglomerate of police and press set into motion by the "mugging" (4–5). He is still, unmistakably, a *criminal*: he beats the insulting blond man (4–5), smokes marijuana (8), has incited riot (275–84), and has participated in the arson of the Harlem tenements (543–49). Yet he has reshaped the dynamics of the lam into a relation he controls, or claims to control. His assertion of invisibility functions as a tactic, a means of denying his previous position at the receiving end of the accusatory gaze, and, hence, like Sweet the Monkey, who "could make himself invisible," he takes himself out of the police's eye even as he goes on the lam.

In a sense, the narrator can in his home claim to be *home* without any of the trappings and designations by which homes are gridded, secured, subjected. He asserts a space within the public geography without specifically asserting which space. Important in the transitory project Ellison's narrator proposes is the notion of in-between spaces. The "hole" is itself one of these, a location without a location. The narrator's introductory monologue suggests others: the yokel who "simply stepped inside of his opponent's sense of time" to knock him out (8); the careful articulation of how invisibility allows IM to perceive jazz— it "gives one a slightly different sense of time, you're never quite on the beat. Sometimes you're ahead and sometimes behind. Instead of the swift and imperceptible flowing of time, you are aware of its nodes, those points where time stands still or from which it leaps ahead. And you slip into the breaks and look around" (8). In these rents in space and time, Invisible Man opens the possibilities within the grids that constrain the everyday. These grids include time and space, discipline, law, economic and racial hierarchies.

In *The Practice of Everyday Life*, against the "the social hierarchization which organizes scientific work on popular cultures and repeats itself in that work," Michel de Certeau speaks of a desirable tactic for living everyday life, *la perruque*, "the wig." "*La perruque* is the worker's own work disguised as work for his employer. It differs from pilfering in that nothing of material value is stolen. It differs from absenteeism in that the worker is officially on the job. *La perruque* may be as simple a matter as a secretary's writing a love letter on 'company time' or as complex as a cabinetmaker's 'borrowing' a lathe to make a piece of furniture for his living room," explains de Certeau (25). Belligerently, de Certeau locates the *perruque* in the very spaces in which Foucault locates the testing and dissemination of disciplinary practices: "practices analogous to *la perruque* are proliferating in government and commercial offices as well as in factories. . . . Not only workshops and offices, but also museums and learned journals penalize such practices or ignore them" (26). To do so proposes the *perruque* as an alleviation of the instrumentalizing sweep of Foucauldian models of discipline; if it true that "the grid of 'discipline' is everywhere becoming clearer and more extensive," de Certeau writes, "it is all the more urgent to discover how an entire society resists being reduced to it, what popular procedures (also 'minuscule' and quotidian) manipulate the mechanisms of discipline and conform to them only in order to evade them, and finally, what 'ways of operating' form the counterpart, on the consumer's (or 'dominee's') side, of the mute processes that organize the establishment of socioeconomic order" (xiv).

De Certeau's frustration with Foucauldian models and his struggle to articulate the "minuscule" and "quotidian" resistances of the everyday are congruent with the Invisible Man's eventual recognition and acceptance of his own flight from the minutely structured and gridded spaces and relations that have been created by an empowered racism or a racist power. IM's universe is not Ellison's; Ellison always referred to Oklahoma as an anchor, a memory of boundless possibility. (If we credit Ellison's nostalgic remembrance to the carelessness of childhood, we might then reflect on the ways in which other, less hopeful individuals, both actual and fictive, have been deprived of that anchor, the fantasy childhood of infinite promise.) IM's universe is underlain by the horror of the briefcase dream; it establishes certain instrumentalisms that he is largely helpless to resist.

The main issue that de Certeau helps raise and elucidate in Ellison is this: how do we read Invisible Man's "hibernation?" As merely a retreat from the grids and policing of the everyday, particularly severe in their racist strain? Or as a sort of resistance—one that cannot be subsumed by the same power relations that turn Bledsoe into a sort of yea-saying cannibal and Tod Clifton into an emblem of black senselessness, of "random rioting?" IM himself appreciates the delicacy of political readings of his position: although he offers "Who knows but that, on the lower frequencies, I speak for you?" as the final bell in an epilogue addressed directly to the reader (581), he also sounds the personal: "What *is* the next phase?" he wonders (576) and explains that he "carried his sickness and . . . for a long time I tried to place it in the outside world" (575).

De Certeau makes a distinction between two ways of operating, *strategies* and *tactics*, and his distinction builds directly upon the geographical calculus undergirding Foucault's models of discipline; it also resembles the language of Houston A. Baker Jr.'s essay on Richard Wright and black placelessness. De Certeau writes, "I call a *strategy* the calculation (or manipulation) of power relationships that becomes possible as soon as a subject with will and power (a business, an army, a city, a scientific institution) can be isolated. It postulates a *place* that can be delimited as its *own* and serve as the base from which relations with *exteriority* composed of targets and threats (customers or competitors, enemies, the country surrounding the city, objectives and objects of research, etc.) can be managed" (36). De Certeau defines tactics as "determined by the absence of a proper locus. . . . The space of a tactic is the space of the other. Thus it must play on and with a terrain imposed on it and organized by the law of a foreign power" (37). By this definition, the operations of fugitive African-Americans from slaves to Bigger Thomas have been tactical; they have operated in what Baker calls the absence of PLACE.

Fred Daniels and Invisible Man both acknowledge their suspension in "the space of the other," in "a terrain . . . organized by the law of a foreign power." I would argue that IM's adoption of a den in which to hibernate (a natural process, but also volitional; a passive stage, as IM notes, but also, he "couldn't be still. . . . damn it, there's the mind, the *mind*" [573]) represents an attempt to move from tactical to strategic operation. Lest we confuse the notion of a comfortable *home* with what de Certeau calls "a *place* that can be delimited as its *own*," let me add that the somewhat belligerent placement of IM's nest—in a border area, drawing power from the grid—represents an aggressive means of *managing* the other and the threats it represents.

The distinction I am making between this home and any other (comfortable, one's property) depends further upon the business of narration that both reflects the consciousness that makes this project possible and as well helps give the home its importance, its value, through the voicing of its existence and meaning: " 'Ah,' I can hear you say, 'so it was all a build-up to bore us with his buggy jiving. He only wanted to listen to him rave!' " (581). *Voicing* is what Fred Daniels was denied; silenced by the churchgoers' revulsion and the policemen's derision and violence, his underground experience goes to waste, so to speak, as his body washes back into the sewers. The first-person narration that manages *retroactively* to turn the eye of surveillance upon the rabbits, upon the explosive appearances and actions that compose Ellison's Harlem, is also the narration that creates a strategic relation between the character/narrator and his experiences. Mirrors or reflections function to calm or encourage the narrator through the novel; the moments at which he gathers himself after fleeing or spreads his seven tainted letters of reference out "like a hand of high trump cards" (163) pass quickly, leaving the narrator's object-visibility unchanged. The prologue and epilogue, by contrast, present a sustained self-reflection, one that, in isolation, changes the narrator's relation to the public gaze and that, in recouping tradition and *time*, disrupts the strategic rule of place over the narrator.

The ambiguity of the ending, in this reading, resides also in that self-authorizing move toward narration. If the task of telling the story represents a gathering up of subject and object positions and a self-reinvention of sorts—a taking oneself *off* the lam—its product instantly reestablishes a position of specularity for the narrator insofar as he becomes a represented entity in his own story. After narration, in other words, more policings ensue, from the ones the narrator antici-pates—"I can hear you say, 'What a horrible, irresponsible bastard!'" (14)—to others he does not, including this writing of mine. Ellison's novel finally draws our attention to the nature of narration, its foren-sic power, its making visible of a person, or, as Foucault would have it, a soul.

In closing, I would reflect upon how the special problems of the black fugitive suggest limits to white American myths of mobility, both law abiding (tourism, transiency) and criminal (the lam). White American "road stories" as diverse as *On the Road*, *Lolita*, and *Easy Rider* have been discussed in terms of establishing marginal perspec-tives upon the American landscape and culture. Yet we do not as often consider the degree to which American privileges of mobility are—and have always been—racially coded or how the Western landscapes that have been variously described as constitutive of American character are sparsely populated by African-Americans, either in their recent his-tory or in present-day demographics. Two black characters people *The Petrified Forest*'s Black Rock Bar-B-Q during the tense visit of Duke Mantee: Joseph, the Chisholms' chauffeur, and Slim, one of Duke's three henchmen. Two exchanges between the men emphasize the chasm between the stiff, timorous chauffeur and the brassy desperado: after Joseph asks Mr. Chisholm's permission to accept a drink, Slim taunts him mercilessly. Yet Slim, gun in hand, is no more comfortable in the desert West than is Joseph; repeatedly he pleads with Duke to "lam on out of here," despite the white outlaws' comfort. If 1934 was too early for Dillinger and Mantee, two white outlaws evading massive man-hunts, to feel the pressure in this rundown outpost, Slim's prescient restlessness nevertheless hints at an acute reading of the relative safety of space. If myths of the West have figured as central contributors to our national character, then the lingering effects of a domestic cultural geography that continues to dictate black place even into the twentieth century must inevitably alter what it means, for black citizens, to be an American.

afterword

The fugitive remained a vital and changing figure throughout the second half of the twentieth century. An inventory of fugitive tales released as American films in the 1990s confirms the continuing popular appeal and adaptability of stories of running from the police. The situation of the lam occasioned high-budget blockbusters (*The Fugitive, True Romance, U.S. Marshals*), self-important epics (*Thelma and Louise, Natural Born Killers*), low-budget thrillers (*U-Turn, Kalifornia, Love and a .45, Kiss or Kill*), comedies (*House Guest, Nothing to Lose, For Richer or Poorer*), male buddy flicks (*Fled*), female buddy flicks (*Boys on the Side*), lesbian twists on the thriller (*Bound*), romances between cop and robber (*Out of Sight*), puppy-love parental-defiance teen movies (*The Chase, Excess Baggage*), and so on. This list omits other films in which a chase scene or evasion of police merely plays a part (*Goodfellas, Speed, In the Line of Fire, Boyz N the Hood*, among others). The decade saw several high-profile fugitive cases, including the summer 1997 lam of serial murderer Andrew Cunanan and the culmination of the search for the Unabomber, arrested in April 1996 when his brother recognized the antitechnology diatribe he pressured the *New York Times* and *Washington Post* into publishing. No flight attracted as much attention as that of O. J. Simpson. Simpson's June 17, 1994, flight from his attorney's custody and the "chase" he led through the canyonlike freeways of Los Angeles stopped traffic and brought thousands of Angelenos to the roadway to witness the event, revel in the media spotlight, and wish Simpson well. The bizarre spectacle obliterated scheduled programming on major networks for half a day, attracting a combined viewership that approached Super Bowl numbers and setting the stage for the highly public trial that followed.

In these and other fugitive stories from the last 50 years, the internal borders of the United States have proven increasingly irrelevant. Borders with Canada (for draft dodgers and in Ishmael Reed's *Flight to Canada*) and Mexico (in Jim Thompson's *The Getaway* and the films *Butch Cassidy and the Sundance Kid* and *Thelma and Louise*) offer the dominant venue of escape for late-twentieth-century fugitives. Notably, a barren and antique Western landscape, photogenic and foreign yet familiar, shelters an *escapist* tendency in other flight stories: the booby-trapped idyll of *Badlands,* the feverish pilgrimage of *Close Encounters of the Third Kind,* the iconic poses of *Natural Born Killers,* or the sepia-tone nostalgia of *Butch Cassidy.* Louise's refusal to enter Texas, where years ago she may have been raped, highlights internal borders and interprets them not in jurisdictional but associative terms. Concretely speaking, the machinery of surveillance functions well against Thelma and Louise even in the empty West, conjuring a wall of police vehicles to hem their antique Thunderbird against the edge of the Grand Canyon. But their decision to crash—presumably to die—in the canyon betrays the enduring symbolic capacity of Western landscapes and archetypes to frame and valorize certain types of outlawry.

For this reason, it was curious to see U.S. President George W. Bush evoking the Old West with his "Wanted: Dead or Alive" notice to terrorist Osama bin Laden in the wake of the September 11, 2001, hijackings and attacks on Manhattan and the Pentagon. These attacks have precipitated a transnational search for al Qaeda–trained operatives which placed the manhunt front and center among news headlines once again, but which also effected a furtherance of U.S. anticriminal jurisdiction and intensified the interrogative aspects of American security.

The ease with which the hijackers, like judo fighters, used American training and rerouted American airliners in order to strike against American targets was, as the event sank in, deeply unsettling. It caused an understandably panicked rush to incrementally bolster extant airline security procedures and standards. Yet these specific security issues pointed to a more profound threat: the terrorists' conversion of ubiquitous systems into explicitly destructive forces. A flurry of articles throughout autumn 2001 critiqued American systems in terms of similar convertibility (so many, and with such sudden revelations of danger, that one wished the reporters would just quiet down). The airline industry understandably suffered sharp curtailments due to passenger unease, and small airports near Washington stayed closed well into

2002. Other news stories established the vulnerability of U.S. nuclear plants; the dangers inherent in the storage of spent nuclear fuel; the potential that small planes, crop dusters, or insecticide spray trucks could distribute chemical or biological agents; the vulnerability of reservoirs and bridges; the destructive possibility of trucked hazardous material. The spate of anthrax-laden mail claimed several lives and caused the shutdown of Congress and its office buildings as well as numerous post offices while spilled anthrax spores were cleaned up or neutralized. While it is true that damage caused by computer worms and viruses and wreaked by hackers had focused attention upon the negative convertibility of Internet and E-mail networks, time may prove the most profound accomplishment of the attacks to be a downturn in the broad public confidence in the systems and networks inherent to nationalization and globalization.

This fear is, like the crime panics of the past, potentially productive. Reduced airline travel and travel abroad have been the most conspicuous effects, perhaps, of this fear, the existence and pervasiveness of which cannot be denied despite the earnest, vigorous flag-waving which at least rekindled American enthusiasm. This specific crime panic enabled acceptance of clumsy, picayune, uneven security searches at airports. It countenanced severe use of powers of arrest: on October 10, 29 days after the attacks, the *Washington Post* reported that 614 people had been "arrested or detained," many on minor immigration or traffic charges, and that 220 remained in custody, while a court order forbade release of their names (McGee and Eggen). This fear quashed reservations about covert paramilitary action and funded increased espionage and special operations work. It supported the obliteration of the fundamentalist Islamic Taliban government in Afghanistan. It witnessed the establishment of a penal colony in Cuba and the semantics by which the prisoners were designated "detainees" in order to circumvent Geneva Convention standards for treating prisoners of war. It accepted the disappearance of a hard-won federal budget surplus, a good portion of which went into the assault on Afghanistan and the tightening of domestic security. It stockpiled antibiotics against the threat of anthrax, though as of this writing only a handful of poisoned letters had been found. It reopened formerly stalled discussions about the possibility of national identification cards involving sophisticated biometric "signatures." It asserted, once again, the oneness of all America: "United We Stand" became the tag line of many declarations of symbolic resurrection.

This is a powerful fear, though not an insensible one. It endorsed the manhunt that was to follow. The identification and apprehension of al Qaeda–trained terrorists may reduce the threat of future attacks in the United States or abroad. Yet this manhunt is by several measures more complex than any of its precedents. It sought to apprehend an unspecified number of potential terrorists in nations across the globe, many of them relatively unfriendly to the United States. In effect, this manhunt proposed an exponential step beyond J. Edgar Hoover's effacement of intranational jurisdictional borders; it proposed the reach, by hook or by crook, of U.S. law enforcement across the world. Where nations failed to recognize the legal and moral authority of U.S. law enforcement (coupled with the international coalition swiftly assembled in the wake of September 11), U.S. and allied military and paramilitary forces took on the function of law enforcement, compensating for what they lacked in mandate with force of might. A cost-benefit analysis may become a factor in evaluating the application of force to future international pursuit and extradition stalemates; the costs of using force to retrieve suspected murderer Samuel Sheinbein from Israel, for example, may appear too high, but in other cases, notably the forcible extradition of Panamanian leader Manuel Noriega for drug trafficking, the United States has already asserted a transnational extension of its ability to track and apprehend suspected criminals.

Another complicating factor in this manhunt is the imagined nature of al Qaeda operatives. John Torpey has recognized the passport and other personal identification documents as crucial technologies by which states expropriate the "means of movement" from individuals, and inventions by which the citizen is defined, embraced, penetrated, and surveilled (4–20). The al Qaeda organization's reported use of stolen and fake passports confused the already nebulous identity of the enemy in this American war and destabilized the assumed ties between individual and state agency in violence, even as the war in Afghanistan sought to reassert them. Arranged in cells that may function independently and benignly and then suddenly strike, this enemy poses a Deleuzean nightmare for American apprehensive efforts. The criminality of their training may be a central legal question in years to come. Is it merely the training that makes a potential terrorist prosecutable, or must a trainee manifest criminal intent or association? In a nation devoted to its freedom of speech, what sanction will be lowered against terrorist knowledge? As the September 11 incidents showed, where hijackers effected their attacks with apparently no more formidable (or detectable) weapons than box-cutting knives, the project of sniffing out a terrorist who is prepared to remain dormant for years before acting may require extraordinary lengths of surveillance. Or luck.

Like the establishment of a policing network through the 1930s and 1940s, the security measures of the coming years will, even as they focus upon lawbreakers, recruit the subjection of all U.S. citizens, residents, and visitors. Integral to that participation will be a renewed effort to define the discourse surrounding law, lawlessness, and security. George Bush's September 18, 2001, "Wanted: Dead or Alive" comment seemed initially clumsy posturing. Worse, it seemed a symbolic misstep to invoke a mythic past in which contestation of the force of the law— and law's weakness relative to the exigencies of survival in a Western wilderness—made the marshal's badge a tenuous mark of authority. Rather than asserting control, it presaged a drama to follow.

On the other hand, Bush's remark, which came at the dawn of a precipitous upswing in his popularity and approval ratings, may have succeeded because of its simplicity. From the gut-wrenching aftermath of the attacks, his comment gained him mythic access—to discursive traditions as well as to control, allowing him to operate in a streamlined, mythicized space, far above the bureaucracy of the recently disgraced FBI. It shucked the horror and complexity of the moment, the nagging history wherein the United States had helped to arm its present enemies, and the dour chaperonage of a rancorous Congress. The sheriff metaphor was integral to Bush's ascent in approval polls and his formation of a global imperative against terrorists. He superimposed the presidency, the military, and the badge of the police: thus far the nation's fear has defended the consolidation. Framing the American response as a manhunt, appropriating the role of J. Edgar Hoover, and drawing upon the symbolic reservoir of the West, the President presented the shocked public with a story it was sure to recognize and follow.

The fugitive, this book has argued, is a figure peculiarly subject to representational mediation and whose story has served at various moments to rearticulate the multiple relationships between individual and nation. In 1934 John Dillinger became the first fugitive prominent and mobile enough to exercise the engines of the coalescing federal police network. In the first years of the twenty-first century, bin Laden has already emerged as the Dillinger of the transnational era, a figure who both mobilized and justified unprecedented policing alliances, strategies, and technologies and who inspired a new reconceptualization of the criminal. The hunt for bin Laden will provide the narrative via which new ideologies of policing, criminality, surveillance, and security are disseminated and ultimately by which the category of citizenship will be continually revised. As in the case of Dillinger, those meanings will inevitably find contestation; indeed, American deployments of the figure of bin Laden have already been contested well outside the radical Islamic world. If the episode of John Dillinger is any guide, the American efforts to shape perceptions of bin Laden, to recruit consensus around the securitization and surveillance he has triggered, and to apprehend and enact justice upon the fugitive himself represent crucial moments, foundational texts, in the mapping and implementation of a globalized future.

works cited

"Air, Land, Sea Drive on Crime Planned." *New York Times* 4 May 1934: 1+.

Alexander, Jack. "Profiles: The Director—I." *New Yorker* 25 September 1937: 20–25.

"All in a Week: Choate Says We Live in 'Fool's Paradise.'" *Newsweek* 12 May 1934: 9.

"All Speak American." *New York Times* 21 June 1934: 22.

Althusser, Lewis. *Lenin and Philosophy and Other Essays.* Trans. Ben Brewster. New York: Monthly Review Press, 1971.

Anderson, Edward. *Thieves Like Us. Crime Novels: American Noir of the 1930s and '40s.* Ed. Robert Polito. New York: Library of America, 1997. 215–377.

Andrews, William L. *To Tell a Free Story: The First Century of Afro-American Autobiography, 1760–1865.* Champaign-Urbana: University of Illinois Press, 1986.

"Asks Capital for Horse So He Can Get Dillinger." *New York Times* 27 June 1934: 40.

"At the Observation Post." *Literary Digest* 4 August 1934: 11.

Atwood, Albert W. "A Concrete Approach to the Problem of Crime." *Saturday Evening Post* 10 March 1934: 23+.

"Bad Man at Large." *Time* 7 May 1934: 18–21.

Baker, Houston A., Jr. "On Knowing Our Place." *Richard Wright.* Ed. Henry Louis Gates, Jr., and K. A. Appiah. Amistad Literary Series. New York: Amistad/Penguin, 1993. 200–25.

"Bandit's Escape in Tradition." *New York Times* 11 March 1934: 14.

"Behind John Dillinger." *Washington Post* 24 April 1934: 8.

Belasco, Warren. "Commercialized Nostalgia: The Origins of the Roadside Strip." *The Automobile and American Culture.* Ed. David L. Lewis and Laurence Goldstein. Ann Arbor: University of Michigan Press, 1980. 105–22.

Bell, Bernard W. *The Afro-American Novel and Its Tradition.* Amherst: University of Massachusetts Press, 1987.

Bennett, Juda. *The Passing Figure: Racial Confusion in Modern American Literature.* Modern American Literature Series 6. New York: Peter Lang, 1996.

Bercovitch, Sacvan. *The Rites of Assent: Transformations in the Symbolic Construction of America.* New York: Routledge, 1993.

Bergman, Andrew. *We're in the Money: Depression America and Its Films.* New York: NYU Press, 1971.

"Berlin Press Sees 'Lesson' in Dillinger." *Los Angeles Times* 25 April 1934: 2.

Bibb, Henry. "Narrative of the Life and Adventures of Henry Bibb, an American Slave, Written by himself." *Puttin' on Ole Massa.* Ed. Gilbert Osofsky. New York: Harper and Row, 1969. 51–171.

Black, Leonard. *The Life and Sufferings of Leonard Black, a Fugitive from Slavery. Written by Himself.* New Bedford, Massachusetts: Benjamin Lindsey, 1847. 9 December 2001 <http://docsouth.unc.edu/neh/black/menu.html>.

Bland, Sterling Lecater, Jr. *Voices of the Fugitives: Runaway Slave Stories and Their Fictions of Self-Creation.* Westport: Greenwood Press, 2000.

Bluefarb, Sam. *The Escape Motif in the American Novel: Mark Twain to Richard Wright.* Columbus: Ohio State University Press, 1972.

Bold, Christine. *The WPA Guides: Mapping America.* Jackson: University Press of Mississippi, 1999.

Brown, Richard Maxwell. "Desperadoes and Lawmen: The Folk Hero." *Media Studies Journal* 6 (1992): 150–61.

Brown, William Wells. "Narrative of William Wells Brown, a Fugitive Slave, Written by Himself." *Puttin' on Ole Massa.* Ed. Gilbert Osofsky. New York: Harper and Row, 1969. 173–223.

"Bruce Takes Issue with Hoover Figures." *New York Times* 23 April 1929: 3.

Burger, William Henry. "The Contribution of the United States Coast and Geodetic Survey to Geodesy." *Centennial Celebration of the United States Coast and Geodetic Survey.* Washington: GPO, 1916. 81–91.

Burns, Robert Elliott. *I Am a Fugitive from a Georgia Chain Gang!* 1932. Athens: University of Georgia Press, 1997.

Burns, Vincent G. *The Man Who Broke a Thousand Chains.* Washington: Acropolis, 1972.

Burton, Alan. *Police Telecommunications.* Springfield: Charles C. Thomas, 1973.

Cantril, Hadley, ed. *Public Opinion, 1935–1946.* Westport: Greenwood Press, 1951.

Cash, W. J. *The Mind of the South.* New York: Vintage, 1991.

Cashman, Sean Dennis. *Prohibition: The Lie of the Land.* New York: Free Press, 1981.

"Catch Dillinger and 3 Aids [*sic*]." *Chicago Daily Tribune* 26 January 1934: 1+.

"Chicago Afraid of Herself." *New York Times* 29 October 1930: 24.

The Classic Slave Narratives. Ed. William Henry Gates. New York: Mentor, 1987.

Colvin, D. Leigh. *Prohibition in the United States.* New York: George H. Doran, 1926.

Committee on the North American Datum. *North American Datum.* Washington: National Academy of Sciences, 1971.

Congressional Record 4 January 1933: 1375.

Cook, Fred J. *The FBI Nobody Knows.* New York: Macmillan, 1964.

Cooper, Courtney Ryley. *Ten Thousand Public Enemies.* New York: Blue Ribbon, 1935.

———. Introduction. *Persons in Hiding.* By J. Edgar Hoover. Boston: Little, Brown, 1938. vii–xix.

Craft, William. *Running a Thousand Miles for Freedom; or, The Escape of William and Ellen Craft from Slavery.* London: William Tweedie, 1860. 9 December 2001 <http://docsouth.unc.edu/neh/craft/menu.html>.

"Crime Rise This Year Shown in 772 Cities." *New York Times* 29 September 1930: 12.

"Crime-Ridden America Blushes for Its Jails." *Literary Digest* 17 March 1934: 39.

"Crime: Congress Speeds Bills as Gangsters Remain Headliners." *Newsweek* 5 May 1934: 10–11.

"Crime: Dillinger and Company Catch up with Recent Rumors." *Newsweek* 7 July 1934: 9–10.

"Crime: Dillinger's Latest Dash from Justice Caps Week of Nationwide Blood and Lawlessness." *Newsweek* 28 April 1934: 10.

Cromie, Robert, and Joseph Pinkston. *Dillinger: A Short and Violent Life*. New York: McGraw-Hill, 1962.

Crowther, Bosley. "A Native's Return: Jimmy Cagney, the Old 'Public Enemy,' Is a Gangster Again in 'White Heat.' " *New York Times* 11 September 1949, sec. 2: 1.

———. "The Screen in Review." *New York Times* 3 September 1949: 7.

Cruse, Harold. *The Crisis of the Negro Intellectual*. New York: William Morrow and Company, 1967.

Darrow, Clarence. *Crime: Its Cause and Treatment*. New York: Thomas Y. Crowell, 1922.

Davis, Charles T., and Henry Louis Gates Jr. *The Slave's Narrative*. New York: Oxford University Press, 1985.

Dayan, Joan. "A Residue of Liberty: Prisons and the Law." Gothic Americas: From Plantation to Penitentiary. MLA Convention. Sheraton Centre Hotel: Toronto. 29 December 1997.

"Death of Dillinger." *Time* 30 July 1934: 14.

de Certeau, Michel. *The Practice of Everyday Life*. Trans. Steven Rendall. Berkeley: University of California Press, 1984.

Demaris, Ovid. *The Director: An Oral Biography of J. Edgar Hoover*. New York: Harper's Magazine Press, 1975.

de Toledano, Ralph. *J. Edgar Hoover: The Man in His Time*. New Rochelle: Arlington House, 1973.

"Dillinger Back in Indiana Jail." *Los Angeles Times* 31 January 1934: 3.

"Dillinger Break Recalls Escape of Tom O'Connor." *Chicago Daily Tribune* 4 March 1934: 3.

"Dillinger Eludes Hunt in 4 States; 'Kill' Order Issued." *New York Times* 5 March 1934: 1+.

"Dillinger Escapes Jail; Using a Wooden Pistol He Locks Guards in Cell." *New York Times* 4 March 1934: 1+.

"Dillinger Escapes Posses after Two Running Fights; Two Killed, Five Wounded." *New York Times* 24 April 1934: 1+.

"Dillinger Excites Interest Abroad." *New York Times* 25 April 1934: 3.

"Dillinger Gang Guarded by Own Machine Guns." *Los Angeles Times* 27 January 1934: 2.

"Dillinger Gangsters' Four Month Campaign of Slayings and Robberies Is Traced on Map" (illustration with caption). *Chicago Daily Tribune* 27 January 1934: 28.

"Dillinger Gets out with Wooden Pistol." *Miami Herald* 4 March 1934: 1+.

"Dillinger Is Being Trailed about Chicago." *Cumberland Evening Times* 8 March 1934: 1+.

"Dillinger Just Pawn of Crime, Darrow's View." *Washington Post* 25 April 1934: 11.

"Dillinger: Negro Has Story to Tell; Dies with Lips Sealed." *Newsweek* 24 March 1934: 14.

"Dillinger Plays a Part in Three Escape Plots." *Chicago Daily Tribune* 5 March 1934: 2.

"Dillinger Plays Raleigh for Moment in Flight." *Los Angeles Times* 24 April 1934: 2.

"Dillinger Robs Bank, Kills Policeman." *Chicago Daily Tribune* 16 January 1934, 1+.

"Dillinger 'Rose' in 6-Month Spurt." *New York Times* 4 March 1934: 24.

"Dillinger Seen on South Side." *Chicago Daily Tribune* 9 March 1934: 1+.

"Dillinger Sped East." *Los Angeles Times* 30 January 1934: 2.

"Dillinger: The Killer (Maybe) Escapes Police Once Again." *Newsweek* 7 April 1934: 10.

"Dillinger's Escape." *Los Angeles Times* 6 March 1934: 4.

"Dillinger's Father Is Visited by Son." *Miami Herald* 24 April 1934: 7.

"Dillinger's Gang Called 'Kill-Crazy.' " *New York Times* 26 December 1933: 28.

"Dillinger's Trail Long." *Los Angeles Times* 23 July 1934: 1.

"Dillinger's Trail Lost." *Los Angeles Times* 5 March 1934: 1.

Dorman, Robert L. "Revolt of the Provinces: The Regionalist Movement in America, 1920–45." *The New Regionalism*. Ed. Charles Reagan Wilson. Jackson: University Press of Mississippi, 1998. 1–17.

Douglass, Frederick. *Narrative of the Life of Frederick Douglass, an African Slave*. 1845. *The Classic Slave Narratives*. Ed. Henry Louis Gates Jr. New York: Mentor, 1987. 243–331.

"Down the Spillway." *Baltimore Sun* 26 April 1934: 12.

Durgnat, Raymond. "Paint it Black: The Family Tree of the *Film Noir*." *The Big Book of Noir*. Ed. Ed Gorman, Lee Server, and Martin H. Greenberg. New York: Carroll & Graf, 1998. 1–13.

Editorial. *Los Angeles Times* 11 March 1934: 12.

Editorial. *Washington Evening Star* 5 March 1934: A-8.

Ellison, Ralph. *Collected Essays*. Ed. John F. Callahan. New York: Modern Library, 1995.

———. "The Essential Ellison." *Conversations with Ralph Ellison*. Ed. Maryemma Graham and Amritjit Singh. Jackson: University Press of Mississippi, 1995. 342–377.

———. *Invisible Man*. 1952. New York: Vintage, 1989.

Erben, Rudolf. "The Western Holdup Play: The Pilgrimage Continues." *Western American Literature* 23 (1989): 311–22.

"Escape Is Pictured by Kidnaped Guard." *Miami Herald* 4 March 1934: 8.

Fabre, Michel. *The World of Richard Wright*. Jackson: University Press of Mississippi, 1985.

"Federal 'Teeth' Asked in Gang War." *New York Times* 20 March 1934: 46.

Flanigan, Daniel J. *The Criminal Law of Slavery and Freedom, 1800–1968*. New York: Garland, 1987.

Fleming, Philip B. "40,000 Miles of Auto Heaven." *Magazine* August 1945: 25+.

Foucault, Michel. *Discipline and Punish: The Birth of the Prison*. Trans. Alan Sheridan. New York: Vintage, 1979.

———. *The History of Sexuality: An Introduction, Volume I*. Trans. Robert Hurley. New York: Vintage, 1990.

Franklin, John Hope, and Loren Schweninger. *Runaway Slaves: Rebels on the Plantation*. New York: Oxford University Press, 1999.

Friedman, Lawrence M. *Crime and Punishment in American History*. New York: Basic Books, 1993.

"A Fugitive from Georgia's Prison System." *New York Times Book Review* 31 January 1932: 4.

Gallup, George H., ed. *The Gallup Poll: Public Opinion, 1935–1971*. New York: Random House, 1972.

Gara, Larry. *The Liberty Line: The Legend of the Underground Railroad*. Lexington: University of Kentucky Press, 1961.

Gentry, Curt. *J. Edgar Hoover: The Man and His Secrets*. New York: Norton, 1991.

"Gibe at Raid on Dillinger." *New York Times* 25 April 1934: 2.

Girardin, G. Russell, and William J. Helmer. *Dillinger: The Untold Story*. Bloomington: Indiana University Press, 1994.

Glueck, Sheldon. "The Place of Proper Police and Prosecutory Work in a Crime Reduction Program." *Proceedings of the Attorney General's Conference on Crime, Held December 10–13, 1934 in Memorial Continental Hall, Washington, D.C.* Washington: Bureau of Prisons, 1936. 52–63.

"Gone Again." *Baltimore Sun* 4 March 1934: 8.

Gun Crazy. Dir. Joseph H. Lewis. United Artists, 1949.

"Hardly a Crime Wave." *New York Times* 10 March 1934: 6.

Hepworth, Mike, and Bryan S. Turner. *Confession: Studies in Deviance and Religion*. London: Routledge and Kegan Paul, 1982.

Hibbs, Ben. "Is the Sheriff a Back Number?" *Country Gentleman* December 1933: 10+.

Hobsbawm, Eric. *Bandits*. 1969. New York: New Press, 2000.

———. *Primitive Rebels: Studies of Archaic Forms of Social Movement in the 19th and 20th Centuries*. 1959. 2nd ed. New York: Praeger, 1963.

Hoover, J. Edgar. "The Crime Wave We Now Face." *New York Times Magazine* 21 April 1946: 26–27.

———. "Detection and Apprehension." *Proceedings of the Attorney General's Conference on Crime, Held December 10–13, 1934 in Memorial Continental Hall, Washington, D.C.* Washington: Bureau of Prisons, 1936. 24–34.

———. Foreword. *Ten Thousand Public Enemies*. By Cooper. New York: Blue Ribbon, 1935. vii–ix.

———. "In the Fight against Crime." *True Detective Mysteries* February 1933: 3+.

———. *Masters of Deceit*. New York: Pocket Books, 1958.

———. "National Bureau Here Has Records of All Criminals." *Washington Post* 24 May 1925: 12.

———. "Our 'Achilles' Heel." *Vital Speeches* 15 October 1946: 10–11.

———. *Persons in Hiding*. Boston: Little, Brown, 1938.

Hopkins, Richard J. "Prohibition and Crime." *North American Review* 222 (1925): 40–44.

Hubbard, Gardiner G., and Marcus Baker. "Geographical Research in the United States." *National Geographic* 8 (1897): 285–93.

Hyams, Joe. *Bogie: The Biography of Humphrey Bogart*. New York: New American Library, 1966.

I Am a Fugitive from a Chain Gang! Dir. Mervyn LeRoy. Warner Bros., 1932.

I Am a Fugitive from a Chain Gang! Ed. John E. O'Connor. Wisconsin/Warner Bros. Screenplay Series. Madison: University of Wisconsin Press, 1981.

"In Today's News." *Miami Herald* 4 March 1934: 6.

"In Today's News." *Miami Herald* 24 April 1934: 6.

"Indiana Police 'Box Score' Records Fight on Gang." *New York Times* 12 January 1934: 15.

"John Dillinger Sr. Glad of Escape, but Worried about Son." *Chicago Daily Tribune* 4 March 1934: 3.

Kahn, Karl M. "Behind the Record." *Washington Times* 27 April 1934.

Kaltenborn, H. V. "Radio and Crime." *Proceedings of the Attorney General's Conference on Crime, Held December 10–13, 1934 in Memorial Continental Hall, Washington, D.C.* Washington: Bureau of Prisons, 1936. 111–19.

Kantor, MacKinlay. "Gun Crazy." *Author's Choice: 40 Stories.* New York: Coward-McCann, 1944. 352–77.

Kasinsky, Renee Goldsmith. "Patrolling the Facts: Media, Cops, and Crime." In *Media, Process, and the Social Construction of Crime.* Ed. Gregg Barak. New York: Garland, 1994. 203–34.

Kastor, Elizabeth. "Chasing a Nightmare: The Search for a Serial Killer Generates an Instinctive Thrill." *Washington Post* 18 July 1997: B1+.

Keller, William W. *The Liberals and J. Edgar Hoover: Rise and Fall of a Domestic Intelligence State.* Princeton: Princeton University Press, 1989.

Kemp, Philip. "From the Nightmare Factory: HUAC and the Politics of *Noir.*" *The Big Book of Noir.* Ed. Ed Gorman, Lee Server, and Martin H. Greenberg. New York: Carroll & Graf, 1998. 77–86.

Kinnamon, Kenneth. "*Native Son:* The Personal, Social, and Political Background." *The Critical Response to Richard Wright.* Ed. Robert J. Butler. Critical Responses in Arts and Letters 16. Westport: Greenwood Press, 1995. 15–20.

Kitses, Jim. *Gun Crazy.* BFI Film Classics. London: British Film Institute, 1996.

Klapp, Orrin E. *Heroes, Villains, and Fools: The Changing American Character.* Englewood Cliffs: Prentice-Hall, 1962.

Koppes, Clayton R. "Hollywood and the Politics of Representation: Women, Workers, and African Americans in World War II Movies." *The Home-Front War: World War II and American Society.* Ed. Kenneth Paul O'Brien and Lynn Hudson Parsons. Contributions in American History 161. Westport: Greenwood Press, 1995. 25–40.

Krutnik, Frank. *In a Lonely Street: Film Noir, Genre, Masculinity.* London: Routledge, 1991.

Kyvig, David E. *Repealing National Prohibition.* Chicago: University of Chicago, 1979.

Lane, Winthrop. "Crime and Punishment." *New York Herald Tribune Books* 17 January 1932: 4.

———. "Georgia Savagery." *The Survey* 15 March 1932: 696–97.

"Legal Briefs: Two Dillinger Aides to Die; Third Gets Life." *Newsweek* 31 March 1934: 20.

Leonard, V. A. *Police Organization and Management.* Police Science Series. Brooklyn: Foundation Press, 1951.

———. *The Police Communications System.* Springfield: Charles C. Thomas, 1970.

Leuchtenberg, William E. *Franklin D. Roosevelt and the New Deal, 1932–1940.* New York: Harper Torchbooks, 1963.

Levy, Newman. "The Crime Situation." *Harper's* 154 (1927): 262–64.

Lichtenstein, Alex. *Twice the Work of Free Labor: The Political Economy of Convict Labor in the New South.* New York: Verso, 1996.

Mancini, Matthew J. Introduction. *I Am a Fugitive from a Georgia Chain Gang!* By Robert Elliott Burns. 1932. Athens: University of Georgia Press, 1997. v–xxiv.

"Manhunt." *Newsweek* 3 April 1950: 53.

Margolies, Edward. "Wright's Craft: The Short Stories." *Richard Wright.* Ed. Henry Louis Gates Jr. and K. A. Appiah. Amistad Literary Series. New York: Amistad/Penguin, 1993. 75–97.

Martin, Olga Johanna. *Hollywood's Movie Commandments.* New York: Arno Press, 1970.

Matovina, Millard T. "F.M. Radio Gives Greater Range with Less Power." *American City* December 1943: 15.

Maxfield, James F. *The Fatal Woman: Sources of Male Anxiety in American Film Noir, 1941–1991.* Madison, New Jersey: Fairleigh Dickinson Press, 1996.

McGee, Jim, and Dan Eggen. "Probe Narrows to 220 Detained after Attacks." *Washington Post Online* 10 October 2001: A01. 28 February 2002 <http://www.washingtonpost.com/ac2/wp-dyn?pagename=article&node=&contentId=A33982-2001Oct9>.

McGilligan, Patrick. "Introduction: 'Made It, Ma! Top of the World!'" *White Heat.* Ed. McGilligan. Wisconsin/Warner Bros. Screenplay Series. Madison: University of Wisconsin Press, 1984. 9–36.

"Meek Dillinger Is Jailed." *Chicago Daily Tribune* 31 January 1934: 1–2.

Mendenhall, T. C., and Otto H. Tittmann. "A Brief Account of the Geographic Work of the U.S. Coast and Geodetic Survey." *National Geographic Magazine* 8 (1897): 294–99.

"Milksop Enforcement." *Miami Herald* 6 March 1934: 6.

Miller, D. A. *The Novel and the Police.* Berkeley: University of California Press, 1988.

"More Patrol Cars for Milwaukee." *American City* January 1945: 11.

Mullen, Bill. "Popular Fronts: Negro Story Magazine and the African American Literary Response to World War II." *African American Review* 30 (1996): 5–15.

Mulvey, Laura. *Visual and Other Pleasures.* London: Macmillan, 1989.

Murphy, Paul L. "Societal Morality and Individual Freedom." *Law, Alcohol, and Order: National Perspectives on National Prohibition.* Ed. David E. Kyvig. Contributions in American History 110. Westport: Greenwood Press, 1985. 67–80.

Nash, Jay Robert. *Citizen Hoover.* Chicago: Nelson-Hall, 1972.

———. *The Dillinger Dossier.* Highland Park: December Press, 1983.

"The News-Week at Home." *Newsweek* 26 May 1934: 9.

Newton, Michael, and Judy Ann Newton. *FBI Most Wanted: An Encyclopedia.* New York: Garland, 1989.

Nordheimer, Jon. "Dalton Trumbo, Film Writer, Dies; Oscar Winner Had Been Black-listed." *New York Times* 11 September 1976: 22.

"Not a Comedy." *Washington Post* 5 March 1934: 8.

"Not Beelzebub, but 'Just a Dumb Crook.'" *Literary Digest* 30 June 1934: 10.

"Noted Killer Dillinger and Jailer from Whom He Escaped." *Cumberland Evening Times* 3 March 1934, city ed.: 1.

Osgood, Herbert L. *The American Colonies in the Seventeenth Century.* Vol. 2. Glouces-ter: Peter Smith, 1957.

Osofsky, Gilbert. "Puttin' on Ole Massa: The Significance of Slave Narratives." *Puttin' on Ole Massa.* Ed. Gilbert Osofsky. New York: Harper and Row, 1969. 9–44.

"Outlaws Rob Bank, Kill a Policeman." *New York Times* 16 January 1934: 42.

Packard, Vance. "Hot Spots of Crime." *American Magazine* August 1946: 34+.

"Pals Expect Delivery." *New York Times* 5 March 1934: 3.

Pennington, James W. C. "The Fugitive Blacksmith, or Events in the History of James W. C. Pennington." *Great Slave Narratives.* Ed. Arna Bontemps. Boston: Beacon, 1969. 193–267.

The Petrified Forest. Dir. Henry Blanke. Warner Bros., 1936.

Photo illustration. *Newsweek* 28 April 1934: 11.

"Police Hunt Gang Trio." *Los Angeles Times* 28 January 1934: 2.

Potter, Claire Bond. *War on Crime: Bandits, G-Men, and the Politics of Mass Culture.* New Brunswick: Rutgers University Press, 1998.

Powers, Richard Gid. *G-Men: The FBI in American Popular Culture.* Carbondale: South-ern Illinois University Press, 1983.

———. *Secrecy and Power: The Life of J. Edgar Hoover.* New York: Free Press, 1987.

"Press Comment on Hoover Speech." *New York Times* 23 April 1929: 28.

"The Price of Crime." *Coronet* September 1952: 99–114.

"Primaries: Red Fire, Burning Words—The Campaign Is On." *Newsweek* 19 May 1934: 8–9.

"Progress in Surveying the United States." *National Geographic Magazine* 17 (1906): 110–12.

"Prosecutor Posing with Dillinger Is a Shock to Loesch." *Chicago Daily Tribune* 1 February 1934: 3.

"Public Enemies: Dillinger, Sankey, Floyd Act No. 1 Role." *Newsweek* 10 February 1934: 14.

"Public Enemy: One More Jail Fails in Holding Dillinger." *Newsweek* 10 March 1934: 10.

"R. E. Burns Dead; Fled Chain Gang." *New York Times* 7 June 1955: 33.

Record, Wilson. *The Negro and the Communist Party.* New York: Atheneum, 1971.

Richard Wright. Ed. Henry Louis Gates Jr. and K. A. Appiah. Amistad Literary Series. New York: Amistad/Penguin, 1993.

Rippy, J. Fred Jr. "FM Radio Serves Cars for Fire, Police, Water and County." *American City* September 1944: 15.

Robb, David. "Naming the Right Names: Amending the Hollywood Blacklist." *Cineaste* 22 (1996): 24–29.

Robinson, Warren F. *The G-Man's Son at Porpoise Island.* Chicago: Goldsmith, 1937.

Roosevelt, Franklin D. "An Address." *Proceedings of the Attorney General's Conference on Crime, Held December 10–13, 1934 in Memorial Continental Hall, Washington, D.C.* Washington: Bureau of Prisons, 1936. 17–20.

Ruhmann, Lony, Steven Schwartz, and Rob Conway. "Gun Crazy, 'The Accomplishment of Many, Many Minds.'" *Velvet Light Trap* 20 (1983): 16–21.

Ruth, David E. *Inventing the Public Enemy: The Gangster in American Culture, 1918–1934.* Chicago: University of Chicago Press, 1996.

"Says 'We Will Get Him.'" *New York Times* 24 April 1934: 2.

Schaub, Thomas. "Ellison's Masks and the Novel of Reality." *New Essays on Invisible Man.* Ed. Robert O'Meally. *The American Novel.* Cambridge: Cambridge University Press, 1988. 123–56.

"Seek Dillinger Gang Hideout." *Chicago Tribune* 5 March 1934: 1+.

Sherwood, Robert Emmet. *The Petrified Forest, Acting Edition.* New York: Dramatists Play Service, 1962.

Silver, Alain, and Linda Brookover. "What Is This Thing Called *Noir?*" *The Film Noir Reader 2.* Ed. Alain Silver and James Ursini. New York: Limelight Editions, 1999. 261–68.

Silverman, Kaja. *Male Subjectivity at the Margins.* New York: Routledge, 1992.

Slotkin, Richard. *Gunfighter Nation: The Myth of the Frontier in Twentieth-Century America.* New York: Atheneum, 1992.

Smith, Valerie. "Alienation and Creativity in the Fiction of Richard Wright." *Richard Wright: Critical Perspectives Past and Present.* Ed. Henry Louis Gates Jr. and K. A. Appiah. New York: Amistad/Penguin, 1993. 433–47.

"Sociology." *Times Literary Supplement* 13 October 1932: 740.

"Speaking of Pictures." *Life* 10 March 1947: 20–22.

"Speed Dillinger East by Air." *Chicago Daily Tribune* 30 January 1934: 1–2.

Sperber, A. M., and Eric Lax. *Bogart.* New York: William Morrow, 1997.

Spurr, David. *The Rhetoric of Empire.* Durham: Duke University Press, 1993.

"States' Rights and Crime." *Houston Post* 26 April 1934: 6.

"Steps in Dillinger's Notorious Career." *Chicago Daily Tribune* 4 March 1934: 2.

Stepto, Robert B. *From behind the Veil: A Study of Afro-American Narrative.* Urbana: University of Illinois Press, 1979.

Still, Bayrd. *The West: Contemporary Records of America's Expansion Across the Continent: 1607–1890.* New York: Capricorn, 1961.

Stimson, Henry L. "An Address." *Proceedings of the Attorney General's Conference on Crime, Held December 10–13, 1934 in Memorial Continental Hall, Washington, D.C.* Washington: Bureau of Prisons, 1936. 8–15.

"Stop Encouraging Bandits!" *Collier's* 2 June 1934: 70.

Sullivan, William C. *The Bureau: My Thirty Years in Hoover's FBI*. New York: Norton, 1979.

Tannenbaum, Frank. *Crime and the Community*. Boston: Ginn and Company, 1938.

Tanner, Laura E. "Uncovering the Magical Disguise of Language: The Narrative Presence in Richard Wright's *Native Son*." *Richard Wright: Critical Perspectives Past and Present*. Ed. Henry Louis Gates Jr. and K. A. Appiah. New York: Amistad/Penguin, 1993. 132–48.

Tatum, Stephen. *Inventing Billy the Kid: Visions of the Outlaw in America, 1881–1981*. Albuquerque: University of New Mexico Press, 1982.

Taylor, William R. *Cavalier and Yankee: The Old South and American National Character*. New York: George Braziller, 1961.

"Text of President Hoover's Address." *New York Times* 23 April 1929: 2.

Theoharis, Athan G. *The FBI: An Annotated Bibliography and Research Guide*. New York: Garland, 1994.

———. *J. Edgar Hoover, Sex and Crime: An Historical Antidote*. Chicago: Ivan R. Dee, 1995.

Theoharis, Athan G., and John Stuart Cox. *The Boss: J. Edgar Hoover and the Great American Inquisition*. Philadelphia: Temple University Press, 1988.

They Live by Night. Dir. Nicholas Ray. RKO, 1948.

Thompson, Jim. *The Getaway*. 1958. New York: Black Lizard–Vintage, 1994.

"Three States Hunting Dillinger." *Chicago Daily Tribune* 4 March 1934: 1+.

Tindall, George B. "The Benighted South: Origins of a Modern Image." *Virginia Quarterly Review* 40:2 (1964): 281–94.

———. *The Emergence of the New South, 1913–1945*. Baton Rouge: Louisiana State University Press, 1967.

Toland, John. *The Dillinger Days*. New York: Random House, 1963.

"Topics of the Day." Illustration. *Literary Digest* 14 August 1934: 8.

Torpey, John. *The Invention of the Passport: Surveillance, Citizenship, and the State*. Cambridge: Cambridge University Press, 2000.

Tuska, Jon. *Dark Cinema: American Film Noir in Cultural Perspective*. Contributions to the Study of Popular Culture Series. Westport: Greenwood Press, 1984.

"22 Who Saw Killing Identify Dillinger." *New York Times* 1 February 1934: 3.

"Two Crimes Solved?" *Washington Post* 9 March 1934: 8.

"Ubiquitous Outlaw." *Baltimore Sun* 23 April 1934: 8.

United States. Department of Justice. *99 Facts about the FBI: Questions and Answers*. Washington: GPO, 1981.

———. *FBI Facts and History*. Washington: GPO, 1990.

———. Library of Congress Archive of Folk Song. *A List of Songs Concerning John Dillinger*. Washington: Library of Congress, 1970.

"Urschel Abductor Captured in Texas on a Lonely Ranch." *New York Times* 15 August 1933: 1+.

"A Vital Network." *American City* June 1946: 17.

"Wanted: America's Most Dangerous Criminals." *Coronet* December 1950: 115–17.

"Watch Here for Dillinger." *New York Times* 5 March 1934: 3.

White Heat. Dir. Raoul Walsh. Warner Bros., 1949.

White Heat. Patrick McGilligan, ed. Wisconsin/Warner Bros. Screenplay Series. Madison: University of Wisconsin Press, 1984.

Whitehead, Don. *The FBI Story.* New York: Random House, 1956.

"Wickersham Would Change Dry Law." *New York Times* 17 July 1929: 1.

Wilson, Woodrow. "Address by the President of the United States." *Centennial Celebration of the United States Coast and Geodetic Survey.* Washington: GPO, 1916. 141–44.

Wood, C. Leland. "New Radio Doubled Police Efficiency." *American City* November 1943: 15.

Wright, Richard. "The Man Who Lived Underground." 1944. *Richard Wright Reader.* Ed. Ellen Wright and Michel Fabre. New York: Harper & Row, 1978. 518–76.

———. *Native Son.* 1940. New York: Perennial/Harper, 1993.

index

CPSIA information can be obtained at www.ICGtesting.com
Printed in the USA
LVOW07s2205240616

494061LV00001B/26/P

9 781604 731835